AFFIRMATIVE ACTION
IN HIGHER EDUCATION

AFFIRMATIVE ACTION IN HIGHER EDUCATION
A Sourcebook

Lois VanderWaerdt

DISCARD

GARLAND PUBLISHING, INC. • NEW YORK & LONDON
1982

Library of Congress Cataloging in Publication Data

VanderWaerdt, Lois.
  Affirmative action in higher education.

  Bibliography: p.
  Includes index.
  1. College teachers—United States—Selection and
appointment. 2. Affirmative action programs—United
States. 3. Discrimination in employment—United States.
I. Title.
LB2331.72.V36   331.13′3   80-9041
ISBN 0-8240-9313-5   AACR2

Printed on acid-free, 250-year-life paper
Manufactured in the United States of America

To Dr. Dorothy Selz,
Professor of English, University of South Dakota,
1915–1981

ACKNOWLEDGMENTS

Many people have provided guidance and support in the development of this book; however, I thank particularly Dr. Robert Gard for his editorial assistance, Dr. Blanche Touhill for urging me to write the book, and members of my staff: Barbara Couture, Peggy Carter, and Linda Oppland.

CONTENTS

AFFIRMATIVE ACTION
IN HIGHER EDUCATION

Chapter One

THEN AND NOW: AN INTRODUCTION

Affirmative action has substantially changed employment practices affecting faculty and staff on college and university campuses. Fifteen years ago, faculty and staff positions might be filled by a professional acquaintance of the dean or department chairman. Advertisements were needed only if no known candidates were available. Mentoring was common, particularly for white males. Seldom were women or members of minority groups given the encouragement and job opportunities available to their white male colleagues. Since few senior faculty or staff were women or members of minority groups, many promising female and minority scholars lacked both role models and the encouragement to continue their studies. Hence a cycle was perpetuated which ensured that the best jobs went to the protégés of departmental scholars who were usually white males. The "old boy" network reigned supreme.

Into this relaxed academic milieu came the Civil Rights Act of 1964, amended in 1972 to apply to educational institutions. The legislative history of the amendment contained substantial data documenting discrimination in institutions of higher education. A House Report summarized the Congressional view of the widespead and persistent discrimination in higher education employment:

> There is nothing in the legislative background of Title
> VII, nor does any national policy suggest itself to support
> the exemption of these educational institution employees--
> primarily teachers--from Title VII coverage. Discrimination
> against minorities and women in the field of education is as
> pervasive as discrimination in any other field of employ-
> ment.... The committee feels that discrimination in edu-
> cational institutions is especially critical. The committee
> cannot imagine a more sensitive area than educational in-
> stitutions where the Nation's Youth are exposed to a
> multitude of ideas that will strongly influence their future
> development.

Prior to the enactment of this amendment, institutions and educational leaders seemed to support the fight against discrimination and voiced little opposition to the passage of the amendment. Subsequently, however, many institutions and academicians resisted changes in their procedures and practices which would permit more women and minorities to be considered for faculty and administrative positions. The early 1970's brought numerous articles decrying the amendment as a threat to academic standards, predicting that vast numbers of unqualified women and minorities would have to be hired to comply with government regulations. These traditional and conservative scholars failed to make the

inductive leap to understand that discrimination causes *less* qualified
people to be hired because significant groups of qualified people are
not considered for positions. They also failed to understand that hiring
less qualified candidates because of race or sex is a *violation* of the
law.

In spite of the backlash against affirmative action, colleges and
universities found it advantageous to comply with government regulations, at least to the extent of staffing affirmative action offices
and searching nationally to fill faculty and many staff positions.
Minorities and women filed charges of discrimination by the score, and
institutions found it essential to assign staff to process these charges
and to provide data for government investigators. The more enlightened
institutions set up procedures designed to document their affirmative
action efforts and to ensure fair treatment to applicants of both sexes
and all races.

After nearly a decade of affirmative action, however, women and
minorities who have been hired have been not only numerically and
proportionally few, but frequently better qualified than their majority
group male counterparts. Many studies have shown that women are held
to a higher standard of performance than men and that, although a woman
who is distinctly superior may be hired or promoted, women who are merely
average generally do not fare well against comparably qualified men.*
Although colleges and universities have scrambled to accomplish a representation of women and minorities on par with the national average, and
to provide equal opportunity, few institutions have stepped boldly
forward to take affirmative action to dramatically increase the representation of women and minorities on their campuses.

As the backlash against affirmative action subsides and a brief
historical perspective becomes possible, colleges and universities that
wish to do so may move forward with effective affirmative action programs.
Designed to be a resource book for institutions that wish to improve
their present programs or that are faced with government investigations
or compliance reviews, this book provides a comprehensive view of the
components of a successful affirmative action program.

An effective affirmative action program is designed to provide equal
consideration for all applicants for faculty and staff positions, for
all faculty members in the tenure and promotion process, for administrators and staff members seeking promotions and upgrades, as well as for
students seeking admission, financial aid, and equality in academic

---

*See L. Lewis, *Scaling the Ivory Tower* (Baltimore, 1975), pp. 123, 129,
137, 143; J. Farley, "Academic Recommendations: Males & Females as
Judges and Judged," *AAUP Bulletin*, May 1978; L. Fidel 25 *American
Psychology* 1094 (1970); Lewin and Ducker, "Women in Academia" 173
Science 892; J. Abramson, *The Invisible Woman: Discrimination in the
Academic Profession* (San Francisco, 1975), p. 119; R. Kantor, *Men and
Women in the Organization* (New York, 1977), pp. 200 ff.; G. Ezorsky,
Response to presentation of G. Roche, in *Affirmative Action in Employ-
ment in Higher Education* (1975), p. 215. See also P. Goldberg, "Are
Women Prejudiced Against Women?" *Transaction*, April 1968, pp. 28-31;
S.L. and D.J. Bem, "Training the Woman to Know Her Place: The Power
of a Non Conscious Ideology," *Women's Role in Contemporary Society*
(1972).

and athletic programs. Such a program encourages positive supervisory practices and ensures equitable disciplinary procedures. The affirmative action program includes an informal means of resolving potential grievances and a more formal grievance mechanism.

Appendix 1-1 summarizes the laws and regulations that affect affirmative action programs and that are designed to provide equal opportunity for all employees, prospective employees, and students regardless of race, sex, color, national origin, religion, age, handicap, or veteran status. Appendix 1-2 explains in more detail each of the federal laws affecting higher education.

Several indices may be used to gauge the success of an affirmative action program. Although some disgruntled employees, applicants for employment, and students will file charges of discrimination regardless of the effectiveness of the affirmative action program, a substantial decrease in such charges is both a goal of an affirmative action program and a measure of its success. Another measure of the success of the program is the increased numbers of members of protected groups who are hired and retained. The tangential benefit of this increase is that the presence of minorities and women in and of itself generates interest in the institution by other members of these groups. Seeking to escape the isolation of tokenism, women and minorities will gravitate toward an environment where they will have demographic peers and where they perceive they will have greater opportunities. An improved view of affirmative action on the campus is reflected in the increased numbers of both employees and administrators who visit the Affirmative Action Office to solicit the advice and counsel of the Director--thus providing an opportunity to "front end" problems that may arise.

A successful program can be affected by numerous factors over which a Director of Affirmative Action has little or no control. A lawsuit lost or a charge resolved through a consent decree or settlement can convince even the most ardent unbeliever of the value of an affirmative action program. Activism by members of protected groups results in more awareness of the presence of these groups, influences hiring, and helps in combating institutional discrimination based on race, sex, age, or handicap. High-level administrators who are members of protected groups influence the campus by their visibility as well as by their support for affirmative action. They can demonstrate that support by the procedures they follow, the hires they make, and by the verbal support they provide when such opportunities arise.

In short, affirmative action is not an isolated phenomenon that can be delegated to an Affirmative Action Office and forgotten. Affirmative action must involve the entire campus and, to succeed, must be supported by administrators beginning at the very top. Attitudes cannot, of course, be legislated or decreed. Procedures can be developed and educational programs can be presented, however, which encourage non-discriminatory treatment of all employees, prospective employees, and students. This book is devoted to that premise.

Chapter Two

CRITERIA FOR AN EFFECTIVE AFFIRMATIVE ACTION OFFICE

Effective Affirmative Action Offices at colleges and universities have commonalities, even though they may follow different models. This chapter discusses organizational arrangement and staffing which combine these commonalities.

Reporting directly to the chief academic officer (the president or chancellor) on the campus allows the Affirmative Action Office to operate from a position of strength. Doing so enhances the prestige of the office and demonstrates the institution's commitment to affirmative action. A direct reporting relationship is logical because affirmative action responsibilities cut across organizational levels (faculty, staff, students). Direct reporting permits impartial attention to all units and individuals.

At some institutions, affirmative action responsibilities are decentralized: the Director of Affirmative Action is responsible for faculty hiring and the Director of Personnel is responsible for staff hiring. Usually these offices report to different branches of the campus hierarchy. This arrangement causes problems if the two directors do not agree on basic philosophies and procedures or if neither has the responsibility for campus-wide coordination of the institution's affirmative action program. A stronger model assigns such coordination to a Director of Affirmative Action, who is then responsible not only for employment matters but also for the institution's affirmative action program for students.

The direct reporting relationship strengthens the affirmative action program because it assures a hearing for affirmative action at a central decision-making level and permits access to the chief academic officer by the Director of Affirmative Action. A director who takes full advantage of this relationship to discuss affirmative action problems and the approaches to alleviate those problems not only can test the waters of the chief academic officer's support, but can also receive from him/her valuable advice on implementing proposed solutions. Chief academic officers achieved their positions at least partly because of their political acumen, and their suggestions on how to accomplish difficult goals or their advice as to which goals are impractical can be valuable. A director who initiates discussions with the chief academic officer on a regular basis will lay the foundation for a strong professional relationship between the two administrators and hence a more effective program. A director wishing to maximize the effectiveness of these discussions will approach them with a firm grasp of any relevant facts, a clear statement of the problem, and perhaps a proposed solution.

Sensitivity toward affirmative action and level of knowledge of affirmative action varies greatly among chief academic officers. Whatever the views of the chief academic officer, these views affect the affirmative action program. In some instances, the director may argue passionately and logically for a course of action different from that ultimately chosen; however, the director reports to the chief academic officer and must accept his/her decision once it is made. A director acting in an official capacity is part of the system--not a zealot trying to change the system from the outside. A significant part of the director's job involves working creatively within the views of high-ranking academic administrators and, if necessary, discovering the means to gradually adjust these views for better harmony with affirmative action.

Most chief academic officers want to show their support for their campus's affirmative action program in tangible ways. The following are some ways in which the chief academic officer can enhance affirmative action:

1. Highlight the institution's affirmative action efforts and successes in public speeches and in meetings with faculty and staff on campus.

2. Become informed (through the director) of departments which are underutilized and question, perhaps directly to the department, hires and promotions in those departments which do not contribute to the goal achievement.

3. Take advantage of opportunities to appoint or nominate women and minorities to committees,* for fellowships, for leadership programs, and for positions on the chief academic officer's staff.

4. Meet with community leaders and lobbying groups to engage their assistance in recruiting applicants for employment and for admission as students, in fund raising, and in suggesting ways of resolving problems.

5. Support professional development programs on campus designed to heighten sensitivity to affirmative action and improve administrative and supervisory skills.

6. Participate actively in such programs when they are presented for top-level administrators.

7. Be open to new ideas and to changing long-held conceptions.

*A caveat: Tenure and promotion decisions at most colleges and universities are based on research, teaching, and service. When the representation of members of protected groups is small, women and minorities may be appointed to a disproportionate number of committees. The result may be adverse to their tenure and promotion opportunities, as time spent serving on committees cannot be spent doing research. Officials faced with the dilemma of ensuring representation of women and minorities on committees must be sensitive to this phenomenon. An evaluation should be made of which committees are key to the campus, and members of protected groups first utilized on these committees.

8. Look to the director as an expert and as an advisor
   in developing an effective affirmative action program.

9. Choose a director who has the skills described in this
   chapter and who is capable of making well-reasoned
   recommendations which can be acted upon.

10. Provide an adequate staff and budget so that the affirma-
    tive action program can be implemented successfully
    and expeditiously.

Direct reporting provides a unique opportunity to capitalize on a
chief academic officer's support of affirmative action or to lobby for
the stronger support of a reluctant chief academic officer. A director
who moves forward with the full support and participation of the chief
academic officer will produce a successful program. In keeping with this
view, the time a director and chief academic officer spend in discussions and conversations can be a learning experience for both and can
result in a successful collaborative effort. The chief academic officer
may not fully support every recommendation the director makes; however,
conversations and memoranda clearly detailing the director's position
on a matter may result in a climate more in harmony with affirmative
action in the future.

A final word about the direct reporting relationship: a director
who aspires to use a successful affirmative action program as a stepping
stone to higher administrative positions can find no better mentor
than a chief academic officer with whom a successful working relationship has been established. Conversations with the chief academic officer
about affirmative action problems and approaches to resolving these
problems provide a unique opportunity for the director's professional
growth. The role of Director of Affirmative Action is similar to that
of the chief academic officer: both are under pressure from a variety
of constituencies and are charged with an overview of the entire institution. The major difference is the respect and prestige associated
with the position of the president or chancellor. The broad view of
decision-making that a chief academic officer must take provides a study
in power, in constituent relations, and in determining appropriate
times to fall back or to stand firm.

The staffing and budgetary requirements of an Affirmative Action
Office depend upon the size of the institution and the stage of development of the institution's program. A program in its initial stages of
development or one at an institution which has significant problems
should be staffed more fully and perhaps should emphasize different
skills than one in which the program is well established and running
smoothly. On small campuses, the affirmative action responsibilities
are frequently included with the personnel responsibilities or with a
staff position reporting to the chief academic officer. Even on such
a campus, however, someone with a thorough knowledge of affirmative
action should initially develop the program and continue to work closely
(perhaps on a consulting basis) with the staff person who maintains
the program. On large campuses, the affirmative action staff may be
supported by a network of Equal Employment Opportunity Counsellors
or by Equal Employment Opportunity Committees which assume some affirmative action responsibilites within their departments, units, or build-
ings.

An Affirmative Action Office appropriate for an institution with
800 to 1500 employees includes a director, a staff assistant or assistant

director, a secretary, and several part-time employees with specialized skills. Larger institutions will require several staff assistants or a larger cadre of part-time employees as well as additional clerical support. The clerical staff will have normal secretarial responsibilities and excellent typing skills, but must also have the ability to lay out charts and graphs artistically and clearly. The staff assistant in such an arrangement is responsible for gathering data, designing formats for its presentation, and for some preliminary analyses. Strong supervisory and communication skills are essential to the staff assistant's repertoire of abilities.

Students majoring in business, economics, or mathematics have the basic training required for the mathematical, statistical, and computer-related analyses inherent in much of the work of the Affirmative Action Office. Persons with degrees in economics, mathematics, business, and political science have the required statistical skills; however, the frequency and depth of analysis required in the Affirmative Action Office probably does not merit staffing the office for this skill except on a part-time basis. Students who have initiative and interest in the work can refine skills valuable in their own careers as well as to the Affirmative Action Office. Students can be paid out of the part-time payroll or out of work-study monies. Much of the data-related work of the Affirmative Action Office can be divided into projects performed by these students and coordinated by a staff assistant. Students working under the supervision of a staff assistant may do analyses of availability and utilization as well as studies of salary equity, turnover, promotions, and applicant flow. Most information that is distributed will not include conclusions or speculation about the reason for under-utilization or concentration, but rather will present the data and perhaps suggest ways to remedy any apparent problems.

When many of the formulae for analyses are developed and the major tasks of the Affirmative Action Office are routinized, the primary work load will shift to the staff-assistant level. Once that occurs, the director's responsibilities can be revised to include additional faculty or administrative responsibilities. As the staff assistant's responsibilities increase, of course, so should the salary for that position and perhaps the monies allocated for part-time and student staff.

The staffing of the Affirmative Action Office is keyed to the director, who, contrary to modern myth and practice, must have both specialized training and specific professional skills in order to function effectively as an agent of change within the organization. A qualification that is frequently stated in recruiting ads is a "demonstrated commitment to equal opportunity." Unfortunately, this qualification frequently translates to membership in a protected group. A composite profile of affirmative action officers indicates a numerical domination by racial minorities and women--a disproportionate representation in view of the distribution of the requisite skills in the general population.*

*See M. Reul, "EEO in Higher Education," *Forum*, October 1980, pp. 11-13; L. Liss, "AA Officers--Are They Change Agents," *Educational Record*, Fall 1977, pp. 418-428.

Some institutions state this qualification more broadly, referring to an "ability to empathize with the diverse positions of minority and majority groups, administrators and grievants, academics and nonacademics." The fallacy of this requirement becomes apparent upon closer analysis: although members of protected groups tend to trust "one of their own," whether black, female, or handicapped, most majority group males are probably most comfortable with other majority group males. Hence it is impossible to hire someone demographically acceptable to all constituencies. The appointment of a member of a protected group to the position of Director of Affirmative Action has, unfortunately, been used to appease pressure groups, often without regard to hiring the person most likely to be an effective change agent within the institution. Many campuses have taken a present faculty or staff member who is female and even more often is a member of a racial minority and assigned him/her the campus's affirmative action responsibilities. But affirmative action skills are not genetic. Being born black, Hispanic, or female is not a qualification for an affirmative action position. Campuses that fall into this trap do a disservice both to the members of protected groups and to their own affirmative action programs. Clearly, the director should be selected not because of membership in a majority or minority group but because of qualifications and skills essential to the position.

Legal knowledge is an essential qualification for a Director of Affirmative Action. Although, theoretically, anyone with strong academic and adminstrative skills can learn the basics of affirmative action, directors who are lawyers have a distinct advantage over those who are not. Many institutions specify that a Juris Doctorate (JD) is desirable or preferred; some require it. The job market for lawyers is such that institutions will not find it difficult to attract a competent lawyer with specific expertise in equal employment law to an affirmative action position.*

A lawyer approaches the laws and regulations with a level of understanding that permits a more sophisticated and creative approach to compliance with those laws and responsibilities. A lawyer will see where exceptions can be made to standard operating procedures and where charges of discrimination or lawsuits are likely to arise. A lawyer will be more adept at developing forms, guidelines, and memoranda not only because of a more sophisticated understanding of the regulations but also because a lawyer is trained to seek practical solutions to legal and regulatory requirements. A lawyer will grasp the potential impact on the institution of court decisions, agency rulings, or trends in the law and can make appropriate adjustments designed to protect the institution. A lawyer will command a respect from administrators and faculty that will contribute to necessary institutional change.

When grievances and charges of discrimination are filed against the institution, investigative and analytical skills acquired through

*A 1981 study by Dr. Richard Fields of Indiana University of affirmative action officers at 207 four-year institutions found that the study of law as a recommended area of preparation for future affirmative action officers has replaced psychology/counseling as the number-one-ranked item by practicing affirmative action officers. The study also found that law and the interpretation of court decisions have increased in importance as a duty of affirmative action officers since 1974.

legal training will prove valuable. Investigative skills may also be acquired from experience as a government investigator or compliance officer.

Government experience provides an understanding of compliance with laws and regulations from the bureaucratic point of view, knowledge that can be valuable in the investigations and compliance reviews that are a part of the director's job. Unfortunately, most government investigators have neither the degrees nor the faculty experience necessary for a position as a director at an educational institution. Some agencies have benefitted from the job market for lawyers to the extent of being able to hire lawyers for compliance positions as well as for the more traditional legal positions. The combination of legal training and a year or two of governmental experience is advantageous for any institution of higher education. Resolution of grievances and charges of discrimination require negotiation and mediation skills which may be acquired through legal training, experience as a government investigator, experience in labor relations, or experience in educational administration. Mastery of the techniques of nonthreatening inquiry and the ability to negotiate and mediate are essential skills in investigating and resolving grievances and charges of discrimination. The way in which these skills are utilized is described more fully in Chapter 8.

Because administrators and supervisors must learn good equal employment opportunity management practices, the director must have sufficient programming and organizational skills to plan successful management training programs. If the director does the actual training, knowledge of affirmative action and teaching ability are also necessary. A lawyer will have the legal and regulatory knowledge as well as the ability to make ideas and concepts clear to program participants (just as a lawyer must be able to persuade a jury). Faculty members or persons qualified for faculty appointments are likely to have the teaching skills necessary to developing and presenting a successful management training program focusing upon affirmative action.

Although prior administrative experience is an advantage to a director, the Affirmative Action Office is a relatively small department and other skills are far more important to a successful affirmative action program. The director must have or quickly acquire an understanding of academic hiring, promotion, tenure, and merit salary processes as well as a rudimentary knowledge of wage and salary administration for staff. At the level necessary for a well-functioning Affirmative Action Office, these concepts are not difficult to grasp; a director with the other skills herein described will be able to handle this area with sufficient expertise after a short time on the job.

Although actual academic administrative experience may not be essential to the success of a director, an understanding of the vagaries of academe gained by experience as a faculty member is essential. Faculty experience not only may be a measure of intellectual excellence and scholarship; it also may enhance the director's acceptability on campus when working with the academic administrators and faculty members. An appointment both as an administrator and as a faculty member strengthens the effectiveness of the director, particularly if the director uses that faculty appointment to actually teach a class in his/her academic discipline. Faculty status legitimizes the director's participation in campus governance, on campus committees, and in departmental activities. Contact with faculty and administrators as a faculty member not only enhances the director's credibility on affirmative action

matters, it also communicates to the campus community a caring about
the institution as a whole, beyond the more narrowly perceived frame-
work of affirmative action. The result will be a more hospitable environment in which affirmative action can flourish.

As with any administrative or faculty position, intangible and
often subjective factors such as the ability to communicate verbally
and in writing with people who possess widely differing levels of
understanding are important for a Director of Affirmative Action. On
most campuses, the director will need to communicate with employees who
have doctorates and those who do not have high school diplomas. These
communications will often take place in emotionally charged situations.
The parallel communication skill is in writing ability, since responses
to government agencies, memoranda explaining affirmative action, and
an affirmative action plan must be carefully phrased. Clearly, communication skills are job-related. Fortunately, candidates' vitae will
provide numerous indices of this qualification: a well-written resumé
and letter of application, publications and other indices of scholarship, an undergraduate major in a liberal arts discipline requiring
strong communication skills (history, philosophy, English, political
science, or economics, for example). The ability to answer questions
clearly and directly during the interview process is another indication
of the candidate's communication skills.

A job description focusing on these qualifications would include
the following specific elements: law degree required; liberal arts
undergraduate degree preferred; experience in investigation and negotiation; knowledge of Equal Employment Opportunity laws and regulations
essential; qualification for faculty status in an academic department.
A director with these qualifications will produce an affirmative action
program that will effect changes and improvements in many aspects of
campus life.

Equal opportunity is a field concerned with laws and regulations
and charged with feelings and emotions. Equal opportunity policies
have engendered animosity, resistance, and confusion. If equal opportunity is to prevail, the institution's commitment must extend to carefully defining the qualifications required for the position of director,
filling that position based upon those qualifications, providing an
adequate budget for an effective affirmative action effort, and supporting the program at all administrative levels.

Chapter Three

THE AFFIRMATIVE ACTION PROGRAM

Whether or not an institution has in place a well-functioning affirmative action program, this chapter provides suggestions relevant either to initiating a program or improving an existing one. Even in an institution with an established Affirmative Action Office, a new director has an opportunity to change campus perceptions about affirmative action. As the director frequently becomes the personification of the program, respect for the director often is synonymous with respect for the program. Hence a director must carefully lay the foundations for the affirmative action effort by making the program a cooperative campus endeavor. The foundations of such a program are laid through group meetings and individual conferences with department heads, deans, and other ranking administrators, as well as with individuals who are members of protected groups. Although an organizational chart is valuable in determining formal avenues of support, knowledge gained informally is often the key to real power on campus and to the support which will create a domino effect once it is gained.

Many people regard the Director of Affirmative Action as an adversary regardless of the constituency of which they are a part. Members of protected groups may be suspicious of someone who is not of "their" group or of anyone who has an "establishment" job. Administrators, especially those who are majority group males, may view the Director of Affirmative Action as the personification of overregulation by government or of undesirable change on campus. A director faced with these reservations will need to apply his/her best diplomatic and decision-making skills in order to win the allegiance of key people on campus. A key element in campus support for affirmative action will be the perception of campus leaders regarding the "reasonableness" of the director's decisions and the "understanding" of higher education s/he demonstrates. Although the support of the chief academic officer is essential, the support of faculty members, who view themselves as independent thinkers, must be considered as a uniquely academic dynamic. This collegial attitude can be used effectively in meetings with key individuals and campus groups. A willingness on the part of the director to serve on campus committees and to contribute positively to those committees--even when their relationship to affirmative action is only tangential--will reap benefits for the affirmative action program because such participation brings affirmative action into the mainstream of campus life.

A substantial number of meetings will deal clearly and directly with affirmative action. Such meetings provide the director an opportunity to explain laws and responsibilities and their practical effects on campus life, to provide an outlet for immediate reactions and problems, to solicit advice, or to suggest alternative means of dealing with campus

problems. Just as the chief academic officer's advice can be extremely
useful, so too can the advice of other campus groups. Councils of deans,
chairpersons, or department heads, for instance, can provide knowledge-
able and articulate suggestions for developing and maintaining a viable
affirmative action program. The advice of these groups may be solicited
through meetings or by circulating drafts of guidelines or memoranda
for discussion. In developing campus guidelines on sexual harassment,
for instance, a tactful director will understand that while a dean who
is primarily concerned with protecting male professors from frivolous
charges of sexual harassment by female students can hardly be classed
as a campus liberal, s/he is philosophically representative of many
members of the academic community. Guidelines and procedures for dealing
with sexual harassment must consider this point of view not only because such protections should be provided, but also because if they
are not, the guidelines or procedures are unlikely to be accepted or
implemented on campus.

   Although people have strong feelings about affirmative action,
even the most recalcitrant faculty and administrators now realize that
affirmative action is a part of academic life and that it has not
destroyed either the concept or the fact of quality education. A moderate
approach for the affirmative action program will gain the allegiance
even of some campus skeptics. The Affirmative Action Office should
serve the campus community rather than be an advocate for a particular
point of view. Members of protected groups are served because the office
provides advocacy for campus equity, a forum for discussion of grievances,
and an internal grievance procedure wherein the director can apply
mediation and negotiation skills to bring about an acceptable result
without escalation to a formal charge with an outside agency. The
Affirmative Action Office is also an office dedicated to improving
employment conditions on campus so that procedures are more fair and
open. These "services" are obviously of substantial benefit to all
members of the academic community, not only to those designated as
"protected."

   The Affirmative Action Office serves the administrative, faculty,
staff, and student constituencies on campus by developing procedures
designed to protect decision-makers from liability in charges of discrimination and lawsuits, as well as by recommending particular courses
of action for both usual and unusual circumstances. Communicating to
the campus community the "service" function of the Affirmative Action
Office can be an important part of meetings with groups and individuals
throughout the institution.

   The position of the Affirmative Action Office between members of
protected groups and the institution is most evident in the "staff"
role played by the director, who must be able to listen to beliefs and
problems of all constituencies without threat of later reprisal because
of a "line" decision. The director must also be able to advise people
in adversary roles, sometimes on both sides of the same issue. The
arrival of grievant and supervisor in the Affirmative Action Office
only hours apart, both seeking confidential advice, calls for skill,
tact, and diplomacy from the director. Both parties must receive advice
they perceive as sensible, and neither must know the other is coming or
has been to the Affirmative Action Office. Sometimes one party will
wish to meet in another location to preserve confidentiality. A director
with a faculty appointment and another office elsewhere on campus will
find that office very convenient upon such occasions.

   An advisory affirmative action committee can assist in the initial

stages of the program by developing policy, by reviewing documents and
forms, and by serving as a barometer of campus concerns. A committee
comprised of faculty members, staff, and students--and including representatives of the protected groups on campus--will provide a far different perspective for a director who will otherwise spend a disproportionate amount of time with other administrators. Even a director who
has been appointed from within the campus ranks will come to know
people who can provide valuable suggestions and support but whom s/he
probably would not have known except for this committee. The Affirmative
Action Committee can provide informal assistance in establishing the
Affirmative Action Office's credibility as a problem-solving force on
campus. The campus grapevine can be an effective source of power and
confidence or can sabotage affirmative action efforts. An Affirmative
Action Office seen as a purely administrative office will be less
successful than one known for its problem-solving skills and service
functions. Perception of the office as a source of both formal and
informal assistance to faculty and staff can be enhanced by the Affirmative Action Committee.

Simultaneously with gaining the cooperation of campus constituencies
must come an assessment both quantitatively and qualitatively of campus
strengths and weaknesses. The qualitative aspects, by nature less
scientific, require an analysis of campus problems as perceived by
members of protected groups and persons in the administrative hierarchy.
Do minorities complain that they lack opportunities for promotion? Do
minority and female students complain of racism/sexism in the classroom? Do females lack role models in leadership positions on campus?
Do people complain that no one listens to their problems or tries to
do anything about them? The answers to these and other questions
provide an indication of the qualitative perceptions of affirmative
action on campus.

The quantitative assessment begins with a campus profile showing
departments where the members of protected groups are employed. The
methodology for the development of these data is detailed in Chapter 6.
This analysis, coupled with insight into the needs for qualitative
change on campus, will lead to a formalized campus program. This campus
program differs from the formal Affirmative Action Plan prepared for
review by the Office of Contract Compliance (see Chapter 7) in its
broader focus upon needs and solutions to campus problems rather than
upon format and mathematical formulae.

The Affirmative Action Committee can assist both in identifying
problems and in developing a program for campus change. If, for
example, many administrators and faculty members believe that affirmative
action means the lowering of academic standards, even an explanation
of the law and appropriate cases complete with Supreme Court citations
may be unconvincing. More convincing to faculty and staff who hold this
belief may be the development of a campus policy, stating that only the
best qualified are to be hired. Appendix 3-1 contains an illustration
of one such statement which can be adopted through the normal campus
governance system. Although the nature of faculty and administrative
positions may make the determination of who is the best qualified an
issue upon which reasonable people may differ, adopting a best-qualified policy allays fears and diffuses hostility toward affirmative action. It does not affect the legal responsibilities of the campus: no
less an authority than the Supreme Court has clearly stated that affirmative action does not mean hiring less-qualified people. In fact, if less-
qualified members of protected groups are hired, the institution may

be subject to charges and lawsuits alleging reverse discrimination.

Illustrations of campus programs to improve the quality of campus life are found in Chapter 10, in which a management training program and a plan to improve classroom atmosphere are discussed. Each campus will demonstrate different forms of discrimination, and an effective affirmative action program will include execution of a campus plan to rectify these problems.

Chapter Four

PROCEDURES FOR FACULTY HIRING

An Affirmative Action Office staff responsible for campus-wide affirmative action spends much time on the hiring process, evaluating in statistical studies and analyses what has occurred and participating extensively in the process itself. Campus administrators with a clear idea of their responsibilities not only will be more cooperative with affirmative action efforts but will fulfill their own affirmative action responsibilities with greater confidence. Thus a major project for the Affirmative Action Office is the development of forms, procedures, and guidelines responsive both to the uniqueness of academe and to the applicable laws--guidelines which allow comparable responses to similar situations.

Academic decision-making, characterized by the process of consultation within departments and by decentralization, may result in decisions made without knowledge of institutional "common law." These traditional decision-making mechanisms did not create legal hazards for the institution until the advent of the Civil Rights laws and the doctrine of comparability in which courts weigh the allegations of discrimination against the treatment of majority group males in comparable situations. This phenomenon makes crucial an institution's responding to similar situations in a similar manner.

One response to the need to develop institutional "common law" and to inform administrators in the hiring chain of those procedures is the preparation of memoranda and guidelines which, though not officially adopted institutional policy, usually will be followed when situations arise to which they apply. Appendix 4-1 is an Index to such a guide, which, distributed to all administrators in the hiring chain, may be included in a chairperson's handbook, if one exists, or filed in departmental files under hiring procedures. The memoranda are included in this guide for easy reference and accessibility by the administrators who need this information. The memoranda can be expanded, revised, or amended as needed, perhaps as a result of discussions between the director and groups of chairpersons or deans. Such memoranda cover a variety of subjects from reassigning part-time faculty to full-time positions to discrimination against members of protected groups in the tenure and promotion process. They respond to perceived campus needs and to the qualitative aspects of the campus affirmative action program.

Guidelines developed in consultation with appropriate campus groups also provide procedural continuity in the hiring process. The director may prepare a draft of such guidelines, circulate the draft, and discuss it at meetings and with key individuals such as department chairpersons, deans, and members of the Affirmative Action Committee. If the groups and individuals who will use the guidelines and procedures or who will be affected by them participate in the development of these documents,

they will be more cooperative in implementing them. The final product
will also be of a higher quality because of the valuable suggestions
and recommendations these groups and individuals contribute. Any guidelines, procedures, or memoranda should be organic: as the need for
changes becomes apparent, changes should be made. The drafting and
consultation process takes four to six months, and the documents may
be used for one or two years before all the minor problems are adjusted.
The campus will have more consistent procedures and thus will be less
vulnerable to lawsuits and charges of discrimination as a result of
developing such guidelines.

Because search committees play a significant role in the hiring
process and because search committees may be comprised of faculty and
staff who are not experienced in the hiring process, searches are a
fertile area for the development of guidelines and procedures. The
following are areas addressed in these guidelines: when a search should
be conducted, how extensive it should be, how applications should be
generated, how the workload of a search committee may be divided, and
how the work of the search committee relates to the responsibilities
of the hiring official. Appendix 4-2 contains an Index to Guidelines
for Search Committees and a checklist to assist the committees.

The director may meet with each search committee at its first
meeting. A copy of the guidelines shared with the committee at that
time provides an opportunity for committee members to become aware of
the services and information the Affirmative Action Office provides.
The director may discuss the subjective nature of many of the decisions
the committee will make and the tendency of both males and females to
rank members of protected groups lower than equally qualified majority
group males. Evidence is accumulating that search committees may work
to the disadvantage of the candidacies of members of protected groups,
and the director will wish to sensitize the committee to that possibility.

Although the guidelines follow the search from initiation to completion, unusual situations may occur and the director may assist the
committee greatly upon those occasions. If the committee is to interview six candidates for a dean's position, for example, and an internal
candidate ranks eighth or tenth, should that candidate be interviewed?
Does the answer change if such a candidate is local but not internal
or if such a candidate is a member of a protected group? Committees
can expend enormous amounts of time wrestling with such questions. The
Director of Affirmative Action can suggest relevant considerations to
the committee or can recommend a resolution to such issues. Central to
the resolution is an awareness that the committee is a *search* committee,
not a *selection* committee. The responsibility for the *selection* lies
with the hiring official. Hence the search committee may generally be
advised that when in doubt about whether to interview someone, especially
a local candidate for whom interview expenses are minimal, the decision
probably should be to interview that person. Likewise, when the committee
is in doubt as to whether to place a candidate's name on the list of
recommendations for the hiring official, the decision should cut toward
inclusion. This is particularly true if the candidate is internal or
is a member of a protected group.

The Director of Affirmative Action can provide much assistance to
both hiring officials and search committees. S/he can become the campus
expert on hiring by developing guidelines and preparing memoranda, by
participating in the hiring process, and by encouraging practices and
procedures that are consistent and hence less likely to result in law-

suits and charges of discrimination. In addition to developing memoranda and guidelines, the director will develop forms and procedures
to provide consistency in the hiring process, documentation on a routine
basis of hiring decisions and the reasons for them, and an opportunity
for hiring officials to focus upon job-related reasons for selection
and rejection of applicants. Concurrently with development of procedures
for campus departments, the Affirmative Action Office will develop an
Intra-Office Monitoring System that dovetails with the campus-wide
procedures. The intra-office responsibilities, illustrated in Appendix
4-4, contain a Monitoring Form developed to log key information on
faculty hiring and to ensure that consistent procedures are followed
for each new hire. The forms referenced on the intra-office checklist
are shown on the Index in Appendix 4-1 and are used by individuals in
the hiring chain throughout the campus.

The campus-wide procedures will begin when the position is funded
and terminate when the hire has been administratively approved. Appendix
4-3 illustrates this procedure with a flow chart. Many affirmative
action problems can be forestalled if they are identified before a
crisis stage is reached. If the Affirmative Action Office does not
participate in the hiring process until after an offer has been made
to a candidate selected by a department, the effectiveness of the
affirmative action program may be substantially hampered. The strongest
position for the Affirmative Action Office is clearly to receive notification at the time the position is opened.

The hiring process begins when a department or hiring official has
an opening, is authorized to begin recruiting, and notifies the Affirmative Action Office of the vacancy (Appendix 4-5). Once notified that a
vacancy exists, the Affirmative Action Office begins monitoring that
opening by logging it on the Intra-Office Monitoring System and by
incorporating it into the Goal Achievement Log (Appendix 4-6). The
department proceeds with its recruitment procedures, which have been
filed in the Affirmative Action Office (see Appendix 4-7).

By receiving early notification of faculty openings, the Affirmative Action Office becomes a central point for information about academic
vacancies on campus; a natural result of this is the development of
another recruiting device, a Job Register, illustrated in Appendix 4-8.
The Job Register can be prepared on a monthly or bi-weekly basis, depending upon the number of vacancies and the deadlines for receipt of
applications. Some of the information requested on the Notification
Form is designed specifically for preparation of the Job Register, so
that the Notification Form serves a dual purpose. The Job Register can
be distributed campus-wide to deans and chairpersons, posted on bulletin
boards, mailed to other institutions, mailed to organizations serving
applicants from protected groups or to individuals who may wish to be
informed of openings on campus. The Job Register has benefits in addition to its utility as a recruiting device: it gives the Affirmative
Action Office visibility on a regular basis and promotes the office as
one serving the academic community.

Although actual recruiting for faculty positions is generally a departmental responsibility, the Affirmative Action Office monitors this
part of the hiring process and collects demographic data on the applicants. The tool for gathering this information is the Data Collection
Card illustrated in Appendix 4-9. This card represents the Affirmative
Action Office's interface with prospective faculty members when, as
applicants, they are asked for the demographic information needed for
maintaining data on applicant flow. Because requests for this informa-

tion have brought letters of outrage and refusals to provide the data from numerous applicants, requests must be carefully phrased and limited to essential data. The Data Collection Card illustrated not only has a proven record of use for more than four years without a single objection, but during that time has had an overall return rate exceeding that of previous instruments. The name of the applicant is included so that accurate applicant flow can be determined for each position. If the name is not included on the card, the applicant flow can be analyzed only by department, by school, or by institution--an analysis destined to be far less effective in identifying problem areas.

The card is sent by the academic department with a letter acknowledging receipt of the candidate's application and vita. The card is mailed to the Affirmative Action Office by the applicant. There, the data is logged and the information shared with the department on a statistical basis only. It is not used by the department in the selection process. Appendix 4-10 is a Demographic Data Summary which is sent to the department whenever a position has been filled. The form combines information from the Data Collection Cards and from the Administrative Approval Form (discussed below), provides a reminder of the department's utilization as compared with availability, and details the effectiveness of the recruiting sources used for that position.

Although federal regulations encourage using the ethnic media for recruiting applicants, most minority and female applicant flow for faculty positions is generated from the same sources as applicant flow for majority group males: the professional journals of the academic discipline and personal contacts by department members. The Affirmative Action Office can evaluate the effectiveness of a department's recruiting efforts by reviewing the sources indicated by applicants returning the Demographic Data Cards or by changing slightly the name or address to which the applicants are asked to reply in each publication in which an ad is place: Dr. R.K Smith or Dr. Ruth K. Smith or Dr. R. Kane Smith. The name or address to which the vita is sent will provide information as to the recruiting source to which each applicant is responding. This analysis becomes important if an Impact Ratio Analysis (see Chapter 7) indicates a disparity between applicant flow and availability. Applicant flow and the related forms are discussed in Chapter 6 as part of the data collection activity and the personnel activity report.

Academic departments must maintain applicant pools as a part of normal recruiting procedures so that if a vacancy arises unexpectedly, a number of qualified applicants will be considered for that vacancy. Departments faced with a late resignation or high student demand for a particular course may consider applicants of both sexes and all races even when specific advertising is not possible if the department has a previously generated applicant pool. Most applicant pools of this type consist predominantly of unsolicited vitae received by the department. This rather unscientifically developed applicant pool may not contain sufficient numbers of members of protected groups for affirmative action to be a viable consideration in the hiring process. Hence, a substantive contribution to generating applicants for academic positions can be coordinated by the Affirmative Action Office in the form of a "pool ad," published in local or regional newspapers on an annual basis for the expressed purpose of generating applicants whose vitae will be placed in departmental applicant pools. Such an ad provides an opportunity for members of all demographic groups to be considered for vacancies that may arise. The ad must be carefully phrased so that the respondents to the ad are fully aware that positions may not presently

be available in their specific disciplines. Appendix 4-11 illustrates
a pool ad which can be used as a recruiting device.

The key document for academic hiring is the Administrative Approval
Form, illustrated in Appendix 4-12, which provides documentation and
assurance that the proper procedures have been followed in the hiring
process. This form can also be called an Affirmative Action Approval
Form, but since the signatures of several other administrators are
required, that is not only inaccurate but places an undesirable onus
on affirmative action as being the source of yet another form. The form
illustrated is characterized by the use of codes to present necessary
information in as concise a format as possible. Coding the reasons for
nonselection or providing a concise list of standard reasons not only
simplifies the paperwork involved in the approval process, but also
focuses departments and search committees on job-related reasons for
rejecting applicants and for the selection of the recommended candidate.
All of the coded reasons are relatively objective and are legitimate
reasons for not selecting an applicant (see Appendix 4-13).

Because some legitimate reasons will not be coded, departments may
create their own reasons in some instances. When reviewing reasons for
nonselection created by the department and requiring the exercise of
professional judgment, the director must review for job-relatedness
and for nondiscrimination toward members of protected groups. The review
will include special scrutiny for such reasons as candidate selected
had "better communications skills" or "better leadership qualities."
If lack of communication skills is used only for minority group applicants and never for majority group applicants, or if lack of leadership
skills is used only for females, some subtle discrimination may be
occurring, and the director may wish to discuss these reasons with the
department chairperson or dean.

A catchall that departments may favor is "candidate selected was
better qualified than this applicant." That reason is so general as to
be no reason at all. The director may wish to educate chairpersons not
to use so vague a reason by calling them and discussing the reasons
with them whenever such vague reasons appear. Often such conversations
will uncover more specific reasons that are both more objective and
clearly job-related. Memoranda discussing the subtleties of reasons
for nonselection are included in Appendix 4-14.

The reasons for nonselection are a key documentation effort that,
as part of the daily business records of the institution, may be admitted
into evidence during litigation. Thus another factor for the director
to consider in reviewing an Approval Form is whether any of the applicants can sue the institution over this hire. Obviously, if all the
applicants for a position are demographically similar, the likelihood
of the institution's being sued is substantially decreased. Some positions (in the sciences, for example) may have only oriental male applicants; other positions (in women's studies, for example) may have only
white female applicants. If such a situation occurs, a problem may be
indicated in the applicant flow or recruiting area; however, lopsided
applicant flow frequently is related to the availability in that particular subspecialty. If demographic similarity in applicant flow occurs
with regularity only in certain departments or contrary to the availability data, the director will wish to discuss the problem with the
department. That is a different problem, however, than the department's
selection for a particular position.

The Approval Form should always be examined in light of the relationship between a department's utilization and availability. A depart-

ment's failure to make a hire in an underutilized area may be the
result of the absence of qualified candidates in the applicant pool,
the superior qualifications of the person selected, the voluntary with-
drawal from consideration of an attrative member of a protected group,
or the inability to meet salary or other requirements necessary to
attract such a person to the institution. The director should carefully
analyze such phenomena, perhaps in consultation with the department
chairperson, because each goal which is not met must be explained in the
Affirmative Action Plan (see Chapter 7).

The effective use of the Approval Form for affirmative action purposes depends in part upon its placement in the administrative process.
Once a department has selected a candidate, the department is usually
anxious to make a formal offer. The checks and balances provided by the
review process create numerous potential bottlenecks which can delay a
department's making that offer. As nothing raises the ire of faculty
members like administrative delays, the acceptance of the affirmative
action program is related to the expeditious processing of the Approval
Form. The entire approval process can take less than a day if all administrators who must review the form give it priority. In situations
where time is of the essence, Approval Forms can be hand-carried through
the process in a matter of hours. A key to the success of the approval
process from the vantage of affirmative action is that the director
reviews the process for affirmative action consideration *before* a formal
offer is made. An efficient approval system balances affirmative action
and the department's legitimate desire to process new-hires expeditiously.

Problems which surface in the approval process are best resolved
at the lowest possible level. If the reasons for nonselection are inappropriate, for example, the director will consult with the chairperson,
and the department may submit a new form containing acceptable reasons.
If the problem with the Approval Form is substantive rather than procedural, more delicate maneuvering is required. The director who has
established the Affirmative Action Office as part of the academic
community will often be alerted through the campus grapevine to hires
requiring special review. Only rarely, when affirmative action has been
most blatantly ignored, will the director be able to stop a hire that
a department has recommended. The director's goal should be, of course,
to ensure nondiscriminatory treatment for all, but also to use any
irregularities that occur as opportunities to educate those in the
hiring chain against future such irregularities.

The educational process can occur in meetings involving those in
the hiring chain at which the irregularities or subtleties of discrimination are fully discussed, or in a memorandum detailing the problems
with the hire. If the problems are not resolved informally, the director
may wish to send the Approval Form forward unsigned with an accompanying
memorandum. The director's power is to recommend only. Those in the
hiring chain are the decision-makers. The director's responsibility is
to advise and to advocate the best course of action to the chief academic officer, who is the final link in the hiring chain.

Although the hire recommended by the department may be approved in
spite of the director's not certifying that affirmative action has been
considered, the issues raised in a thoughtful and persuasive memorandum
may forestall a similar situation's arising in the future. Certainly,
all involved in the process will be more aware of affirmative action
and the significance of the process. Hence, even if the director's
recommendation is not followed, the affirmative action program may be

enriched in the long term.

The real key to the approval process is fair treatment for all applicants. Discrimination not only subjects the institution to charges and lawsuits, but also violates precepts of fair treatment--an inequity which is anathema to all free thinking people. Although the spirit of affirmative action cannot be legislated or regulated, procedures designed to provide fair treatment and a review of hiring decisions contribute greatly to providing true equality of opportunity.

The majority of academic positions, both faculty and administrative, will be filled in the customary manner: the position will be announced by advertising in the appropriate journals; a search committee or departmental selection committee will screen the applicants and make a recommendation to the hiring official. This process normally takes three to six months. For a variety of reasons (usually related to the academic calendar), these normal procedures may be impractical or even impossible to follow in some instances. A system which waives the normal search procedures, though not affirmative action considerations, is a practical means of dealing with these exigencies. A waiver system must be used with restraint and only in extraordinary situations, as illustrated in the guidelines in Appendix 4-15.

A waiver is not used in filling tenure-track positions. Instead, a visiting title is used, and if a regular position is funded for the following year, the visiting person can compete for the tenure-track position along with other applicants in a national search. Because members of protected groups do not always surface at the most opportune times, the waiver permits an institution to take advantage of an opportunity to hire such a person, probably with a visiting appointment, when s/he applies. The waiver system also expedites the hiring of distinguished professors who may visit the campus for a semester or a year.

The academic calendar places a restriction on hiring that occurs in few other employment situations. This restriction provides an opportunity for the Director of Affirmative Action to find creative solutions to staffing simultaneously with fully considering affirmative action. The pool ad, used formally to replenish applicant pools, and the waiver system effectively balance affirmative action considerations with these staffing needs.

A cornerstone of an effective affirmative action program is a system providing essential checks and balances as well as proper documentation without becoming so bureaucratic as to antagonize the department chairpersons whose cooperation is crucial to the program's success. Judgments balancing those factors must be made in setting up a workable system of academic hiring.

A judgment may be made, for instance, to treat full-time academic appointments differently from part-time appointments. Part-time forms and procedures may be simpler because part-time positions are valued differently both in terms of prestige and money. The director may decide that, whereas the purpose of the Approval Form for full-time positions is both monitoring of procedures and documentation, the purpose of a part-time hiring form (Appendix 4-16) is primarily documentation. If the overall process results in a suitable percentage of women and minorities being hired, the part-time form adequately documents who was hired and who was considered. The form is kept as a record in the Affirmative Action Office and need not complete the full round of signatures the full-time form must complete.

The director may decide to keep the Approval Form for full-time positions as simple and straightforward as possible. Through the extensive use of codes, the form illustrated in Appendix 4-12 replaced an eight-page form. Departments actually provide more information on the two-page form, but because the format is more acceptable, antagonism to the bureaucracy of the affirmative action forms has evaporated.

Judgments of this nature are a staple of life for a director who is setting up a new affirmative action program or making substantial changes in an existing program. Such judgments are best made in the collegial atmosphere of academe by consultation with appropriate groups and individuals on campus. Sharing a draft of a proposed form with the persons who will be using the form is not only a wise move politically but will probably improve the quality of the final product. Even in the development of forms, procedures, and guidelines, mainstreaming the affirmative action program into campus life will result in a stronger and more effective program.

Chapter Five

AFFIRMATIVE ACTION AND SUPPORT STAFF

Although centralization of the employment relations services for personnel is common in smaller institutions and is on the increase in larger colleges and universities, many institutions presently assign the responsibilities for academic and for staff personnel to different offices. When academic personnel responsibilities are decentralized, the Affirmative Action Office has major oversight responsibilities for faculty hiring. Many of these responsibilities parallel those of a Director of Personnel in charge of employment relations for staff. Under the usual division of responsibilities, the Director of Affirmative Action will have campus-wide responsibilities for faculty hiring and for affirmative action and the Director of Personnel will be responsible for staff hiring. The Directors of Affirmative Action and Personnel thus will have many opportunities to work together.

Because the mere existence of an Affirmative Action Office may be threatening to a Director of Personnel whose procedures and responsibilities antedate the Affirmative Action Office, the Director of Affirmative Action must once again use diplomacy, tact, and frequently a great deal of patience to establish a satisfactory relationship with the Director of Personnel and with the staff of that office. In some instances the personnel director's resistance may exceed the perseverance of even the most determined affirmative action director. If such a situation exists the Director of Affirmative Action has a number of alternatives. S/he can concentrate on other affirmative action matters until the climate changes, solicit guidance from the chief academic officer as to how to elicit the personnel director's cooperation, or arrange meetings that include others in addition to the Directors of Personnel and of Affirmative Action. A recalcitrant director may be reluctant to appear uncooperative in the presence of members of the Affirmative Action Committee, for instance, or in the presence of the person to whom s/he reports.

The role of the Director of Affirmative Action should not be to take over functions appropriately housed in the Personnel Office but rather to work with the Director of Personnel to ensure that relevant information is being documented and that procedures compatible with affirmative action are being followed. This relationship implies some monitoring of the Personnel Office by the Affirmative Action Office, but it also implies a close working relationship between the directors and with their respective staffs. Indeed, administration of affirmative action matters and administration of staff employment require many similar skills. Hence the Directors of Personnel and of Affirmative Action can form a natural alliance to improve the programs in both jurisdictions.

In consultation with the Director of Personnel, the Director of

Affirmative Action will develop systems to monitor the employment processes affecting staff personnel. Notice of staff positions which are open should routinely be posted in key places on campus and distributed to organizations specializing in placement of members of protected groups. Posting which does not generate sufficient or demographically representative applicant flow is usually followed by or occurs simultaneously with local or regional advertising. The key to avoiding charges of discrimination at this stage of the hiring process is consistency. If posting and advertising is a routine part of filling job vacancies, complaints from potential applicants alleging denial of opportunities to apply for jobs are unlikely to occur.

The Director of Affirmative Action should review the employment application form so that it can be purged of irrelevant or potentially discriminatory questions. Many applicants are sufficiently enlightened to observe and be offended by questions that may be discriminatory. Since the first impression an applicant has of an institution is frequently through the employment application, this form should be representative of the nondiscriminatory treatment the applicant would expect to receive as an employee of that institution. Questions that may be offensive or of questionable legality should be expunged from the application form. Such questions include: race, sex, marital status, age, date of birth, disability, veteran status, military record, spouse's name, spouse's occupation, citizenship, type of visa, and arrest record. Some states and institutions have adopted, as official law or policy, standards similar to the Pre-employment Inquiry guidelines included as Appendix 5-1.

Appendix 5-2 contains an Application for Employment form focusing on employment-related information. This suggested form includes information regarding military service under specialized training skills and the employment record. The form focuses on the contributions of older applicants who may not have been in the workforce for a time as well as on recent graduates or applicants with a more traditional employment history by including community activities as well as extracurricular collegiate activities and by including leadership roles and volunteer activities among "other qualifications."

When an applicant is hired, information traditionally requested on the Application for Employment is necessary for institutional record-keeping or for payroll and insurance benefits. Once a person is hired, the institution is free to ask many questions that are ill-advised on the Application for Employment. Appendix 5-3 illustrates a supplemental data form which provides employee information essential to the institution but not asked on the Application for Employment.

The interview process, as well as the employment application, must be both bias-fee and sensitive to the prospective employees. Most interviewers in Personnel Offices are trained professionals familiar with appropriate interview techniques and questions. Workshops and conferences offer refresher courses and a personnel director who understands affirmative action can suggest to his/her staff interviewing techniques that are not discriminatory.

Department heads, however, present a different problem. Because their expertise is in areas other than employment interviewing, they must be sensitized to the interview process. As the key for interviewers in both the Personnel Office and in the departments is to focus on job-related inquiries, a training program such as that described in Chapter 10 may prove a wise investment of an institution's time and money.

The preemployment process often includes tests, particularly for clerical positions. The Equal Employment Opportunity Commission (EEOC) and the Office of Contract Compliance (OFCCP) define a test as "Any paper and pencil or performance measure used as a basis for any employment decision." Tests include measures of general intelligence, mechanical or clerical aptitudes, dexterity and coordination, knowledge and proficiency, interests, attitudes, personality and temperament. As a general rule, any tests given as part of the qualification process must be validated if they result in the disproportionate elimination of members of protected groups. Because validation studies are difficult, expensive, and sometimes impossible, many institutions choose the "bottom line" approach, one which both the EEOC and some federal courts have accepted. Instead of validating each step of the hiring process, the institution develops an overall process that results in suitable percentages of minorities and women being hired. The institution uses unvalidated tests, but makes adjustments at other stages in the hiring process to insure unbiased hiring. The "bottom line" rather than a particular step along the way justifies the process as nondiscriminatory.

Alternatively, the Directors of Personnel and of Affirmative Action may choose to validate individual tests to determine whether they have an adverse impact on members of protected groups by using the Impact Ratio Analysis described in Chapter 7. Although tests which do not have a discriminatory impact on members of protected groups may be used without validation, use of a test that may have a discriminatory impact requires validation in accordance with the Uniform Guidelines on Employee Selection Procedures (Appendix 5-11). Proof of validation is based on procedures such as those described in "Standards for Educational and Psychological Tests and Manuals," published by the American Psychological Association, 1200 Seventeenth Street, N.W., Washington, D.C. 20036. Validation studies should be performed by experts because of their highly technical nature. Both the American Psychological Association and the American Board on Counseling Services, Inc. (1607 New Hampshire Avenue, N.W., Washington, D.C. 20009) provide names of such experts.

Testing is compatible with higher education's concern with high-quality employees. Administrative offices obviously have an interest in good office skills. Math or science departments may need typists especially adept at statistical typing. Obviously, skilled employees are needed to staff maintenance crews and craft positions. Job-related testing is an efficient means of determining an applicant's qualifications. Institutions must use tests cautiously, however, because of the laws and regulations in this area. The key is to ensure the job-relatedness of tests and a nondiscriminatory selection rate if nonvalidated tests are used. All tests must be given by the Personnal Office; individual departments should not create their own unvalidated tests. A department with needs for personnel with specialized skills may work with the Personnel Office to develop tests meeting testing requirements.

A personnel director who works cooperatively with the Affirmative Action Office in developing affirmative action oversight for staff can make a substantial contribution to the program, since the Director of Personnel, not the Director of Affirmative Action, is likely to have the best opportunities to funnel members of protected groups into positions on campus. Most institutions have an established system for hiring nonacademic staff; illustrations included herein are part of one such process.

Just as with faculty hiring, affirmative action must be intrinsic to staff hiring and considered from the beginning of the hiring process. A flow chart included as Appendix 5-4 illustrates the hiring process

and affirmative action participation in that process. The hiring process for staff begins when the department notifies the Personnel Office
of a vacancy. The Personnel Requisition (Appendix 5-5) initiates the
posting and advertising process described earlier in this chapter, and
provides for a description of special skills desired for the position.
A personnel staff member will discuss these qualifications with the
department to ensure job-relatedness. In many institutions, initial
screening occurs in the Personnel Office, although departments make
the final selection. The Personnel Office has control over who is referred to departments for interviews and has an opportunity to question
departmental choices that might have been discriminatory.

The Personnel Office documents its own interview process by the
Personnel Referral Form illustrated in Appendix 5-6. This form provides
essential documentation both for monitoring the Personnel Office's
affirmative action responsibilities and for investigating grievances
and charges of discrimination should they occur. The form is a business
record, admissible in court on the issue of how an applicant was treated
procedurally and perhaps substantively. The Personnel Referral Form
should include as part of the disposition a reason for nonreferral,
so that the personnel interviewer's action is also part of the record.
Cooperation between the Affirmative Action Office and the Personnel
Office on referrals to departments will increase the likelihood that
hiring goals are met. A current copy of the Goal Achievement Log
(Appendix 5-7) provides the Personnel Office with current information,
and a departmental hiring goal that provides leverage will increase
the likelihood that goals are met.

An Applicant Referral Form (Appendix 5-8) is sent to the department
for each applicant referred for consideration and interviewing. For
affirmative action purposes, the most important item on the form is
the reason for nonselection of the applicant (item 20). Department heads
must learn to choose employees and to reject applicants for reasons
that are both job-related and nondiscriminatory. A training program
described in Chapter 10, an orientation session dealing specifically
with this form, development of standard reasons for nonselection
similar to the coding for faculty positions, and discussions with individual department heads who submit inappropriate reasons are mechanisms
for this educational process. The key role of the Personnel Office
becomes apparent in that office's monitoring of reasons for nonselection,
especially in areas of underutilization of minorities or women, because
the Affirmative Action Office will examine Applicant Referral Forms
only for positions in departments with unmet goals at the end of the
Affirmative Action Plan year. The knowledge of and commitment to affirmative action of the Director of Personnel and his/her staff is crucial
to affirmative action for administrative and support staff.

Because the Personnel Office monitors departmental hiring for staff,
the role of the Affirmative Action Office is primarily one of analysis
after the hiring has occurred. The Affirmative Action Office receives
the information indicated on the flow chart from the Personnel Office
on a monthly or bi-weekly basis. An Intra-Office Monitoring System for
staff (Appendix 5-9) for use within the Affirmative Action Office will
ensure that all information necessary for the Affirmative Action Plan
and for other analyses has been received in the Affirmative Action
Office. A collaboration between the Personnel Office and the Affirmative Action Office regarding these data is required so that affirmative
action analyses can be performed. The directors of these offices must
establish a system that is practical for their institution for providing

the following information to the Affirmative Action Office on a regular
basis:

1. Job postings and job descriptions for all open positions.

2. Demographic Data Cards (Appendix 4-9) returned to the
   Affirmative Action Office by applicants (those not mailed
   may be collected in the Personnel Office and forwarded
   to the Affirmative Action Office).

3. Copies of the Personnel Referral Form (Appendix 5-6)
   on which applicants for each position are listed and
   the applicant selected is indicated.

4. Copies of the Applicant Referral Form (Appendix 5-8)
   for all positions for which a goal was not met.

5. Copies of the Termination Log kept in the Personnel
   Office and illustrated in Appendix 5-10.

Demographic data for staff applicant flow analysis is collected
just as for faculty: by providing a Data Collection Card for each
applicant who requests an application for employment. Information provided by the card illustrated in Appendix 4-9 is logged and analyzed
as described in Chapters 6 and 7.

In addition to information on the hiring and promotion process,
the Personnel Office will keep data on terminations. The Affirmative
Action Office must have access to this information, perhaps in a format
similar to that illustrated in Appendix 5-10. This information is
essential for developing the Affirmative Action Plan and for analyzing
staff turnover with a view toward identifying potential problem areas.
Analyses prepared in the Affirmative Action Office and based on such
information allow the Personnel Office to perform its work more effectively.

The benefits for the institution of cooperation between the
Personnel Office and the Affirmative Action Office are substantial.
Both directors can enhance the efforts of their own offices through such
a collaboration. Difficult as it may be initially to establish a
workable system involving both offices, the end result will be a stronger
and more effective affirmative action program.

Chapter Six

COLLECTING AND DEVELOPING DATA

The collection and analysis of data is detailed work which must be
performed accurately and is probably the most time-consuming task in
the Affirmative Action Office. In all but very small institutions, at
least one person will work full-time on data collection and analysis.
Because the work is divisible into projects, several people, perhaps
students with mathematical and statistical skills, can work simultaneously on different projects. Students are capable of working
responsibly with confidential personnel data, but the privileged
nature of this information must be discussed with all employees who
will have access to it. This chapter is devoted specifically to developing a data base from which studies and analyses can be conducted and
which has the following components: data control boxes, computer-
generated reports, and a system of logging and tallying personnel
activity information.

The key to a manually developed data base is a card file containing
a card for each employee; developing the data base is tedious but pays
big dividends at later stages in the analysis of data. Three card
files or "data control boxes" will be developed: one for faculty, a
second for staff, and a third organized by position number. The project,
utilizing several staff members simultaneously, involves transferring
key information from employee personnel files to 5 x 8 index cards.

Information for the cards exists wherever the personnel files are
kept. In institutions which decentralize these functions, the Affirmative Action Office may have to work with several different offices
in order to develop and to update the cards for affirmative action
purposes. If card files existing in other offices contain the essential
information and are easily accessible, the Affirmative Action Office
should consider making an arrangement with these offices for access
instead of preparing its own files. Appendix 6-1 illustrates typical
cards from faculty and staff files. To make key information readily
accessible, the cards are color-coded by sex (white cards for male,
green cards for females) or by EEO categroy (white cards for administrators, blue cards for professionals, etc.). Each card contains the
following information for each employee: name, birth date, race, sex,
citizenship, education level, service date, tenure and promotion dates
(for academic appointments), position title, and salary history. The
third file, organized by position number and also illustrated in
Appendix 6-1, provides a history of each job and insight into which
jobs, job groups, and EEO categories have historically been "male jobs,"
"female jobs," or "minority jobs."

The cards will be useless unless they are updated regularly. Each
institution has its own system of recording personnel changes. Updating

the cards may be as simple as gaining access to new employee information forms and to staff change forms on a daily basis in cooperation
with offices such as personnel, academic affairs, budget, or payroll.
Appendix 6-2 illustrates a staff change form from which data is extracted
for updating the cards. A comparison with the information recorded on
the Data Control Cards (Appendix 6-1) shows the type of information
extracted from this form. With the cooperation of an office in which
the new employee information forms and the staff change forms are filed,
the Affirmative Action Office can maintain current data control boxes.

Although a manual data system may be most efficient for a small
institution, larger institutions may have little choice but to use a
computer-based system. Often multi-campus systems adopt a computer
system as the best means of acquiring uniformity among the campuses
in reporting data. A computer system can be an efficient tool for the
Affirmative Action Office in the preparation of studies and analyses.
The data base is stored in the computer, just as the manual data base
is stored in the data control boxes described above. The information
in a manual system is retrieved by pulling cards and extracting the
necessary information from them; the information in a computer system
is retrieved on a computer report.

In some institutions the data base "resides" in either the payroll
department or the personnel department. The Affirmative Action Office
is thus a user of the data rather than an owner of the data base. When
the information required by the Affirmative Action Office comes from
a data base owned by payroll or personnel, that department's data takes
precedence. Payroll information takes priority, for example, because
it is more important that employees get paid than for the race and
sex of employees to be added to a data base. Hence the data needed to
generate information required by the Affirmative Action Office may not
be updated with the same frequency as the data required for the payroll
function. Because the needs of the owner (payroll and/or personnel)
may be different from those of the user, the Affirmative Action Office
may have to negotiate with both the owner and the computer center to
acquire usable information. The goal is an accurate computer-generated
report containing information necessary to prepare affirmative action
reports and analyses. The report is the product of what is stored in
the data base. Obviously the degree of control over the information
is greater for owners than for users. Thus owning the data base results
in quicker access to usable computer reports for the Affirmative Action
Office.

Although a computer system can be an efficient means to retrieve
data for reports and analysis, a manual data base may also be necessary
to correct an edit run or otherwise to ensure report accuracy. A manual
data system is often more accurate and more current, especially if the
Affirmative Action Office is not a data owner. If checking an edit run
against an accurate manual data base takes more time than simply using
a manual data base, adjustments in the system are essential. The major
advantage of a computer system is economy of time. Usually the director
of the computer center will recognize that an inaccurate data base is
an institutional problem, not just an affirmative action problem; other
offices such as admissions, financial aid, and budget are likely to
have user/owner problems similar to those of the Affirmative Action
Office. The computer center can facilitate resolution of these problems
by initiating meetings and/or training sessions with both users and
owners of data in order to improve the usefulness of computer reports.
Developing accurate report data for the Affirmative Action Office may

take several years of diligent effort by many people.

As the Affirmative Action Office wrestles with developing the computer system into a useful tool, someone in the institution will surface who can cut through the red tape. This person may be located in the computer center, in faculty personnel, in staff personnel, or in payroll, but efficient utilization of the computer requires finding that person and establishing a working relationship with him/her.

As users of computer-generated information, the affirmative action staff must have a rudimentary knowledge of computers. The computer center may suggest ways for the affirmative action staff to acquire the necessary skills or to familiarize themselves with the idiosyncrasies of the institution's program. Once the format of the report is defined, the report can be used in much the same manner as a manual data base, but much more efficiently.

Information can be provided in a variety of formats. Appendix 6-3 illustrates a format providing data on full-time faculty and staff members. To tap computer information, the employee's name and social security number are required. In addition, the printout includes the employee's department, title, educational level, race, sex, age, citizenship, starting date, change of title date, tenure date (if faculty), and salary. All of these data are used to develop the formal Affirmative Action Plan described in Chapter 7 and to produce additional studies and analyses. Once this information has been included in the data base by the owner, reports can be requested which provide lists and counts of all tenured black faculty, all females above a certain salary range, or all members of a given department. Computer reports are an efficient means to illustrate such information.

A computer report shows what is in the data base on a given day. In requesting the report, the director and staff assistant can choose any day that is logical. October 30, for example, would include new faculty and would provide sufficient time for demographic data concerning those new faculty to be added to the data base. An October 30 report also may be used for filing the institutional EEO-6 report, required bianually about January 1. The last day of the fiscal year, too, may be a logical date. New positions are often funded as of the beginning of a new fiscal year, so the last day of the fiscal year is used for the Affirmative Action Plan discussed in Chapter 7. Whatever date is chosen, deadline dates by which additions and corrections must have been added to the data base must be clearly communicated to all personnel with that responsibility. Their cooperation is essential because both human error and a time lag between the date of the personnel activity and the entry of data into the computer can cause a lack of data integrity.

In short, a computer-based system can be an efficient and effective means to store and retrieve demographic data. A computer system instead of or in addition to a manual data system requires some sophistication and knowledge on the part of the user. Staff members can develop these skills on the job with the cooperation of other departments and individuals. Hiring students with computer skills can be an effective means to acquire computer expertise on the affirmative action staff.

One of the first uses of these data, whether located in data control boxes or in a computer system, is creation of a series of faculty and staff profiles. A profile is a demographic picture of a department or a job group on a given day. The format for a departmental profile may be a computer report or a summary developed from the information in the data control boxes. Whether the profile is developed manually or by

computer, each department should be asked to verify the information
pertaining to that department. This step ensures accurate information,
involves the departments in preparing the Affirmative Action Plan and
related studies, and provides statistical credibility for later studies.
A department which has verified a profile of the department's employees
will be more reluctant to challenge the accuracy of later reports and
analyses from the Affirmative Action Office. A departmental profile
for an academic departmental is illustrated in Appenddix 6-4. A summary
of minority representation developed from the profiles and spanning
a nine-year period shows changes occurring over that period (see
Appendix 6-5).

The "truth telling" inherent in such a summary can be a boon to
affirmative action. Correct information widely distributed is an indication of openness and of the institution's willingness to change those
areas where women and minorities are numerically underrepresented. The
public dissemination of this information also acts as a means of exert-
ing subtle pressure on departments to recruit and hire more members
of protected groups and as a means of complementing departments which
have successfully hired and promoted women and minorities. Eventually
the Affirmative Action Office will prepare the availability and utilization analyses detailed in Chapter 7, providing additional perspective
on the information presented in the summary.

A final component of the data base essential to an effective program
and required for an Affirmative Action Plan developed in conformity
with Revised Order 4 addresses itself to logging applicant flow, new
hires, promotions, terminations, and offers of employment. Although
this information is sometimes included in a computer data base, more
likely this information will be developed manually. The information,
eventually summarized in Personnel Activity Reports and analyzed by
using Impact Ratio Analysis as discussed in Chapter 7, must be collected
and logged for both faculty and staff.

Applicant flow for faculty positions will be developed from two
sources: the Demographic Data Cards (Appendix 4-9) and the listing of
applicants on the Administrative Approval Form (Appendix 4-12). This
information, tallied on a Demographic Data Summary (Appendix 4-10) and
on the Applicant Flow Data Log (Appendix 6-6), becomes the Affirmative
Action Office's record of the applicant flow for each faculty position.
Because this demographic information is provided voluntarily, the data
will include a number of people whose race and sometimes sex is unknown.
These individuals are logged and tallied as unknowns and eventually
distributed among the known categories.

Applicant flow for staff positions is developed primarily from the
Demographic Data Cards (Appendix 4-9). Some personnel offices log
demographic data on applicants by a visual scan, but this is not as
accurate as using the cards. Demographic data logged during an interview in the Personnel Office (Appendix 5-6) and combined with information on the data collection cards provides both broader coverage and
greater accuracy. The Data Collection Cards connect the applicant with
the position applied for, allow the applicant to respond to the information request (thus including applicants who do not "look" black or
Hispanic or handicapped), and provide for an analysis of the effectiveness of the recruiting sources used for that position.

Since the Personnel Office is usually responsible for generating
applicant flow for staff positions, applicant flow information should
be shared primarily with that office. A Termination Log (Appendix 5-10)

permits the same kind of applicant flow analysis to be performed for staff positions as was described above for faculty positions. The log, kept chronologically for each EEO category, summarizes the applicant flow information gathered from all sources, and is shared with the Personnel Office on a routine basis, either monthly or quarterly. The frequency will depend upon the number of positions filled and the degree to which generating applicants who are members of protected groups is a problem.

Faculty new hires are compiled from the Administrative Approval Forms (Appendix 4-12) and logged on the Affirmative Action Office's Intra-Office Monitoring Form (Appendix 4-4). That form provides the demographic data necessary for summarizing new hire activity, as "applicants name" is synonymous with "new hire." A New Hire Summary is part of the Personnel Activity Report in the Affirmative Action Plan (Chapter 7). Faculty promotions resulting from the tenure and promotion process are available from the Office of Academic Affairs or Office of the Provost or from the faculty profile (Appendix 6-4). Faculty terminations usually coincide with the academic year and are determined by comparing faculty profiles for successive years; this information is logged (Appendix 5-10) and summarized on the Personnel Activity Report in the Affirmative Action Plan. Reasons for termination include expiration of appointment, terminal year after denial of tenure, resignation, retirement, or disability. Offers of employment that are declined are recorded on the Intra-Office Monitoring Form and summarized on the Personnel Activity Report. Offers of employment may provide evidence of good faith attempts to meet goals set in the Affirmative Action Plan.

New hires and promotional information for staff is compiled from the Staff Change Forms (Appendix 6-2) and the Personnel Referral Form (Appendix 5-6). This information, logged on the Applicant Flow Data Form (Appendix 6-7) is summarized in the Affirmative Action Plan on the Personnel Activity Report (Chapter 7). Staff terminations are logged by the Personnel Office and shared with the Affirmative Action Office on a regular basis. This information, verified by the Staff Change Forms (Appendix 6-2), is summarized on the Personnel Activity Report. Offers of employment for staff positions are logged on the Personnel Referral Form (Appendix 5-6) and summarized on the Personnel Activity Report.

The Personnel Activity Report, the Utilization Analysis, and the Workforce Analysis, mandated by Revised Order 4, are developed from the data base described in this chapter. These data also form the basis for studies of potential problem areas such as equal pay, turnover, and distribution of minorities and females by department and by level. Whenever possible, studies should cover at least a three-year period to add perspective to the analysis.

Chapter Seven

THE AFFIRMATIVE ACTION PLAN, REVISED ORDER 4,
AND THE OFFICE OF CONTRACT COMPLIANCE PROGRAMS

One of the areas targeted for change in the early months of the Reagan Administration was affirmative action. Because the obligations of federal contractors are controlled by executive order, and changes therefore require little public debate, the requirements of formal affirmative action plans prepared to comply with Revised Order 4 are likely to undergo significant changes.

In the fall of 1981, the Reagan Administration proposed numerous substantive and procedural changes that would affect higher education's Affirmative Action Plans. These proposed changes have been indicated in this chapter. The Women's Equity Action League estimates that only 19% of the institutions required to have an Affirmative Action Plan in 1980 would have to write a Plan if the $50,000 threshold is raised to $1,000,000. Less than 30% of currently protected faculty members would find themselves at schools with Affirmative Action Plans if the proposed rule is finalized. Public comments were received on the proposed changes until November, 1981, with final publication anticipated in the spring of 1982.

One proposed change, which would substantially affect the contents and format of affirmative action plans, is for good faith affirmative action efforts or broad performance standards to become the standard for review rather than the statistical parity which has characterized Revised Order 4 since its inception.

Although this approach has been described as naive and as a step backward in efforts to overcome the legacy of discrimination, the view of the current administration makes some changes in this area likely. The proposed changes focus upon reductions in record-keeping and in the affirmative action requirements for small contractors as well as elimination of "unnecessary confrontations" or less of a "police approach" to fighting job discrimination.

Resources listed in the bibliography such as the *Fair Employment Report*, the looseleaf services, and the *Federal Register* will provide current information on these changes.

Historically the affirmative action plans of institutions of higher education had been reviewed by the Department of Health, Education, and Welfare's Office of Civil Rights. On October 8, 1978, the responsibility for reviewing the affirmative action plans of institutions of higher education shifted to the Office of Contract Compliance Programs (OFCCP), changing substantially the format requirements and the level of substantive review for institutional Affirmative Action Plans. This chapter discusses the development of a plan conforming with the format required by Revised Order 4. An institution with at least $50,000* in government contracts must develop such an Affirmative Action Plan. The

*The Reagan Administration proposes raising this threshold to $1 million.

39

$50,000 is an aggregate amount, so several small contracts totaling
$50,000 give the OFCCP jurisdiction for a review. A review by the OFCCP
includes both an analysis of the Affirmative Action Plan and a personnel
and employment audit, because the agency sees a high correlation between
the Affirmative Action Plan and the substantive aspects of an institution's program. A review is part of a contractual obligation and is
unrelated to the substantive merits of an institution's program or to
charges of discrimination that may have been filed. An institution that
fails to develop an Affirmative Action Plan that complies with both the
form and substance of Revised Order 4 may be faced with substantial
back pay remedies for affected classes or with debarment from federal
contracts.

The OFCCP focuses on identifying and remedying class-wide situations
rather than upon individual charges of discrimination. The OFCCP does
accept individual charges of discrimination; however, under an agreement with the Equal Employment Opportunity Commission (EEOC), such
complaints are investigated by the EEOC if they fall under one of the
statutes enforced by that agency.

Several resources provide both general and detailed information
on developing an Affirmative Action Plan.

1. *The Federal Contract Compliance Manual* (FCCM) is both a
   common reference source for resolving questions of policy
   or procedure and a uniform body of standards for compliance officers responsible for reviewing Affirmative
   Action Plans. The *FCCM* can be purchased from the Superintendent of Documents, U.S. Government Printing Office,
   Washington, DC 20402, or from Commerce Clearing House.

2. The *Federal Register*, December 30, 1980, contains
   Revised Order 4 including the relevant sections for
   developing the Affirmative Action Plan: 60-2.11 and
   60-2.21-2.26 (see Appendix 7-1). The *Register* also
   contains separate sections on specific types of discrimination that must be addressed in the Affirmative
   Action Plan: Sex, 60-20; Religion and National Origin,
   60-50; Handicap, 60-250; Vietnam Veterans, 60-741.

3. A visit to the local OFCCP office establishes an initial
   positive relationship between the OFCCP and the institution and demonstrates the campus's good faith effort
   in developing an acceptable plan. The reviewer (in OFCCP
   jargon, the reviewer is called an EOS or an "employment
   opportunity specialist") may have questions about idiosyncrasies of academe such as tenuring or collegial
   decision-making described in Chapter 9. The director
   may learn what emphasis the EOS will place on goal
   achievement as opposed to opportunities to achieve
   goals, what format the agency prefers for specific
   sections of the Affirmative Action Plan, or whether
   the Eight-Factor Analysis will be required for faculty
   availability.

4. "A Working Manual," billed as a "complete, step-by-step
   working kit for designing a comprehensive, effective
   Affirmative Action program," contains detailed instructions for developing an Affirmative Action Plan. Primarily
   directed to the uninitiated, the "Manual" lives up to
   its billing. The "Manual" is part of the *Affirmative
   Action Compliance Kit* published by Executive Enterprises
   Company, 33 West 60th St., New York, NY 10023. The other

sections of the *Compliance Kit* are less useful in the
development of a higher education Affirmative Action
Plan.

An Affirmative Action Plan developed to comply with Revised Order 4
is essential to a successful review. Although a document known as the
Gerry Memorandum, issued on December 11, 1978, by the OFCCP to college
and university presidents, attempted to address the unique problems of
academic institutions and to provide a format for Affirmative Action
Plans, that document is no longer applicable to compliance reviews of
higher education. Although a case could surely be made that the OFCCP
should conduct reviews under the format detailed in the Gerry Memorandum,
the requirements of Revised Order 4 are broader and the OFCCP is presently requiring conformity to that Order. The institution will find
that it is both simpler and less costly to follow the requirements of
60-2.11 than to make theoretical arguments for institutional conformity
with the Gerry Memorandum.

The key components of an Affirmative Action Plan developed to comply
with Revised Order 4 (60-2.11) are the development of job groups, and
accompanying availability data, utilization analysis, and goals, as
well as an affected-class analysis, a workforce analysis, a personnel
activity report, and a narrative. The remainder of this chapter considers
these components individually.

The major statistical components of an Affirmative Action Plan
(availability and the utilization analysis) both depend upon the job
groups selected. The Job Group Analysis consists of reorganizing the
faculty and staff profiles (described in Chapter 6) into groups of at
least 50 employees per group (see FCCM 2-150). Because jobs requiring
similar skills must be grouped together, job groups cut across departmental lines. Job grouping begins by dividing EEO-6 categories with
more than 100 employees into subgroups considering common skill requirements, wage rates, and promotional opportunities. Clerical and administrative categories, for example, may be divided into entry-, middle-,
and advanced-level groups. Professional and technical categories with
more than 100 employees are subdivided into disciplines: chemistry,
engineering, nursing, law, accountancy. Faculty are arranged by college,
by division, by department, or by discipline within the department,
depending upon the size of the groups.

Job grouping presents a trap for the unwary because of the linkage
between job groups and goal achievement. Because the OFCCP requires
an explanation for any goal that is not 95% met, the institution will
wish to develop job groups that are large enough for meaningful statistical analysis and for greater flexibility in goal achievement. The
utilization analysis illustrated in Appendix 7-2, for example, separates
the faculty category into divisions because most academic departments
are so small that if one or more minorities or females were in the
department, the utilization would exceed the availability.

Each campus in a multi-campus system must develop its own job groups
not only because campuses vary significantly in size, organizational
complexity, and disciplines, but also because uniform job groups for
all campuses will rarely result in groupings that fit both the numerical
and functional criteria. A campus with a medical facility, for example,
will have a job group for nurses; however, a second campus may have only
a handful of nurses staffing the student health services. Under uniform
job grouping for all campuses, the second campus might have a job group
with only two persons in it. The wiser course for the second campus
is to include nurses with other professionals in a job group large
enough for meaningful analysis.

Once the job groups are established, availability data is developed
for each group. Availability is a mathematical estimate of the propor-

tion and numbers of women and minorities who have the training and
skills necessary to qualify for particular jobs. Although the Affirmative Action Plan must consider all protected groups, availability must
be determined only for females and for minority groups (see *FCCM* 2-160).
The best source of availability for faculty is the annual survey of
doctorates granted by academic discipline. This information is available
each June from the National Research Council (NRC), 2101 Constitution
Ave., Washington, DC 20418. Data for specialized schools such as optometry or nursing or for terminal degrees other than the doctorate
(such as the MFA or the MLS) are available from the National Council
for Educational Statistics, 400 Maryland Ave., NW, Washington, DC 20202.
Professional associations in library science, business, or medicine
may compile data on the groups they represent.

Most faculty positions are filled at the assistant professor level;
a three-year analysis of NRC data provides availability data applicable
to these positions. Unfortunately, the OFCCP may require conformity
to the eight-factor analysis* detailed in 60-2.11. Although this analysis
may be relevant for determining availability for staff positions, especially those within a local recruiting area, it is a less desirable
means of determining availability for faculty positions. The requirement is, however, that each factor in 60-2.11 be *considered*; each
factor is not weighted equally (see Appendix 7-3).

The Utilization Analysis (Appendix 7-2), though a culmination of
several analyses previously completed, is actually a comparison between
availability and the faculty and staff profiles. The test is "yes" or
"no"; if there is no underutilization, that is the end of the process
with respect to that job group. If the job group is underutilized as
to females or minorities, goals are set to correct that underutilization.
A review of the Utilization Analysis in Appendix 7-2 shows the following: job group totals in columns 1-4 are developed from the faculty
and staff profiles; the percentiles in columns 5-6 (labeled "utilization") are based on the numbers in columns 1-4; the availability percentages in columns 7-8 are computed using the eight-factor analysis;
the determinations regarding underutilization in columns 9-10 result
from comparing the percentages in columns 5-6 with those in columns
7-8; the goals projected in columns 11-12 result from an analysis of
underutilized job groups and projected openings in those job groups
over a three-year period.

Goals are required for all job groups in which an underutilization
of minorities or females has been identified (see *FCCM* 2-190). Whether
to set goals is not negotiable. The institution has some flexibility
regarding a timetable for those goals, however, and that schedule should
be as realistic as possible. The Affirmative Action Plan must contain
three types of goals: an ultimate goal equal to the availability (i.e.,
to correct the underutilization), an annual percentage goal (a placement rate of minorities and females into the job group by hire, promotion, or transfer; normally the placement rate will exceed the availability), and an annual numerical goal (the number of openings minorities
or women are likely to fill) (see Appendix 7-4).

The first step in the goal-setting process is a vacancy analysis,
an estimate of the openings likely to occur over a three-year period
in each job group through growth, contraction, and attrition due to
transfers, promotions out of the job group, and terminations. When the
vacancies have been projected, goals of the three types previously mentioned and illustrated in Appendix 7-4 are set. The ultimate goals are
set to achieve parity with the availability within a specified period

---

*The Reagan Administration has proposed changes in the eight-factor
analysis.

of time. Annual goals are based on an analysis of projected vacancies, timetables, and ultimate goals. The annual percentage goal is based on the annual numerical goal. A single goal for minorities is acceptable, according to the *FCCM* 2-190.1b, unless there is "a substantial disparity in utilization of a particular minority group or men and women of a particular minority group."

The Affirmative Action Plan, updated annually, includes an assessment of the goals set the previous year, an analysis of why any unmet goals were not met, a projection of vacancies for the following year, and revised goals for the next three years. Although goal attainment is not the sole measure of compliance, the *FCCM* 2-30.4 states that because goals reflect the probable results of equal employment opportunity, "failure to attain at least 95% of a goal requires that the cause of the failure be determined." In practical terms, the plan must analyze any goals not met and show that a good faith effort was made to meet those goals (see *FCCM* 2-200). Goals may not have been met for a number of reasons. Among these reasons are the following:

1. A projected vacancy did not occur. The goal is carried over as an annual numerical goal for the next plan year.

2. No minority/female applications were received. When applications from members of protected groups are not proportional to the availability in that job group, the problem may lie with insufficient recruiting efforts. The best recruiting device for all demographic groups remains personal contact by departmental members.

3. A minority or female was offered the position but declined. Documentation of this effort is located for faculty on the Administrative Approval Form (Appendix 4-12) and for staff on the Personnel Referral Form (Appendix 5-6). The information is logged on the Intra-Office Monitoring Systems for faculty and staff (Appendix 4-4 and 5-9).

4. The minority/female applicants were not as well qualified as the person selected. Documentation is located on the Administrative Approval Form (Appendix 4-12) and on the Personnel Referral Form (Appendix 5-6).

If the failure to meet goals cannot be explained by good faith reasons, additional analysis and perhaps substantive changes in the institution's procedures or view of affirmative action will be required. An institutional plan for these changes is evidence of a good faith effort to comply with affirmative action requirements. Goal achievement is included in the Affirmative Action Plan as illustrated in Appendix 7-5 and in the Narrative Analysis. This section of the plan is the key to measuring the substantive progress of the campus's affirmative action program.

The Affirmative Action Plan analyzes the institution's affirmative action efforts by department as well as by job group. This section of the plan, known as the Workforce Analysis, lists all employees and their salaries by department, by rank within the department (beginning with the lowest rank), and by salary within each rank (beginning with the lowest salary) (see *FCCM* 2-130). The Workforce Analysis provides the basis for analysis of salary and of demographic distribution. Analysis of this data indicating possible Adverse Impact on members of protected groups must be addressed in the Affirmative Action Plan (see *FCCM* 2-130).

The *FCCM* recommends a formula known as the Impact Ratio Analysis (IRA) for identifying areas within departments of possible Adverse Impact on members of protected groups (see Appendix 7-6). The IRA in-

dicates areas requiring further analysis and is a more precise variation of the Four-Fifths Rule or the 80% Rule.* The IRA assumes that the
institution's personnel actions have a direct relationship to one
another: new hires are related to applicant flow, applicant flow to the
availability, and promotions, training, and terminations to the size
of the institutional workforce. The IRA further assumes a correlation
between a concentration or underrepresentation of minorities or females
in a department and the employee selection procedures. An IRA ratio
of one (1) indicates that minorities or females have been selected at
an equal rate with members of the majority group for hire, promotion,
training, or retention. A ratio of less than .8 indicates a possible
adverse effect: a concentration or an underrepresentation of females
or minorities. Hence an IRA indicating a possible Affected Class calls
for an additional analysis using a formula known as the Job Area
Acceptance Range (JAAR) (see Appendix 7-7). The JAAR specifically
identifies job titles, jobs, lines of progression, or departments from
which minorities or females are being excluded or in which they are
concentrated.

   Both the IRA and the JAAR indicate that Adverse Impact or an
Affected Class may exist; neither provides conclusive proof of an
Affected Class. If either formula indicates a possible Affected Class,
a more meaningful statistical technique such as standard deviation,
cohort analysis, or multiple regression analysis should be applied to
the data (see *FCCM* 7-40.4d). In addition, the IRA should be repeated
for each aspect of the information summarized on the Personnel Activity
Report, because identification of an Affected Class brings into question
the institution's employee selection process. The Personnel Activity
Report is illustrated in Appendix 7-8. Data for this report is kept
and summarized separately for faculty and for staff, as the reporting
periods for these groups are based respectively on the academic year
and on the fiscal year.

   If a possible Affected Class is identified after these analyses,
the institution must develop a meaningful plan to correct the inequity
adversely affecting the members of the Affected Class. This plan is
not part of the Affirmative Action Plan but must be available for inspection by the EOS upon request. The *FCCM* 2-230.2b1 suggests that
institutions with more than 100 employees may be required to prepare
annual "adverse impact determinations" which show the effect of the
selection process for each job group by race and sex. In addition, the
Affirmative Action Plan must address these possible Affected Classes
as "problem areas" in the narrative portion of the plan.

   The institution that has performed this analysis, identified any
problem areas, and incorporated them into the Affirmative Action Plan
will be in a stronger position than the institution that waits for the
EOS to identify Adverse Impact during the review. Identification of an
Affected Class during a compliance review may have serious economic
impact on the institution because minorities and females identified as
members of an Affected Class may be entitled to monetary relief. Between
October 1979 and April 1980, members of Affected Classes received benefits negotiated by the OFCCP during compliance reviews totaling $9.3
million. Substantive problems in the campus program that surface during
a compliance review represent the greatest single impact of OFCCP
reviews on institutions of higher education.

   All of the analyses described above coalesce in the section of the
plan known as the Narrative. The narrative must respond specifically
to each section of the regulations: 60-2.11 through 60-2.25 as well as

*The Reagan Administration has proposed changes in the Four-Fifths Rule.

60-20, 60-50, 60-250, and 60-741. The Standard Compliance Review Report (SCRR) utilized by the agency during a compliance review requires that each item mentioned above be addressed in the Affirmative Action Plan (see *FCCM* 2-A-32). Because the OFCCP has an audit system designed to locate irregularities in the required format, the EOS has little discretion as to the elements included in that format.

The Narrative should be written to show the institution in the most favorable possible light and may include background information designed to inform the EOS about the campus. The campus's recruiting efforts, for example, may be seriously hampered by a salary scale lower than those of other comparable institutions. Discussion of innovative aspects of the institution's affirmative action program or grants relating to the disabled or disadvantaged enhance the narrative portion of the Affirmative Action Plan.

Although the data analyses described in this chapter are required only for racial minorities and women, the institution's efforts to provide affirmative action for members of other protected groups must also be addressed in the Affirmative Action Plan.* The specific elements required for the plan are detailed for veterans in 60-250, Appendix B, and for the disabled in 60-741, Appendix C (see Appendix 7-1).**

The following information regarding Viet Nam-era veterans and the disabled should be accessible for an OFCCP Compliance review.

1. A statement of institutional policy.

2. Copies of any publications that feature the disabled.

3. Copies of any physical/mental requirements that tend to screen out the disabled and that have been reviewed for job-relatedness, business necessity, and safety on the job.

4. Notice to members of these groups asking them to identify themselves. These cards, mailed annually to all employees with a pay check and to all students in the registration material, provide the basis for data collection, mailing lists, pools of promotable employees, and information relevant for training programs (see Appendix 7-9).

5. Copies of the employee application forms of all prospective employees who identified themselves as disabled.

*In addition to the difference in data analysis requirements, the Affirmative Action Plan for veterans and the handicapped must be made available in its entirety to employees; the Affirmative Action Plan based on sex, race, color, religion, and national origin in not subject to such a requirement.

**Although the regulations suggest that the Affirmative Action Plans for veterans and handicapped persons should be separate and independent documents, preparation of two or three Affirmative Action Plans is, for the most part, redundant, especially in higher education where complete Affirmative Action Plans have historically been widely circulated on campus. An important aspect of the pre-review process is negotiating with the local OFCCP an informal agreement to prepare one Affirmative Action Plan for all protected groups.

Disability is indicated on the Demographic Data Card
rather than on the application form. This avoids the
prohibition against preemployment inquiries. Include
a statement of the reasons these applicants were rejected for employment, comparisons of the applicants'
qualifications with those of the persons selected,
and descriptions of the accommodations considered.

6. Copies of the personnel files of disabled employees and
the Data Control Cards showing their employment history.
A log showing the personnel actions and accommodations
made for disabled employees complies with the applicable
regulations (see Appendix 7-10).

Resources that are particularly valuable in ensuring compliance
with federal regulations and affirmative action on campus for the disabled are:

1. *Guide to the Section 504 Self Evaluation for Colleges
   and Universities*, published by the National Association
   of College and University Business Officers (NACUBO),
   One Dupont Circle, Suite 510, Washington, D.C. 20036.

2. *Recruitment, Admissions and Handicapped Students. A
   Guide for Compliance with Section 504 of the Rehabilitation Act of 1973*, available from the American Association of Collegiate Registrars and Admissions Officers
   and the American Council on Education (ACE), One Dupont
   Circle, Washington, D.C. 20036.

The compliance review process begins when the institution receives
a letter from the OFCCP requesting that the institution submit its
Affirmative Action Plan to that agency within 15 days. An OFCCP review
is divided into three phases: the desk audit, the on-site review,
and the off-site analysis. The *FCCM* details the procedures applying
to each phase of the review. (See *FCCM* beginning with section 2-10).
    The Desk Audit, performed by the EOS after the plan has been sub-
mitted for review, identifies potential compliance questions, provides
insight into personnel policies and procedures that may result in a
denial of equal opportunity, identifies areas of underutilization,
assesses the establishment of goals and timetables, identifies areas
for in-depth examination, and assesses initial sufficiency and responsiveness of the Affirmative Action Plan to Revised Order 4.
    Most reviews proceed to an on-site visit by the EOS or by a team of
reviewers who will collect additional information to be reviewed during
an Off-Site Analysis. During the On-Site Review, the director, serving
as the institution's representative, should be present if faculty or
staff members are interviewed, should keep a log of the review, should
confirm all requests and releases of information in writing, and should
obtain a complete list of any and all deficiencies in writing before
beginning negotiations or making any meaningful concessions.
    Although most problems will be resolved during the review process,
the OFCCP has several incremental steps to resolve areas of noncompliance. If the noncompliance is the absence of certain information from
the Affirmative Action Plan, for example, compliance is achieved when
the institution supplies that information. Unless the information is
confidential or represents an unreasonable request by the agency, such

noncompliance is usually corrected informally early in the review process. When problems arise which cannot so easily be resolved, however, the OFCCP attempts to reach a conciliation agreement or to get a letter of commitment from the institution. From the institution's perspective, a letter of commitment is preferable to a conciliation agreement because of the greater flexibility allowed the institution in the contents of the letter. (See *FCCM* 8-110 for the criteria applying to each.) Such an agreement or letter might include back pay,* special recruitment efforts, or other forms of relief for employees against whom the agency determines discrimination has occurred. Although the agency prefers a conciliation agreement or a letter of commitment as a means for resolving substantive or procedural problems, the agency has an enforcement process that is used when conciliation efforts fail. The enforcement process includes an administrative complaint and a hearing before an administrative law judge. An adverse ruling may result in a conciliation agreement, withholding of federal funds, cancellation of government contracts, or debarment from further federal funds. Debarment is the OFCCP's ultimate weapon against discrimination.

*Proposed changes by the Reagan Administration would eliminate back pay as a remedy.

Chapter Eight

GRIEVANCES AND CHARGES OF DISCRIMINATION

Previous chapters have considered primarily the hiring phase of faculty and staff employment because careful development of procedures in the hiring process not only can forestall grievances and charges of discrimination but also can result in those that are brought being resolved to the institution's advantage. Grievances and charges of discrimination, however, may arise not only from new hires but also from promotions, terminations, and from the on-going relationship between administrator/supervisor and employee. In this book "grievances" refers to complaints filed internally and "charges" refers to complaints filed with outside agencies.

Grievances and charges of discrimination will always be with us. Individuals who feel disenfranchised or feel they have been treated unfairly by the institution will use internal grievance procedures if they perceive that these procedures are effective and/or will file charges of discrimination with one of several governmental agencies responsible for investigating such charges. Grievances that fall within the jurisdiction of the various governmental agencies and hence the Affirmative Action Office are those alleging discrimination based on race, sex, color, religion, national origin, age, handicap, or veteran status (see Appendix 1-1 and 1-2). An effective affirmative action program can minimize the number of grievances and charges, ensure that such charges are nonmeritorious, and ensure that situations ripe for class-action relief do not exist. Resolving complaints internally and at the lowest possible level is advantageous for both the institution and the complainant; the procedures and methods of resolving complaints described in this chapter are suggested with that view in mind.

Many administrators consider grievants as troublemakers rather than as employees pressing what may be legitimate complaints. On an abstract level, the freedom to grieve is a corollary to academic freedom, a principle institutions of higher education have long fought to preserve. On a more practical level, some of the greatest gains made in the field of Civil Rights have come through the courts, hence to object to an individual's attempt to rectify a perceived wrong is not entirely consistent with the university's role as an upholder of individual rights. An understanding on that level may make grievances more palatable to administrators, most of whom are academicians accustomed to abstractions and general principles.

An informal process within the Affirmative Action Office designed to handle grievances quickly and fairly and to prevent their escalation to a charge with an outside agency will have three phases: determination of the Affirmative Action Office's jurisdiction over the grievance, a fact finding, and a resolution based on the findings. The first step in an investigation is to get a clear statement in writing from the

grievant of what s/he believes has occurred. This statement can be by
letter or on a form developed for that purpose and illustrated in
Appendix 8-1. Because even grievants with good communication skills may
be unable to describe their grievance clearly and concisely, a personal
interview is an essential component of an informal process. A written
statement, however, is mandatory even in an informal process because
such a statement clarifies the issues the grievant describes, provides
the basis for determining whether the allegations are within the jurisdiction of the Affirmative Action Office, and insures the director
against any embarrassment or criticism should a grievant subsequently
change his/her mind about proceeding with an informal investigation.
If the grievance does not appear to be based on any of the Affirmative
Action Office's jurisdictional grounds, the director should advise the
grievant of other institutional alternatives. The Affirmative Action
Office generally does not become involved in grievances outside
affirmative action jurisdiction.

Once such threshold issues as a written statement from the grievant
and a determination of affirmative action jurisdiction are resolved,
the fact-finding portion of the informal process begins. If the grievant
alleges that his/her salary determination, for instance, was influenced
by sex, the initial step in fact-finding is identifying males, females,
or minorities within the department who are of a different demographic
group than the grievant. For a faculty grievance, the comparable(s),
identified from faculty profile, would be other department members of
the same rank who have approximately the same length of service to the
institution. A cohort analysis of this data is performed (see Appendix
8-3).

Each person who had a voice in the salary determination will be
interviewed. At this stage in the fact-finding, the allegations are only
allegations; their basis in fact has not yet been shown. The director,
as a seeker of truth, will apply skills of nonthreatening inquiry to
any interviews that are a part of the fact-finding process. From the
institution's perspective, clear procedures for salary determinations
that are routinely followed decrease the likelihood of equal pay problems and provide a job-related basis for salary determinations. Dean
Robert Bader has shared the procedures and forms used for a number of
years by the College of Arts and Sciences at the University of Missouri-
St. Louis. These are included as Appendix 8-2.

After identifying the comparables and interviewing the chairperson
and/or dean, the director can develop the Departmental Salary Analysis
Summary illustrated in Appendix 8-3. An examination of this Summary
coupled with information from the grievant, chairperson, dean, and
anyone else who is directly involved will yield an evaluation of the
merits of the grievance. Because the Summary shows quantitative information only, the interview information provides an assessment of the
quality of the work for each departmental member compared. Interview
information should be recorded as memos for file and made a part of the
grievance file.

If the grievance is meritorious, the director's negotiating skills
will focus upon the dean, provost, or whoever has the power to redress
the discriminatory treatment. Part of preparing for such negotiations
is determining an acceptable "fall back" position that can be used to
"save face" for a dean or chairperson who deliberately or inadvertently
made a discriminatory salary judgment. The more compelling the evidence,
the more likely it is that the director will succeed in negotiating
a resolution that will rectify the discrimination. The best setting for

this discussion, as with any discussion in an informal investigation, probably is the office of the chairperson, dean, or provost. Not only will any documents necessary to the fact finding and relevant to the mediation phase be available there, but also the administrator will be more comfortable and less threatened by inquiries and attempts at resolution when they occur in his/her office.

During this negotiating phase, the person to whom the chairperson or dean reports may become involved. The director probably has informed him/her of the grievance when it was filed and perhaps has reviewed the summary privately with him/her. An effective approach is "We have a problem" rather than "Dean Johnson has discriminated against Dr. Smith." Testing the waters with the provost or dean may prevent serious embarrassment during the resolution phase of the grievance process. If, for instance, the person with power to alleviate the discrimination does not perceive that discrimination has occurred despite a thorough investigation and evidence that is compelling to someone expert in the field, the director is unlikely to resolve the grievance informally.

The goal throughout the negotiating phase in a grievance that appears to be meritorious is resolution without the grievant's resorting to filing a formal charge. Enlightened self-interest may be a powerful motivating factor with academic administrators who perceive themselves as proponents of such traditional values as academic freedom. Allowing a provost, a dean, or a chairperson to be perceived as a liberal may provide ego gratification for an administrator wishing to be a leader in fair treatment for faculty. Some administrators respond only to the trump card: the likelihood of the institution's losing a charge or a lawsuit if the discrimination is not rectified informally. If an institution has previously lost a charge or a lawsuit or has made a settlement to a charging party, the likelihood of resolving grievances informally is substantially increased. Until this scenario has occurred, it may be virtually impossible in some institutions to resolve affirmative action-related grievances informally.

The fact finding and internal negotiating completed, the director again becomes a negotiator in a final interview with the grievant. If the grievant believes a fair and thorough investigation has been conducted, s/he will be more likely to accept the director's assessment of the merits of the allegations, even if that assessment suggests that the allegations are nonmeritorious. Using the summary (Appendix 8-3), the director should explain the procedures used for the salary comparison and for the fact-finding process, and should inform the grievant of any alternatives available to the grievant, including filing a formal charge with an outside agency. The decision to file a formal charge or to accept an evaluation of nonmerit clearly rests with the grievant.

No matter how strongly the evidence points to discriminatory treatment, some grievances cannot be resolved internally. The director may discuss this issue with the grievant in the final conversation regarding the grievance. The director's assessment of the merits of the grievance and the likelihood of the grievant's succeeding if s/he files with an outside agency should be a candid one, weighing the professional costs against the likelihood of success. Professional costs of filing a formal charge may be high but frequently are temporary: administrative personnel changes and the climate for affirmative action on campus may change. A grievant should, however, be apprised of the full range of costs and benefits that accompany filing a charge with an outside agency. Grievances and charges which are frivolous or nonmeritorious often result in hostilities toward the affirmative action program that can take great effort to disperse. However, a director should not deter a grievant from filing a formal charge and should fully apprise the grievant of the possible avenues which remain open for possible redress of the grievance regardless of the director's view as to the merits of the case.

One of these avenues is a formal campus grievance procedure. If such a procedure does not exist, the director should begin immediately to develop one, as Title IX and the Executive Order require that such procedures be available. A publication entitled *Title IX Grievance Procedures: An Introductory Manual*, prepared by the Resource Center on Sex Roles in Education and available from the Superintendent of Documents, Government Printing Office, Washington, D.C. 20402, provides complete instructions for developing such procedures.

Campus procedures for sexual harassment must also be developed to comply with the EEOC Guidelines on Discrimination because of Sex (60-20.8). Although the Department of Education has not to date promulgated guidelines on the sexual harassment of students, Title IX is clearly broad enough to encompass this type of sex discrimination against students.*

The EEOC Guidelines' most controversial section imputes liability to the institution not only for acts of which the administration had knowledge but also for acts of which the administration *should* have had knowledge (see *Bundy v. Jackson*). The institution may also be liable for the acts of nonemployees toward employees, though that liability will be determined on a case-by-case basis. Hence any procedures developed to resolve issues of sexual harassment must combine protection for the institution with sensitivity toward both the person who has been harassed and the alleged harasser.

Some protection for the institution is achieved through centralizing the process so that issues of sexual harassment are dealt with consis--tently and incrementally. Because resolving issues of sexual harassment is a more sensitive variation of the work presently performed in the Affirmative Action Office, assigning the responsibilities regarding sexual harassment to that office is both natural and logical.

Sexual harassment is difficult to prove because many such incidents occur in private. Whether or not the alleged harasser admits the incident, the incident should be handled in a manner sensitive to the alleged harasser's rights as well as to the sensitivities of the aggrieved party. Resolutions to sexual harassment cases often will be creative and the resolution will be harmonious with the degree of the offence. Appendix 8-4a contains Suggestions for Resolving Sexual Harassment Problems that stress consistency and incremental discipline. Most sexual harassment cases will be resolved administratively and informally because of the delicacy of the issues involved. Occasionally a case will be filed formally, and campus procedures must anticipate this eventuality. Appendix 8-4b suggests campus procedures in the format of a Policy and Procedure on Sexual Harassment. Such a statement can be published in a brochure; included in general handbooks distributed to faculty, staff, and students; published in campus news sources; and posted on bulletin boards in key locations on campus. The procedures outlined in Appendix 8-4b incorporate sexual harassment issues into existing campus mechanisms and provide for both informal and formal resolution of grievances alleging sexual harassment. (See also Appendix 8-5a and 8-5b.)

Procedures for resolving grievances alleging discrimination of all kinds must be available for both faculty and staff, but the procedures

---

*See P. Franklin; H. Moglan; P. Zatlin-Boring; and R. Angress. *Sexual and Gender Harassment in the Academy* (New York: MLA, 1981).

do not necessarily have to be the same. An existing grievance procedure can be expanded to include discriminatory treatment, or new procedures can be developed. The former method has the advantage of mainstreaming affirmative action into campus life as well as being more effective than a mechanism designed solely to resolve complaints of affirmative action-related types of discrimination.

If the grievance is not resolved during the informal affirmative action fact-finding and the grievance appears to be meritorious, the grievant should consider these more formal proceedings. If the grievant has a case likely to prevail under these procedures and is interested in following it through the courts if necessary to gain redress, it is particularly important to consider formal campus procedures. A finding of discrimination by a campus-hearing panel may be introduced into evidence in a lawsuit to bolster the petitioner's case. If the panel has a record of recommending against grievants, however, this process may be an undesirable avenue of redress from a grievant's viewpoint. Although the regulations require a grievance procedure to be available, they do not require a grievant to use it. A grievant may go directly to a government agency and file a charge.

During an informal fact finding, the grievant should be able to rely upon the Director of Affirmative Action for advice and for a fair effort to resolve the grievance. At some point, however, the grievant may wish to consult with outside legal counsel. A grievant who elects to progress through formal campus procedures, for example, must watch the time restrictions so as to preserve his/her right to file a charge with a government agency (see *Delaware State College v. Ricks*). Hence, the grievant should consider retaining legal counsel if s/he plans to proceed beyond the informal investigation by the Affirmative Action Office. An attorney with expertise in employment discrimination who is consulted early can preserve filing deadlines, phrase the grievance or charge in a manner most conducive to winning a charge or a lawsuit, and advise the grievant on structuring a campus grievance.

Employment discrimination is a specialized and volatile area of the law, and a grievant should consult a lawyer who regularly represents plaintiffs in discrimination cases. Most larger firms represent defendant institutions and companies rather than plaintiffs, but lawyers who represent plaintiffs can be located in a number of ways: the director may be able to offer suggestions, a grievant may know of an attorney who has represented other plaintiffs, the local Lawyers Reference Service or Bar Association may be able to offer assistance.

Lawyers differ widely as to fee arrangements. Many require retainers of $500-$3,000. Attorneys fees may be awarded by the court if the plaintiff wins, but because of the speculative nature of that money, many attorneys require a plaintiff to pay substantial sums of money to finance the lawsuit. Initially, a lawyer may offer consultation on an hourly basis, and a grievant may find it a wise investment to consult and perhaps retain a lawyer if s/he plans to proceed beyond the informal fact finding by the Affirmative Action Office. Most discrimination cases do not, however, result in full trials on the merits in a federal court, and a grievant should not be deterred from consulting a lawyer because of possible future expenses.

In no other area is the dual role of the Director of Affirmative Action more apparent than in handling grievances and charges of discrimination. As long as the grievant is proceeding through campus mechanisms, either formal or informal, the director functions as an advisor and as an advocate for fair treatment. A grievant who files with a government agency becomes a charging party, however, and the director becomes a representative of the institution. Regardless of the director's belief in the merits of the charging party's case, s/he must henceforth refrain from assisting the charging party and approach the case with the best interests of the institution in mind.

Charges may be filed with any of the federal agencies indicated in Appendices 1-1 and 1-2, or with state or local agencies. Although some complainants file simultaneously with several agencies, only one of these agencies will conduct a full-scale investigation. The EEOC, for example, has a policy against duplication and has developed work-sharing arrangements with state and city agencies. Usually the agencies accept one another's findings, but occasionally the secondary agency requires additional information not in the investigating agency's file. The jurisdiction and procedures of state and local agencies vary; these agencies provide copies of the statute and regulations under which they operate upon request. The investigative procedures of federal agencies are available from publishers such as Commerce Clearing House (CCH), from the agencies themselves, or from the Government Printing Office.

1. The Office of Civil Rights' (OCR) procedures are detailed in the *Manual for Investigation of Allegations of Employment Discrimination at Institutions of Higher Education*, published by Commerce Clearing House, 4025 W. Peterson Ave., Chicago, Ill. 60646.

2. The EEOC's procedures are located in the *EEOC Compliance Manual*, also published by Commerce Clearing House.

Charges may be filed with OCR or the EEOC by an individual alleging discrimination against him/herself, by an individual alleging discrimination against a group of which s/he is representative, or by the EEOC alleging systematic discrimination by the institution against an entire class of employees. The EEOC has separate units to investigate individual complaints and those alleging systematic discrimination. If the charging party has made class-action allegations, the charge will be referred to the EEOC's Continued Investigation and Conciliation Unit (CIC). The scope of such an investigation will be much larger, and the agency will review policies and procedures that have a general impact on members of protected groups. These include arrest record inquiries, educational requirements, maternity policies, and other class-oriented issues. The CIC investigation involves both a substantial document request and an on-site investigation. If the agency finds "cause," any settlement will address policy changes as well as any individual misapplication of those policies. During the course of the investigation of an individual charge, the matter may be transferred to the CIC Unit; if the occurs, the institution will be so notified by the agency.

The EEOC also has a Systemic Discrimination Unit*, the work of which

---

*Part of the Reagan Administration's deregulation efforts is to pursue discriminatory practices on a case-by-case basis. The EEOC's Office of Systemic Programs is targeted for dismantling by the administration, an action described by Eleanor Holmes Norton as one which "could not be more directly pointed at women. With women workers greatly concentrated in stereotyped female jobs, only such challenges as commission-

is similar to the former "commisioner's charge" and applies only to private institutions. In cases of Systemic Discrimination, the EEOC is concerned with broad patterns of discrimination rather than the resolution of individual complaints. Investigations are triggered by data supplied on the EEO-6 reports. Private institutions may be charged with Systemic Discrimination if the EEO-6 reports indicate a lower than expected utilization of minorities or women or an expanding workforce without corresponding increases in minority and female representation.

The EEOC attempts to resolve a charge of Systemic discrimination in the same manner as an individual charge--with a negotiated settlement. The agency seeks an agreement by which the institution agrees to end past discrimination, take affirmative action to assure there will be no future discrimination, and provide compensation for identifiable victims of discrimination. If the agency and institution are unable to achieve such a settlement, the EEOC may file a class-action lawsuit against the institution in federal court. Critics have suggested that because only broadly comprehensive efforts will eliminate discrimination, the EEOC should devote significantly more of its resources to the systemic program.

The notice to the institution that a charge has been filed with OCR* comes from the agency in a letter stating the jurisdictional basis for the agency's investigation and the nature of the charge. OCR regulations prohibit release to the institution of a copy of the actual charge unless the agency obtains the consent of the charging party. The institution routinely should request a copy of the actual charge even if the agency's description of the charge appears to be complete. The notice may be accompanied by a request for information regarding the case and by interrogatories which provide the institution with an opportunity to make a preliminary response to the charging party's allegations.

The institution's notice that a charge of employment discrimination has been filed with the EEOC includes a copy of the charge, a notice of a fact-finding conference (see Appendix 8-6), and a questionnaire. The fact-finding conference is an informal proceeding, attended by an institutional representative, the charging party, and an EEOC representative. The proceeding is not adverserial; hence the counsels for the institution and for the charging party are not permitted to cross-examine. All questions and statements are addressed to the agency representative. Each of the charging party's allegations will be discussed and both parties may present their positions. The goal of the conference is to achieve a negotiated settlement. Order 915 describing the Fact-Finding Conference is included as Appendix 8-7.

----

pattern and practice cases stand any chance of breaking these rigid patterns."

*A charge of discrimination filed with either the OCR or the EEOC has similar impact on the Affirmative Action Office. The discussion of charges of discrimination in this chapter encompasses both agencies, indicating distinctions when applicable. Appendices 8-9 and 8-10 contain flow charts illustrating each agency's procedures. Because the OFCCP rarely investigates individual charges, the procedures of that agency are not included. Appendix 8-11 contains the Requirements of Title VII for Common Violations, relevant to charges filed with the EEOC.

If a settlement is not achieved at the fact-finding conference, the EEOC conducts an in-depth investigation. All information submitted in response to agency requests should be documented by letters cooperative in tone and specifically describing the information submitted. All documents should be released through the Affirmative Action Office; individual faculty and staff members should not have the responsibility of determining whether or not specific information should be released. The institution should consider resisting agency requests that are irrelevant, unreasonable, or burdensome for the institution. This decision should be made in consultation with institutional legal counsel, as the end result may be a subpoena. The courts tend to grant such subpoenas unless the information involved is excessive or outrageous in some other respect.

During the investigatory process, numerous employees on campus may be interviewed. The director should schedule these interviews, discuss the charge briefly with the employees to put them at their ease, advise them in any way that is appropriate, respond to their questions, and be present during the interview unless the employee objects. The presence of such a representative is permitted under the procedures of all federal and many state agencies. Hearing the testimony allows the director to make a determination as to the merits of the case, an assessment which may be important in the conciliation phase of the investigation.

After the agency has completed its investigation, the agency will make a determination as to whether there is reasonable cause to believe the charging party has been discriminated against. The OCR provides this information to the institution as a determination letter which may require corrective action even if the finding is not one of cause. The EEOC issues either a "no cause" finding concurrently with a right-to-sue letter, permitting the charging party to sue the institution in federal court, or a determination that the charging party's claim is valid. The latter is the first formal determination made by the agency as to the merits of the charging party's allegations. If the charging party's claim is meritorious, the EEOC will again attempt a negotiated settlement. The institution will receive a Notice of Conciliation Process and an Invitation to Participate in Settlement Discussions.

Both the EEOC and OCR have the authority to conciliate. The stated purpose of the EEOC's conciliation process is "to achieve a just resolution of all violations found and to obtain a written agreement which provides that the Respondent will eliminate the unlawful employment practice and provide appropriate affirmative relief." (*EEOC Compliance Manual* 60.1). The EEOC's conciliation process begins with a conference at which both parties may present proposals and counterproposals. The settlement of an individual charge can include anything both parties agree to that is not illegal. Appendix 8-8 illustrates the format for such a settlement agreement. If a settlement attempt fails, the agency either will sue the institution or will refer the case to a private attorney. Both parties receive a copy of the right-to-sue letter issued by the agency.

The OCR's conciliation process begins after a finding of noncompliance has been established; the position of the agency shifts from that of fact-finder to that of an advocate for compliance with the law. Agency procedures provide for a letter of findings and an opportunity for institutional rebuttal. If the OCR determines the rebuttal does not significantly alter the determination of noncompliance, the agency schedules a conciliation meeting. In general the conciliation remedies advocated by OCR should be in conformity with existing case law; the institution's negotiating tactics will weigh the merits of the case, the difficulty of complying with OCR's proposal, the reasonableness of OCR's position, and the costs resulting from an unsuccessful conciliation. A successful conciliation resolves the case for both parties; an unsuccessful conciliation results in OCR's recommending enforcement, a step which leads to litigation and possibly loss of federal funds.

Although federal agencies attempt to resolve charges through the conciliation procedures described above, state agency procedures may include a hearing. Institutional representation at a hearing is usually by legal counsel; the director often is a witness in the case. Although formal rules of evidence usually do not apply to agency hearings, the hearing is a formal proceeding with exhibits, sworn testimony, and a transcript. Once the charge of discrimination moves to a hearing or to the courts, the role of the director diminishes, probably to assisting institutional counsel in trial preparation and to being a witness at the hearing or trial. Charges of discrimination highlight the dual role of the Affirmative Action Office, as well as the undesirable intrusion of outside parties into institutional affairs. A desirable goal surely is the informal and internal resolution of campus grievances.

Chapter Nine

GOVERNMENT AGENCIES AND INSTITUTIONS OF HIGHER EDUCATION

Nearly every campus has its repertory of stories about the "insensi-
tivity" of federal or state investigators. Many stories originate in
institutional resistance to agency efforts to enforce the antidiscrimination laws. Some stories relate to unreasonable demands made by investigators. Others result from misunderstandings which occurred because
"outsiders" failed to observe courtesies that are routine on campuses
across the country. Neither agency nor institutional personnel come to
this arena with completely clean hands.

Federal enforcement of antidiscrimination laws has been severely
criticized by advocacy groups, by other federal agencies, and by individuals and commissions studying equal opportunity in higher education. A "Report to Associates on Project Activities" by the Project on
the Status and Education of Women (June 1980) made two points:

1. Federal implementation of sex discrimination statutes
   has been lax and inconsistent, arousing complaints from
   both institutions and women's organizations. Despite
   the prevailing and inaccurate notion that HEW* has been
   "forcing" institutions to hire women and "integrate"
   athletics, HEW has been roundly criticized for its
   ineffectiveness by the U.S. Commission on Civil Rights,
   the General Accounting Office (the investigative arm
   of the Congress) and Congressional oversight committees.
   Women's groups sued HEW (and won), charging HEW with
   inefficiency and lack of enforcement.

2. Federal officials all too often lack expertise about
   institutions and the status of women in the higher
   education community.

Others have criticized the OCR in particular and have filed suit
against that agency for poor enforcement.** Agencies have been the victims of the political climate and the courts and have suffered from an
internal malaise that has prevented the completion of many complex

*now the Department of Education

**For detailed critiques of federal enforcement efforts, see J. Abramson,
The Invisible Woman: Discrimination in the Academic Profession (San
Francisco, 1975), pp. 169-198; *Making Affirmative Action Work in Higher
Education*. A report of the Carnegie Council on Policy Studies in Higher
Education (San Francisco, 1975).

investigations. The reviews conducted by OCR in states once operating
segregated systems of higher education, for example, began with substantial document requests and included on-site visits by teams of
investigators. Two years after the reviews were conducted, the agency
finally notified the institutions investigated of the results of that
investigation. In spite of a checkered past, federal agencies can
improve their effectiveness by careful assessment of past problems
and a concerted effort to do better. Although this book is directed
predominantly to campus administrators, this chapter is directed to
federal and state investigators, who, if uninitiated, cannot avoid
the quicksands of academe.

The traditions of most academic institutions originate in western
Europe, particularly England and Germany, and involve a blend of teaching and searching for truth, the latter also called research.* The
Civil Rights Acts sailed into a sea of tradition and collegiality
dating back several centuries, and shortly thereafter the investigators
and reviewers of federal and state agencies began enforcing these laws.
Unfortunately, few of these agency representatives had experience with
higher education beyond their own student experiences--and some did not
have that. The agencies, plagued with high turnover in top positions,
provided little leadership either in hiring qualified investigators
or in developing training programs to enhance investigation skills.
Indeed, job descriptions and interview questions have historically
centered on the community relations activities and on empathy for
protected groups. Fortunately, in recent years some reviewers have been
hired who have investigative and analytical skills, and some leaders
in enforcement agencies have acknowledged the need for emphasizing these
skills rather than those that are less job-related.

Agencies should begin by tailoring procedures, forms, and form
letters to higher education. Letters and notices referring to the campus
as "your firm," for example, should be changed to read "your institution" or "your campus." Letters addressed to "Mr." or "Ms." should be
revised to refer to "Dr.," "Chancellor," or "Dean." A clarifying phone
call to the institution, if the agency is in doubt as to the title or
credentials of the person to whom the letter is being written, would
result in letters demonstrating greater courtesy and sensitivity to
higher education. Agencies should conform to the higher education reporting model, the EEO-6, rather than continuing to request and to use
the industrial EEO-1 model. The review format should include a faculty
category, for example, rather than a sales category.

Although such revisions seem minor, better responsiveness to such
courtesies and peculiarities of academe would enhance the perceptions
institutions have of the sophistication of agencies and investigators.
This sophistication also would increase with greater agency efforts to
understand higher education. The following are basic characteristics
of higher education unique to that type of institution.

1. *Decision-making is collegial rather than hierarchical.*

   Although most colleges and universities appear from organizational
   charts to be traditional hierarchies, all administrators are bound
   by academic traditions requiring consultation with the campus governing body (comprised primarily of faculty members) and with other
   appropriate administrators. The ambiguity of the faculty role in

---

*For a discussion of many of these traditions, see L. Lewis, *Scaling
the Ivory Tower* (Baltimore, 1975).

campus governance is illustrated by *NLRB v. Yeshiva University*
wherein the Supreme Court ruled that for purposes of collective
bargaining, faculty members were members of management.

2. *Decision-making, record keeping, and campus governance are decentralized.*

   In higher education, key decisions regarding employment and
   budgetary matters are made at many different levels. A student who
   wishes to protest a grade, for example, participates in a grievance
   procedure which begins with the classroom instructor and proceeds
   ultimately to the chief academic officer or even the Board of
   Curators, Regents, or Trustees. The grievance may be resolved at
   numerous intermediate steps. Records regarding that grievance will
   be retained at whatever levels the grievance touches: the instructor,
   the department chairperson, the dean, the college committee on
   academic affairs, the senate committee on campus discipline, the
   chief academic officer, and the board. Records of a grievance resolved at the dean's level, for example, will reside in the Dean's
   Office and at the preceding levels the grievance has touched. Only
   in rare cases will the subsequent levels even be aware that a
   grievance has been filed. Hence an agency request during an investigation for copies of all grievances filed by a complainant is often
   a complex request for the institution.

3. *Tenuring* is a system that guarantees life-time employment for those
   who successfully pass through the process.*

   Tenure evolved because of a desire to protect those who would speak
   out on unpopular subjects from suffering the economic reprisal of
   the loss of a job. The concept of academic freedom, long a rallying
   cry among college and university faculty, has been ensured by both
   tenure and due process.
   Historically, proportionately fewer women and minorities have been
   granted tenure, and women have received tenure or a promotion later
   in their academic careers than comparably qualified men. Although
   this information makes the system ripe for an agency investigation
   of an affected class or systemic discrimination, the tenure and
   promotion system is a minefield of potential disaster for the uninitiated. Not only are institutions likely to resist revealing
   this most confidential of information, as the 1980 struggle between
   the University of California and the OFCCP** illustrated, but also,
   decisions at several levels in the tenuring process are made by
   committees. This shared responsibility tends to dilute the responsi-

---

*For additional information on tenure, see B. Smith (ed.), *The Tenure
Debate* (San Francisco: Jossey Bass, 1972), W. Keast, *Faculty Tenure*
(San Francisco: Jossey Bass, 1973), and G. LaNoue, "Tenure and Title
VII," *Journal of College and University Law* 1: 206-221 (Spring 1974).

**On October 3, 1980, one day before an order barring the university
from federal funds totaling $25 million would have gone into effect,
the University of California, Berkeley, agreed to release documents
requested by Department of Labor investigators. The University feared
public disclosure of confidential faculty evaluations and other employment records under the Freedom of Information Act (FOIA). The consent
decree allowed federal investigators to make and remove copies of these
documents on condition that they will be kept confidential unless a
judicial order requires public release.

bility of the individuals participating in tenure and promotion decisions.

4. *Faculty members are hired 6-9 months before the beginning of the academic year.*

Although newly hired faculty members usually begin their jobs with the fall semester, most are hired many months earlier. Advertising and recruiting for faculty positions occurs in the fall of the preceding year; firm commitments are made by both the institution and the faculty member by spring; the faculty member reports for work in August or September. This phenomenon affects the relationship between Faculty Personnel Activity Reports and the Workforce Analysis required by Revised Order 4. Hence, if the Impact Ratio Analysis is used, the applicant flow and new hire data must be coordinated by means other than the budgetary year that is used for staff analysis.

5. *Faculty performance is evaluated based on teaching, research, and service.*

This triumvirate is an academic tradition, all elements of which are difficult to evaluate objectively. Teaching refers to classroom performance. Unfortunately, no one knows for sure what constitutes a good teacher. The result is that judgments about teaching competence are made on the basis of hearsay, student evaluations, or classroom observation. None of these indicators is particularly reliable or scientific, and all may be biased against teachers who are unusual as to style, philosophy, or demographics.

Research may be reflected in the form of books, articles, art objects, musical compositions, or musical performances. Although there is much variation among the disciplines, generally scholarly articles in refereed journals are the best evidence of solid research. Refereed journals exist in most disciplines and publish only articles submitted to them that are determined by experts (referees) to be worthy of publication. Opinions vary greatly regarding the merits of particular articles even among scholars of the same sub-disciplines; hence what is published and the merits of that work is determined by what can most charitably be called professional judgment. There is evidence that journals in general choose a disproportionate number of established male scholars unless the referees do not know the authors' identities.

Service involves committee work within the department, college, campus, or community. Some committees are more prestigious and influential than others; some require more time and effort than others. Service may also include reviewing books for local news media, appearing on local media programs, or participating in professional organizations. Generally service is valued less highly than research and teaching.

Although agencies are often characterized by a bureaucratic concern with format and by a lack of consideration for the institution being reviewed, some discretion is possible and should be used both by the reviewer and by the district or area director. This is not to say that an investigator should not be thorough, but rather that unreasonable burdens should not be placed on an institution.

The "standard access provisions" in the regulations in federal research grants and contracts, for example, demand access to information as a condition of the award, and institutions are legally compelled to provide information requested. The agency can, by using these powers with discretion, not only build some good will with the institution but can do a competent investigative job. A responsible agency will balance the need for the information against the harm produced or the expense created by requiring it. Such an investigator will be responsive to the efforts of the institution to cooperate by considering both the relevancy of the information requested and the alternative modes of obtaining it. Redress for institutions who are subjected to unreasonable harassment by government investigation is available through the courts, but this is in itself a burdensome process.

Agencies can improve the quality of their reviews by assigning reviews of institutions of higher education to persons trained to understand higher education procedures.* Not only will such persons conduct more thorough and efficient reviews, but also they will create less ill will within the institution. Trained investigators will request only relevant information and will assimilate that information in a logical and pertinent manner. They are less likely to possess a cloak-and-dagger mentality or to take the complainant's allegations at face value and more likely to come to the investigation as a neutral truth seeker.

A review will be more effective if the reviewer is well prepared before coming on site for a review. The on-site investigation should be limited to clarifying material previously submitted by the institution and to interviewing campus personnel whose testimony is relevant to the investigation. In fact, an initial analysis of data submitted by the institution should be performed to determine whether an on-site investigation is necessary.

In one documented case, a student alleged discrimination based on race in the distribution of student financial aid. The institution submitted the following information: the student had received eight full semesters of financial aid (the maximum entitlement under federal law); the student's grade point was so low that she not only could not graduate but actually had for some time not made "satisfactory academic progress" and hence should have had her aid cut off prior to her receiving the maximum allowable; and the institution's statistical data showed that members of the complainant's race benefitted from the financial aid disproportionately to their representation in the student body. In spite of this information, which would seem to rebut the complainant's allegations, the agency conducted a full-scale on-site investigation, with an investigator on campus for a full week. Two full days were spent examining documents that did not contain any racially identifiable data. Such practices do nothing to increase the agency's effectiveness; instead they serve to make the agency look foolish and ineffective.

---

*The American Council on Education (ACE) has repeatedly offered to educate and sensitize reviewers assigned to higher education so that the quality of the reviews can be improved from the perspectives of the complaining party, the institution, and the agencies. Federal agencies have, to their discredit, not availed themselves of these opportunities.

Some agencies routinely schedule on-site investigations without affording the institution an opportunity to present evidence which may be sufficient to rebut the complainant's allegations. Not only are some charges nonmeritorious, some are downright frivolous. Agency discretion in limiting the investigation of such complaints by deciding *not* to launch full-scale investigations would enhance institutional good will and perhaps cooperation in future reviews.

Equity and affirmative action have been a part of higher education for nearly a decade, long enough so that governmental agencies and institutions should be accustomed to one another. Institutions should have developed data systems which will retrieve data routinely requested during investigations. Agencies should have developed a sufficient understanding of higher education so that information requests can be relevant and reasonably related to the complaint being investigated. Effective investigations by government agencies can enhance the institution's affirmative action program and can encourage voluntary compliance by even the most recalcitrant faculty member or administrator. Better cooperation by both parties will not only provide more effective and less painful investigations but also will result in greater equity on campus.

Chapter Ten

AFFIRMATIVE ACTION AND CAMPUS LIFE

Many of us look with eagerness to the day when the primary focus of
the Affirmative Action Office will be on improving the quality of campus
life rather than on gathering and analyzing data, although the two
focuses are not entirely unrelated. Developing campus machinery to
handle grievances fairly and expeditiously, for example, not only will
decrease charges of discrimination but also will create a more positive
attitude for faculty and staff who will view the administration as more
responsive to their needs.

Some campus leaders have perceived a backlash against affirmative
action among many white male faculty members and have noted increasing
departmental resistance to the efforts of administrators to promote
the hiring and promotion of more female and more minority group faculty
members. Students recognize discrimination or lack of sensitivity based
on race, sex, age, or handicap. Faculty members, meeting increasing
numbers of students with disabilities, are facing accommodation needs
unheard of a decade ago. Though only tangentially related to a campus's
numerical representation of members of protected groups, these issues
affect campuses across the nation. Because of a position in the campus
hierarchy that cuts across organizational lines, the Affirmative Action
Office is uniquely suited to initiate improvements in the quality of
campus life.

The quality of life for employees, both faculty and staff, improves
when administrators and supervisors better understand their affirmative
action responsibilities and routinely use better management practices.
Although many campuses have training offices associated with the Personnel Office, that office may not emphasize affirmative action-related
programs or may not have the rapport with academics necessary to ensure
their participation. A management training program, well conceived and
well presented under the auspices of the Affirmative Action Office,
effectively promotes better managerial and supervisory skills, a more
positive atmosphere for affirmative action, a better understanding of
affirmative action, and increased visibility and prestige for the
Affirmative Action Office.

Finding an appropriate vehicle for training is a threshold task,
as the vehicle will in large measure determine the approach to the
training. The director can develop his/her own training program; this
has the advantage that the program is then tailored specifically to
the needs of the institution, but the disadvantage is that development
of such a program is difficult and time consuming. The institution can
hire a consultant to present a program; this has the advantage that
supervisors and administrators hear the "truth" from an "expert," but
the disadvantage is that this is very expensive. A consultant-trainer

must be carefully selected so that s/he will have credibility with
academic administrators, and s/he must present an academically-oriented
program. A third alternative is for the institution to purchase a
packaged program and for the director to present it to appropriate
campus groups. Although such a program is expensive, packaged programs
contain films and exercises that are nonthreatening and depersonalized,
enhancing the learning process for participants. Each of the programs
recommended below may be used effectively in a variety of campus settings
including management training. Although a professionally-produced
package is not available specifically for academic institutions,
packages designed for industry can be adapted for academe.

   1. "A Tale of O" is a slide/tape presentation focusing upon the
problems of tokens in organizations. Based on Rosabeth Moss Kantor's
Men and Women in the Organization and distributed by her consulting
firm, Goodmeasure, the program can be presented to administrators and
supervisors with a view toward increasing their understanding of the
problems women and minorities face in departments where they are numerically isolated; to groups of women and minorities to help them recognize the difficulties they face and to teach them coping mechanisms;
to student groups to heighten their awareness of the problems women
and minorities face in the working world. One advantage of the "paper
doll" figures in this program is that it will not become dated. Another
advantage of this presentation is that it is not identifiable with any
particular type of organization; hence it is adaptable to the needs of
custodial supervisors as well as to those of academic department chairpersons. "A Tale of O" has been used successfully in a university setting and is available from Goodmeasure, 6 Channing Place, Cambridge,
Mass. 02138; telephone (617) 492-2714.

   2. *Boomerang* is an eight-hour management training program focusing
on good management skills as they relate to affirmative action. The
program, designed for and set in industry, consists of a trainer manual,
participant manuals, and eight five-minute film vignettes. The subject
matter of *Boomerang* includes job requirements, interviewing, supervision,
performance appraisals, disciplining employees, and termination of
employees whose work performance is unsatisfactory. The program, which
has been used successfully in a university setting, is a high-quality
program that becomes more economically feasible if the cost can be
shared by campuses in a multi-campus system, or by member institutions
in an organization. Although *Boomerang* is most pertinent to supervisors
and administrators, the film vignettes can be adapted to groups of
women and minorities or to student groups, in a manner similar to "A
Tale of O." The vignettes are professionally done and are among the
best training tools in the field. *Boomerang* is available from Leopold
and Associates, 35 E. Wacker Drive, Chicago, Ill. 60601; telephone
(312) 726-1947.

   3. *Breakthrough*, a training program focusing on the work-related
problems of handicapped job applicants, consists of a trainer manual,
participant manuals, and a three-part film. The film shows both negative and positive interviews of a handicapped job applicant as well as
on-the-job accommodations to that disability. The film, set in an office,
is easily adapted to academe. The program can be presented to supervisors and administrators, student groups, or to faculty members. The
program is excellent, perhaps the best in the field of management
training regarding handicapped employees. *Breakthrough* is also available
from Leopold and Associates.

   As evident from the descriptions of these programs, they may be used

in a variety of settings. Although priorities on each campus vary,
beginning with management training will provide both the quantitative
result of fewer grievances and charges of discrimination and the
qualitative result of a better work environment, as supervisors and
administrators learn to make employment decisions for job-related
rather than for discriminatory reasons.

Because management training is relatively new to many academic
administrators, their support and participation must be carefully
enlisted. Even though higher education has a collegial rather than a
hierarchical organization pattern, the participation of upper-level
administrators will enhance the success of the program. A management
training program provides an opportunity for the chief academic officer
to show his/her support for the affirmative action program by attending
and actively participating in the entire program. If the chief academic
officer's only participation is a brief welcome at the beginning, that,
too, will convey a message: that the program is not sufficiently
important to be worked into his/her busy schedule. Although the chief
academic officer's nonparticipation will not be fatal to the program,
word that s/he *has* participated will spread across the campus. Moreover, the program's effectiveness increases when the director/trainer
can say, "When the chancellor participated in this program, s/he observed that...."

Other key participants in an initial session of a management training
program include other high-ranking administrators and deans and directors
of major departments. The optimum group size is between 20 and 30
participants. If the program is an effective one, those who have participated in the initial group can urge their subordinates to participate,
perhaps by letter, and additional groups can be formed in a networking
approach so that eventually all supervisory and administrative personnel
on campus will have participated in a program. Appendix 10-1 contains
an evaluation of the use of the *Boomerang* program on a university campus.

In addition to deciding whether to develop a campus program or to
purchase a packaged program, the director will decide whether to hire
a consultant (who may be a faculty member) to do the training or to
do the training him/herself. Economics may dictate that the director
must make training part of his/her regular duties, but on a large campus
this is probably not a practical alternative. Although the director
already has established rapport and credibility on campus and is knowl-
edgable about both campus problems and affirmative action, training is
adrenalin-producing, time consuming, confrontive, controversial, and
frequently enjoyable. Every group is different, and not only does
training provide an opportunity for the director and other campus administrators to get to know one another better, but also the campus
perceptions about affirmative action will be openly discussed. In nearly
every session, the director will garner ideas that can be utilized to
make a more effective affirmative action program. Management training
both enhances the quality of campus life and provides a vehicle to enhance the visibility and effectiveness of the affirmative action program.

Although institutions of higher education are in the business of
educating and many professors supplement their institutional income
by private consulting, faculty development of any kind is a relatively
recent phenomenon in the campus community. Only when the job market
tightened did the movement to improve the quality of life for faculty
members gain momentum. Faculty-development programs that have evolved
over the last decade have focused on retraining or enrichment so that

faculty members can proceed into fields where the demand for their
skills is greater or they can become administrators. Some programs have
focused on improving teaching or research skills, but the concept of
raising the consciousness of faculty to improve quality of life on
campus is a novel idea. Thus any type of affirmative action program
for faculty is likely to be difficult to implement and to meet with
some resistance.

The development of a training program for faculty will be made
easier by a previously successful management training program. Even
with the faculty, a hierarchical approach may be used, presenting the
program first to deans, next to groups of chairpersons, and finally
to individual departments. If the director has established an ally or
two in each department, and particularly if they are majority group
males, the departmental discussions will go much more smoothly. If the
department chairpersons will call the meetings at which the discussions
are held, faculty attendance will be greater. As with management
training, the campus grapevine will spread the word that the program
is worthwhile. Presentation of such a program to individual departments
will be time consuming and may take several semesters to complete.

The content of a faculty training program will depend upon the
perceived problems on the campus, as identified, perhaps, by the Affirmative Action Committee described in Chapter 3. The director may wish to
discuss the issues identified with students and others on campus to
confirm or to gather additional suggestions and materials necessary for
a credible presentation. An informal training program for faculty members probably will focus on sexism, racism, and discrimination on the
basis of age and handicap in classroom materials and classroom atmosphere.
Numerous tools such as "A Tale of O" and the *Breakthrough* films can
be used to enhance such a presentation, but the most effective format
will be an intelligent discussion of issues relevant to discrimination
in the classroom. The emphasis of the faculty training will be on
educating and consciousness raising rather than on accusations of
wrong-doing. Materials such as those included in Appendix 10-2 serve
to provide information and bases for discussion regarding discrimination in the classroom. Materials such as these will contribute to a
nonaccusatory style of presentation and hence to the success of the
program. The result may be a more sensitive and enlightened faculty
as well as an improvement in the quality of life for students and
faculty of all races, sexes, ages, and abilities.

In addition to developing and presenting training programs to
special groups of faculty, administrators, and supervisors, improvements
in quality of life may focus upon specific protected groups. Affirmative
action programs for the disabled, for example, emphasize physical
accessibility and classroom and workplace modifications as well as
educating faculty, staff, and students to the needs of the disabled.

Special efforts for women and minorites are also compatible with
improving the quality of campus life. Although both women and ethnic
minorities are members of groups that set them apart from the power
structure, the problems in correcting underutilization and in improving
campus life for these groups are different. Most institutions emphasize
recruiting and hiring minorities because there are not enough black
or Hispanic or American Indian faculty or staff. Women, however, are
numerically well represented on campuses. The problem is that they are
secretaries, assistants, instructors, lecturers, and adjuncts. Unfortunately, even enlightened proponents of affirmative action may set

women and racial minorities against each other. Although one-third
of the University of California at Berkeley's academic departments
had no women in tenure-track appointments, the chancellor of that
campus, I. Michael Heyman, declared that affirmative action on that
campus should emphasize ethnic minorities because the "inclusion of
women on the faculty is institutionally seeded now."*

Efforts to improve the quality of life for members of protected
groups will include:

1. Increasing the numbers so that effects of tokenism will
   be alleviated.

2. Providing affirmative action coordinators in each school,
   department, or building.

3. Using recruiters for students, staff, and faculty who are
   members of protected groups.

4. Developing job-related requirements for both faculty and
   staff positions.

5. Presenting programs stressing positive accomplishments
   of members of protected groups.

6. Encouraging a level of discussion on campus of affirmative action issues that will enhance opportunities for
   members of protected groups.

7. Developing policies and procedures for resolving issues
   of concern to members of protected groups such as sexual
   harassment (see Chapter 8).

Quality of life for members of protected groups affects faculty,
staff, and students. Although this book has focused primarily on employment in higher education, student concerns comprise a significant
portion of the institution's affirmative action program. A significant
issue concerning students and their rights under Title IX has been
litigated over the past several years: is Title IX's application limited
only to specific school programs that get direct federal money? This
question has been answered in the affirmative in a case filed by
parents seeking to force the school system to provide golf teams for
both male and female students. (*Othen v. Ann Arbor School Board*). The
question may be rendered moot in a Third Circuit case, *Grove City College
v. T.H. Bell, Secretary of Education*, because of the Reagan Administration's reevaluation and possible modification of the Title IX rules.
Grove City College asserts that Title IX applies only to specific
school programs that get direct school money, not to entire colleges.
The specific question is whether federal grants and loans to students
constitute federal aid to an institution.

The approach indicated by this line of cases would exempt programs
like sports and other extracurricular activities and most academic
programs from Title IX. Because "federal money frees up other money
indirectly subsidizing the entire school programs," Dr. Bernice Sandler,
director of the Project on the Status and Education of Women, argues
that the Grove City approach "asks taxpayers to underwrite discrimina-

Chronicle of Higher Education, Sept. 29, 1980, p. 11

tion against their daughters."* Sandler's view has been termed the "infection theory."

Most affirmative action efforts relating to students will involve developing data (on admissions, degrees conferred, and financial aid), and ensuring compliance with the regulations regarding the handicapped (503 and 504) and with Titles VI and IX. Compliance with these regulations requires analysis of the recruiting, admissions, financial aid, student services, athletic, and academic programs to ensure that they are being administered with equality.

Changes forthcoming by the Reagan Administration will undoubtedly affect the enforcement mechanisms that have characterized Title VI and IX for a decade. Secretary Bell, for example, favors allowing institutions to present plans to correct deficiencies in women's athletic programs as a means of achieving Title IX compliance. Formerly institutions were cited for noncompliance and conciliation agreements were negotiated. The Reagan Administration's "flexible" approach and attempt to reduce the paperwork burden is laudable if the result is more effective enforcement of the laws prohibiting discrimination. Critics fear, however, that such changes represent a relaxation in federal enforcement efforts to the detriment of women and minorities.

The most difficult and frequently controversial compliance with Title IX has involved women's intercollegiate athletics. Equal opportunity for female athletes has been difficult to achieve because of limited institutional resources, vague federal regulations, and institutional resistance. Women's athletics experienced phenomenal growth during the 1970's; the highly capable female athlete is no longer being ignored. The impact of the National Collegiate Athletic Association's (NCAA) January 1980 decision to offer women's championships in all three divisions and to add women to the NCAA governing board is unclear. Recruiting of women athletes at NCAA schools will change drastically, probably to the detriment of the Association for Intercollegiate Athletics for Women (AIAW). During the decade of its existence, the AIAW has been in the forefront of the fight for equality for women in athletics. Given the manner and atmosphere in which the NCAA voted to offer women's championships, a similar advocacy by the NCAA for equality appears unlikely. The deemphasis on Title IX by the Reagan Administration if coupled with the loss of strong organizational advocacy of the AIAW may seriously affect equal opportunity for female athletes. A strong institutional commitment will be essential to ensure this equality in the absence of strong outside pressure.

Many resources are available as guides to compliance and improvement of campus life. Of particular value are publications developed by the Resource Center on Sex Roles in Education, listed in the Bibliography and available from the Superintendent of Documents, Government Printing Office, Washington, D.C. 20202.

These publications include the following:

1. Competitive Athletics: In Search of Equal Opportunity

2. Resource Kit for Title IX

3. Student Guide to Title IX

4. Title IX and Physical Education: A Compliance Overview

*Peer Perspective, 7:2, May 1981.

5. Title IX Grievance Procedures: An Introductory Manual

The *Fair Employment Report*, the looseleaf services, and the *Federal Register* provide additional current information on compliance with Titles VI and IX. Project HEATH has contributed a useful booklet for improving the relationship between faculty members and disabled students: L. Smith, *The College Student with a Disability: A Faculty Handbook*. The Handbook is available from the Government Printing Office, Washington, DC 20402. Ask for #1980 0-327-505:QL4.

The Affirmative Action Office can enhance student life by presenting programs to student groups, participating in student-produced programs, hiring students to work in the Affirmative Action Office, and discussing affirmative action-related questions with students. The primary beneficiaries of the faculty training program described above will be students. Although on many campuses affirmative action will focus on the employee/employer relationship, students' concerns must also be a vital part of the Affirmative Action Office's responsibilities, since students are a major reason for the institution's existence.

The quality of life on campus can be enriched through affirmative action-oriented training programs such as those described in this chapter. A director whose staff can be assigned the data-collection and analysis responsibilities can devote a substantial portion of his/her time to quality-of-life responsibilities. The result will be a better learning and working environment for everyone.

Increasing heterogeneity on campuses across the country is inevitable. Not only are women, ethnic minorities, foreign students, and disabled students enrolling in increasing numbers, but the declining pool of 18 to 21 year olds has forced academic institutions to recruit and to develop programs for older students. Women and minorities with the appropriate credentials for faculty positions are increasing each year. Women are beginning to enter academic disciplines long numerically dominated by men. Many of these changes will occur naturally but often painfully. The Affirmative Action Office can take a leadership role on campus to prepare the campus for these changes and to help the campus better adapt to them.

APPENDICES

APPENDICES

APPENDIX 1-1

MAJOR FEDERAL ACTS AND ORDERS AFFECTING HIGHER EDUCATION

SUMMARY

YEAR	LEGISLATION	BASES OF NON-DISCRIMINATION	ACTIVITY AFFECTED	ENFORCEMENT AGENCY	PRIVATE CAUSE OF ACTION	FEDERAL FUNDS
1963	Equal Pay Act	sex	employment	EEOC	*	
1964	Civil Rights Act Title VI	race, color, national origin	student programs	OCR		*
1964	Civil Rights Act Title VII	race, sex[1], color, religion[1], or national origin	employment	EEOC	*	
1965	Executive Order 11246	race, sex[1], color, religion[1]. or national origin	employment	OFCCP		*
1972	Educational Amendments Title IX	sex	student programs	OCR	*	*
1973	Rehabilitation Act 503 and 504	mental or physical disability	student programs and employment	OCR, OFCCP	*[2]	*
1974	Vietnam Era Veteran's Readjustment Assist. Act (402)	disabled veterans and Vietnam era veterans	employment	OFCCP		*
1974	Age Discrimination in Employment Act (ADEA)	Ages 40-70[3]	employment	EEOC	*	

[1] some exemptions are permitted for institutions owned by religious corporations

[2] conflicting opinions in the federal judiciary

[3] exemption for tenured professors until July 1, 1982

pc

APPENDIX 1-2

FEDERAL LAWS AFFECTING HIGHER EDUCATION

The fair employment laws derive from the federal authority to regulate interstate commerce, from constitutional amendments, and from the early civil rights laws. Enforcement in higher education is by the Equal Employment Opportunity Commission (EEOC), the Department of Education's Office for Civil Rights (OCR), the Office of Federal Contract Compliance Programs (OFCCP) and through the federal court system. In general the laws prohibit discrimination based on race, color, sex, age, religion, national origin, handicap or veterans status. The Executive Orders also require affirmative action: positive steps to increase employment opportunities for members of protected groups. In addition, institutions may be required to take affirmative action as a result of a conciliation or a court order subsequent to a finding of discrimination under Titles VI, VII or IX, the old Civil Rights Acts, or the 5th and 14th Amendments. Affirmative action in higher education involves equity in student related functions (recruitment, admissions, financial aid, and academic programs) and in employment of both faculty and staff. Most of the applicable laws and regulations focus on employment. None of the laws require institutions to hire or retain incompetent employees or employees who perform in an unsatisfactory manner. These laws require that the best qualified person be hired or promoted for a job. The major federal laws and orders prohibiting discrimination are described below. Appendix 1-1 contains a summary of these laws.

1. Civil Rights Acts of 1866 and 1871 - "early" civil rights acts adopted subsequent to the Civil War to protect the employment rights of racial minorities. Often used in conjunction with suits alleging violation of Title VII.

   Enforcement: federal court system

2. Equal Pay Act of 1963 - prohibits an employer from paying persons of one sex at a different rate of pay than persons of the other sex for the jobs requiring substantially equal skill, effort and responsibility. Back pay awards can be doubled if the employer's violation has been "willful".

   Enforcement: EEOC; federal court system

APPENDIX 1-2 (cont'd)

3. Civil Rights Act of 1964, (Title VII) - the major federal law
    prohibiting discrimination in employment. Title VII, one of the
    most complex collections of regulations and guidelines ever issued
    by the federal government, forbids discrimination based on race,
    sex, color, religion or national origin. Title VII covers all
    areas of the employment relationship from advertising open positions
    through termination or retirement.

    The EEOC has issued guidelines which, though they do not have the
    force of law, generally have been upheld by federal courts.

    EEOC Guidelines on Discrimination Because of Sex
    EEOC Guidelines on Discrimination Because of Religion
    EEOC Guidelines on Discrimination Because of National Origin
    EEOC Guidelines on Pre-Employment Inquiries
    EEOC Guidelines on Affirmative Action

    EEOC/OFCCP Guidelines on Hazardous Conditions in the Workplace
    Questions and Answers on Pregnancy Discrimination

    In addition, EEOC is one of five federal agencies that apply the
    Uniform Guidelines on Employee Selection Procedures.

    Enforcement: EEOC; federal court system

4. Civil Rights Act (Title VI) - prohibits discrimination on the
    basis of race, color and national origin in all federally
    assisted programs. Affects student admissions, financial aid,
    and academic programs.

    Enforcement: OCR

5. Executive Order 11246, as amended by Executive Order 11375 -
    requires institutions accepting federal funds to take affirma-
    tive action to increase employment opportunities for minorities
    and women. The institution must have a written affirmative
    action plan which complies with Revised Order 4 to "remedy the
    effects of past discrimination" and to prevent the continuation
    of current discrimination. The institutional obligation is
    contractual. Institutions with an aggregate of $10,000 in
    federal contracts during a 12 month period agree to follow a
    series of rules and regulations that include setting goals and
    timetables for achieving full utilization of women and minorities.

    The OFCCP has issued the following guidelines and orders:

    Revised Order No. 4

    OFCCP Rules and Regulations on the Obligations of Government
    Contractors and Subcontractors

    OFCCP Rules and Sanction Proceedings

    Technical Guidance Memo No. 1 on Revised Order No. 4

    OFCCP Sex Discrimination Guidelines

    Rules on Examination and Copying of OFCCP Documents

    OFCCP Guidelines on Discrimination Because of Religion or
    National Origin

    Enforcement: OFCCP

APPENDIX 1-2 (cont'd)

6. Educational Amendments of 1972 (Title IX) - prohibits sex discrimination in educational programs or activities in institutions
   with federal contracts, grants, and loans. Modeled after Title
   VI, Title IX affects student admissions, financial aid, and academic programs. The greatest impact of Title IX has been on
   intercollegiate athletic programs. Title IX's application to
   employment situations has met with different results in different
   circuits. In Cannon v. U. of Chicago, the Supreme Court ruled
   that individual plaintiffs could being causes of action under
   Title IX.

   Enforcement: OCR

7. Rehabilitation Act of 1973 (503 and 504) - forbids discrimination
   against the disabled and requires institutions to take affirmative
   action to hire and promote qualified disabled persons and to make
   academic programs accessible to disabled persons. Institutions
   are not required to set goals and timetables or to perform utilization analyses but most recruit and consider disabled persons
   for open positions. Institutions must also make such reasonable
   accommodations to the physical or mental limitations of disabled
   employees as providing special equipment or modifying the job.
   The major impact of 503/504 has been on structural changes required
   to make programs accessible for disabled students. Compliance with
   both sections is a responsibility of institutions with federal contracts exceeding $2,500 annually.

   Enforcement: OFCCP and OCR

8. Vietnam Era Veterans Readjustment Act of 1974 (402) - protects
   disabled veterans and veterans of the Vietnam era from employment
   discrimination by institutions holding federal contracts exceeding $10,000 annually. Requires employers to list all suitable
   employment openings with the state employment office.

   Enforcement: OFCCP

9. Age Discrimination in Employment Act of 1974 (ADEA) - protects
   persons who are between ages 40-70 from arbitrary age discrimination in hiring, discharge, pay, promotions, fringe benefits
   and other aspects of employment. The law is designed to promote
   employment of older persons on the basis of ability rather than
   age and to help employers and workers find ways to meet problems
   arising from the impact of age on employment.

   Enforcement: EEOC; federal court system

APPENDIX 3-1

UNIVERSITY OF MISSOURI-ST. LOUIS

Affirmative Action Hiring Policy*

1. The University's goal is the hiring of the best qualified faculty and
    staff members available. None of the items below shall be construed
    to mean that minimally qualified or unqualified persons shall be
    hired/promoted.

2. The University's Affirmative Action policy provides that in departments
    that do not match the appropriate national and/or local availability
    proportions, when a majority group male and a member of a protected
    group are substantially equally qualified, the member of the protected
    group shall be offered the position.

3. When such a department has an opportunity to hire a well qualified member
    of a protected group, the department shall make every effort to do so as
    expeditiously as possible.

*The above policy was developed by the Affirmative Action/Equal Employment
Opportunity Committee and confirmed by vote of the Senate on October 13,
1978.

APPENDIX 4-1

INDEX

APPENDIX 4-2

INDEX TO GUIDELINES FOR SEARCH COMMITTEES

APPENDIX 4-2 (cont'd)

CHECKLIST FOR SEARCH COMMITTEES

____ 1. Select a chairperson.*

____ 2. Determine a meeting schedule.

____ 3. Determine a timetable for the process.

____ 4. Advertising and Posting:**

     ____ a. Notify the Affirmative Action Office (Form 8177)

     ____ b. Place advertising in appropriate journals.

____ 5. Acknowledge applications.

____ 6. Send data collection cards (Form 8377)

____ 7. Preliminary screening of applicants:

     ____ a. List all applicants on Form 8577(2).

     ____ b. Document reasons for rejection on Form 8577(2) for those applicants screened out at this stage.

     ____ c. Rejection letters to candidates screened out.

____ 8. Review credentials.

____ 9. Interview process.

____ 10. Reference checks.

____ 11. Rejection letters to candidates screened out.

____ 12. Submit list of recommended candidates to hiring official.

     ____ a. Document reasons for rejection for those applicants not recommended (8577(2)) and forward to hiring official.

     ____ b. Forward committee files to hiring official.

* usually appointed by the hiring official

** sometimes done by the hiring official prior to convening of the search committee

APPENDIX 4-3

FLOW CHART OF ADMINISTRATIVE APPROVAL FORMS FOR FULL TIME ACADEMIC HIRES

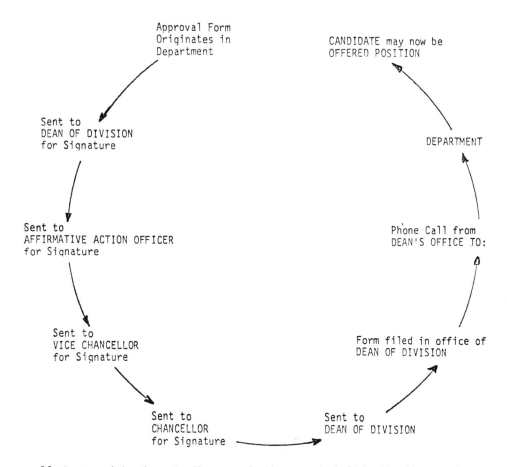

If at any point, there is disapproval, the form is held by the disapproving office until the problems are resolved by the office and the department.

APPENDIX 4-4

INTRA-OFFICE MONITORING SYSTEM - FACULTY

School _____

Department _____

Title _____

Person being replaced _____

1. ___ Position vacancy received.

2. ___ Sent to Missouri State Employment.

3. ___ Position posted in Recruiting and Hires Book and Academic Hires Book.

4. ___ Posted in JOB REGISTER.

5. ___ Posted in SPECTRUM (Campus publication).

6. ___ Utilization/Availability stamped on Chancellor's Job Register.

7. ___ Approval Form received from Department.

8. ___ Utilization/Availability stamped on Approval Form.

9. ___ Survey Cards Compiled.

10. ___ Director's Signature.

11. ___ Sent to Vice Chancellor.

12. ___ Applicant posted in Recruiting and Hires Book and Academic Hires Book.

13. ___ Logged on Applicant Flow Data Chart.

14. ___ Demographic Data Summary Completed.

15. ___ Demographic Data Summary sent to Department.

Person hired _____

Race ___ Sex ___ Service Date ___

Salary ___ Tenure Track ___

Date Offer Declined (if applicable) ___

Application Deadline _____

Person to Contact _____

Address _____

Phone number _____

Search Committee

Chairperson _____ Phone _____

Members:

1.

2.

3.

Person hired _____

Race ___ Sex ___ Service Date ___

Salary ___ Tenure Track ___

Date Offer Declined (if applicable) ___

APPENDIX 4-5

NOTIFICATION OF FULL TIME POSITION VACANCY - (8177)

1. Department _____ 2. School/College _____

3. Title _____
   (Be specific as to area of specialization)

4. Person Being Replaced _____
   (If this represents a new position, so indicate.)

5. Date when employee will begin work _____

6. Description of duties*

7. Qualifications required*

8. If a search/screening committee is involved, list the members, designating a chairperson.

   Person to whom applications should be sent:

   Name _____

   Department _____

   Phone Number _____

   Application Deadline _____

9. Type of search anticipated: National _____ Pool _____ Campus _____

This form should be used for any position which is advertised.

                                        Signed _____
                                        Title _____
                                        Date _____

* Information requested in these items should correspond with   ads used in recruiting.

APPENDIX 4-6

FACULTY GOAL ACHIEVEMENT LOG
ACADEMIC YEAR 198_ - 8_

JOB GROUP _____

DEPARTMENT	POSITION TITLE	GOAL[1]	DATE POSTED	PERSON HIRED[2]	RACE/SEX	EFFECTIVE DATE	GOAL MET?

[1] Minority/female
[2] Include and indicate waivers

pc

APPENDIX 4-7

CENTER FOR ACADEMIC DEVELOPMENT (CAD)
RECRUITING PROCEDURES[*]

INTRODUCTION

The Center for Academic Development was established July 1, 1977.
The main goal of the Center is the retention of promising students. The
objectives of the Center are: (1) to help students overcome basic academic
skill deficiencies, (2) to help students develop effective learning skills,
and (3) to help students develop an organized academic plan leading to
success in a degree program.

The Center is a unit of the Academic Affairs Office. The organizational structure in shown in Appendix I. The three Units of the Center are
as follows, and a descriptive brochure is included in Appendix II.

I.   COMMUNICATIONS UNIT

        a. Reading Lab.
        b. Remedial English Lab.
        c. Writing Lab.
        d. English 09 (Provided by the CAD and administered by
                the English Department.)

II.   MATHEMATICS UNIT

        a. Remedial Math. Lab.
        b. Developmental Math. Lab.
        c. Math 02 (Provided by the CAD and administered by the
                Department of Mathematical Sciences.)

III.   SPECIAL SERVICES UNIT

        a. Program for Disadvantaged Students.
        b. Tutorial Lab.
        c. Advisement.

[*]Prepared by Dr. Edith M. Young, Acting Director and ACE Fellow in
Academic Administration, 1979-1980.

APPENDIX 4-7 (cont'd)

RECRUITING PROCEDURES

The responsibility for recruiting is assigned to the three unit coordinators. The recruiting procedure used by each of the three units is conducted with the approval of the Director. The Director is the hiring official for the Center.

JOB DESCRIPTIONS AND PROFESSIONAL DUTIES

The academic titles listed below are assigned to the professional faculty/staff positions.

Position Title	Title Code
Director	3380
Coordinator/Lecturer	5800
Instructor	5120
Lecturer	5800
Teaching Associate	9100
*Teaching Fellow	9110
*Tutor/Peer Advisor	9430
Educational Assistant III/Coordinator	3577
Educational Assistant II	3576
Educational Assistant I	3575

For a description and listing of the minimum qualifications and professional duties of the faculty/staff positions see Appendix I.

ADVERTISING POSITIONS

Unit coordinators will obtain approval of the Director, the charge to Search Committee, and Affirmative Action Guidelines before initiating the recruiting procedures. After the need to recruit has been established by the Director and Unit Coordinator, a search committee will be established in accordance with the U.M.S.L. Affirmative Action Plan, Procedures, and Guidelines.

---

* Academic Position title assigned to undergraduate/graduate students.

APPENDIX 4-7 (cont'd)

All positions will be listed with the Affirmative Action Office for posting with the Missouri State Employment Office, Spectrum, and the U.M.S.L. Job Register.

The Center will place advertisements in the publications listed below. The position and type of search--local or national--will determine publications selected.

1. St. Louis Post-Dispatch
2. St. Louis Globe Democrat
3. St. Louis Argus
4. St. Louis Sentinel
5. The Chronicle of Higher Education
6. Journal of Remedial/Developmental Education
7. National Association of Remedial/Developmental Studies in Post-Secondary Institutions

APPLICATIONS

Applicant Pool. Unsolicited letters of application and resumes received in the CAD office will comprise the applicant pool file. Unit Coordinators will forward to the CAD office for the applicant pool file applications and resumes received in their office. Applications and resumes will be kept in the file for one year.

When a vacancy occurs, the applicant pool file will be checked for qualified applicants. Applicants possessing minimum qualifications for vacant positions will be notified by letter or phone. Applicants interested in being considered for vacant positions will be requested to update their application for consideration by the search committee. Applicants will be sent an appropriate letter and the affirmative action data card.

Applications in Response to Listing. Applications received in response to listing will be acknowledged with an appropriate letter. The affirmative action data card will be sent to all applicants.

APPENDIX 4-7 (cont'd)

The search committee will evaluate each applicant's credentials carefully.

Interview of Candidates. After careful evaluation of all of the applicants' credentials by the search committee, the committee will determine the candidates. The committee will arrange the interview schedule and provide each individual interviewer with a candidate appraisal form with instructions for completing and returning the form. A copy of the candidate appraisal form is included in Appendix III.

The search committee will invite the Childhood Education Department, English Department, Department of Mathematical Science, Academic Advising Committee, and the Counseling Center to participate in the search process when appropriate.

After the completion of the interview schedule, the search committee will submit an unranked list of all qualified candidates to the Director for consideration. The Chairman of the search committee will also submit to the Director completed affirmative action forms and appropriate letters of rejection addressed to applicants not meeting the minimum qualifications according to the listed job description.

Offer of Appointment. The Director, who is the hiring official, will consider all candidate names submitted, select a candidate, and make an offer in accordance with the Affirmative Action Plan, Policies, and Procedures.

APPENDIX 4-8

THE UMSL JOB REGISTER　　　　　　　　　　AUGUST 1, 1980

The UMSL JOB REGISTER is distributed by the Affirmative Action Office to promote awareness of job opportunities for academic and administrative positions at the University of Missouri-St. Louis. Anyone interested in applying for the positions listed below should do so directly to the hiring department.

DEPARTMENT/UNIT	PROPOSED TITLES AND DESCRIPTIONS	FOR MORE INFORMATION CONTACT
ARTS & SCIENCES		
Chemistry	Assistant Professor of Chemistry (Inorganic)	Harold Harris
	QUALIFICATIONS: Ph.D., with postdoctoral experience desirable. Inorganic chemist with research interests in transition metal chemistry.	324 Benton Hall (314) 553-5311
	DUTIES: Teaching assignments will include courses at intro- ductory through Ph.D. level. Coordinator of undergraduate analytical offerings.	Deadline for Applications: October 20, 1980
Chemistry	Assistant Professor of Chemistry (Physical)	Harold Harris
	QUALIFICATIONS: Ph.D., with postdoctoral experience desirable. Physical chemist with research interests in an experimental area.	324 Benton Hall (314) 553-5311
	DUTIES: Teaching assignments will include courses at intro- ductory through Ph.D. level. Coordinator of undergraduate analytical offerings.	Deadline for Applications: October 20, 1980
Economics	Assistant Professor	William Mitchell
	QUALIFICATIONS: Ph.D. or dissertation stage	408 SSB (314) 553-5351
	DUTIES: Research; teaching in B.A., B.S. and M.A. programs; and departmental and university service.	Deadline for Applications: November 1, 1980

APPENDIX 4-9

DEMOGRAPHIC DATA CARD (8377)

Position Applied For: _____
                              Department   Title

Name_____
              Last   First   M.I.

Source _____
                    (how did you find out about the position)

Age _____ Sex _____ Viet Nam Veteran _____ Handicap _____
                                                              specifiy

Ethnic Category:

_____ White, not of Hispanic Origin—origins in any of the original people in Europe, North Africa or the Middle East

_____ Black, not of Hispanic Origin—origins in any black racial group

_____ Hispanic—origins of Mexican, Puerto Rican, Cuban, Central or South American or other Spanish culture, regardless of race

_____ Asian or Pacific Islander—origins in any of the original peoples of the Far East, SE Asia, the Indian Subcontinent, or Pacific Islands

_____ American Indian or Alaskan Native—origins in any of the original people of N. America who maintain cultural identification through tribal affiliation or community recognition

Since you have recently applied for or been recommended for a position at UMSL, we would appreciate your completing the information requested on this form promptly. Although doing so is voluntary on your part, the information gathered in this manner is vital to the University's Affirmative Action compliance with Titles VII and IX of the Civil Rights Act, the Rehabilitation Act of 1973 and the Viet Nam Era Veterans Readjustment Act of 1974. We appreciate your cooperation.   8377

‖‖‖

FIRST CLASS
PERMIT NO. 9447
ST. LOUIS, MO. 63155

BUSINESS REPLY MAIL
NO POSTAGE STAMP NECESSARY IF MAILED IN U.S.A.

POSTAGE WILL BE PAID BY

Affirmative Action Office
405 Woods Hall
University of Missouri-St. Louis
8001 Natural Bridge Road
St. Louis, Missouri 63121

APPENDIX 4-10

DEMOGRAPHIC DATA SUMMARY - (7979)

Department _____   Position _____

Offer to _____   Race/Sex _____

Applicant Recruiting Source _____   % of cards returned _____

Form 8577 Total Applicants _____

| Total Male Applicants _____ | Minority Male Applicants _____ | Race Unknown _____ | Handicap Indicated _____ |
| Total Female Applicants _____ | Minority Female Applicants _____ | Race Unknown _____ | Handicap Indicated _____ |

Total Applicants from Demographic Data Cards _____

	Recruiting Source	# of Cards Returned	Total Males	Minority Males	Total Females	Minority Females	Handicap Indicated
1.							
2.							
3.							
4.							
5.							
6.							
Total		_____	_____	_____	_____	_____	_____

AVAILABILITY AND UTILIZATION INFORMATION

AVAILABILITY Fem. _____% Min. _____%

UTILIZATION Fem. _____% Min. _____%

APPENDIX 4-11

Part-time and Temporary Positions at the University of Missouri-St.Louis

The University of Missouri-St. Louis occasionally has a need for temporary instructors, lecturers, and other part-time academic personnel. These needs arise because of unexpected student enrollment, unexpected faculty resignations, or illness of faculty members. The positions may be day or evening. In most instances, the minimum degree required is the doctorate.

Although there are no positions available at this time, we are building applicant pools in the disciplines listed below. Applicants should respond only in writing and send resumes indicating their disciplines to the Vice Chancellor for Academic Affairs, Woods Hall, 8001 Natural Bridge, St. Louis, Mo 63121. Vitas will be retained in the applicant pool for one year.

College of Arts and Sciences
- Administration of Justice
- Anthropology
- Art
- Biology
- Chemistry
- Economics
- English
- Foreign Languages
- History
- Mathematical Sciences
- Music
- Philosophy
- Physics
- Political Science
- Psychology
- Social Work
- Sociology
- Speech

School of Business Administration
- Accounting
- Behavioral Management
- Finance
- Legal Environment
- Marketing
- Quantitative Management

School of Education
- Administration, Foundations, and Secondary Education
- Behavioral Studies (Counseling, Special Education, Physical Education, Educational Psychology)
- Childhood Education (Elementary, Early Childhood)

The University of Missouri-St. Louis is an equal opportunity and affirmative action employer and educational institution.

APPENDIX 4-12

ADMINISTRATIVE APPROVAL FORM (8577)

1. Department _____ 2. School/College _____

3a. Title _____ 3b. Person Being Replaced _____

4. Offer of $_____ to 5. _____

6. Effective Date _____

7. Service Basis (academic positions only):

       9 months_____ Regular _____Years Toward Tenure _____

       12 months _____Non-regular_____ FTE _____

8a. New Hire_____ 8b. Promotion (exclusive of academic rank) _____

9. Type of Search: A. National _____   D. UMSL Campus _____

                        B. Metro Area _____   E. Applicant Pool _____

                        C. University-wide _____   F. Other _____

10. Recruiting: _____ as submitted to Affirmative Action Office by department/unit.

               _____ exceptions

11. Number of Applicants: Total____ Fem. ____ Min._____ Hand. Ind.____ Race Unk.____

    Short List: Total____ Fem. ____Min._____ Hand. Ind.____ Race Unk.____

    Interviewed: Total____ Fem. ____Min._____ Hand. Ind.____ Race Unk.____

12. Demographic data on all applicants - page two of this form. Attach additional pages if necessary.

13. SIGNATURES:

    Department Chairperson _____ Date _____

    Dean _____ Date _____

    Approved for Affirmative Action Compliance by Affirmative Action Officer - - - -

    _____ Date _____

    Vice Chancellor _____ Date _____

    Chancellor _____ Date _____

Return of this form signed by the Chancellor or Vice Chancellor is the department's authorization to offer the position to the candidate identified above.

APPENDIX 4-12 (cont'd)

CANDIDATES

DEMOGRAPHIC DATA   8577(2)

Department_____Position_____

Instructions: List all applicants for this position alphabetically. Indicate
                appropriate code in each column. Demographic data not known to
                the department will be filled in by the Affirmative Action Office.
                Indicate person selected by a colored mark in the margin next to
                his/her name. Example: ➡Smith, Jane

NAME	RACE	SEX	AGE	HANDICAP	SHORT LIST	INTERVIEWED	REASON FOR NON-SELECTION
1.
2.
3.
4.
5.
6.
7.
8.
9.
10.
11.
12.
13.
14.
15.
16.
17.
18.
19.
20.

APPENDIX 4-12 (cont'd)

INSTRUCTIONS FOR APPROVAL FORM (8577)

Number one through eight - Self-explanatory. Be specific about title, ie. Assistant Professor of Biology (Microbiology), Assistant Professor of Art History (17th century).

Number nine - See Search Guidelines.

Number ten - Check appropriate space. If you check exceptions, explain any deviations from the procedures submitted to the Affirmative Action Office, including additional efforts you have made.

Number eleven - Indicate numbers as indicated by your records (Affirmative Action Office will complete with data gathered on the cards):

Total _____ Female _____ Minority _____

Handicap Indicated _____ Race Unknown _____

Number twelve - Demographic data on page 2:

a. Indicate race (if known) by the appropriate number. If unknown, indicate so with a "U". See codes for numbers and definitions.

b. Indicate male or female (if known). If unknown, indicate with a "U".

c. Indicate age of candidate.

d. Indicate handicapped candidates with an "H".

e. Indicate which candidates were on the short list and which were interviewed with an asterisk (*).

f. If a candidate was not selected for one of the reasons listed on the code sheet, place the proper number in the designated column. More than one number may be appropriate (see codes for numbers and definitions).

If a candidate was not selected for a reason not listed, select the appropriate item on the code sheet and attach a paragraph explaining that reason (See September 21, 1979, Memorandum on Reasons for Non-selection.) Any reasons not coded must be explained in the manner described in Memorandum No. 2. If several persons are not selected for a position for a similar reason, it is acceptable to categorize them by giving the reasons and then listing the persons to whom it applies.

g. Be sure to include any candidates in the specific area involved whose vitae were unsolicited, were part of your general applicant pool, and/or arrived prior to the official announcement of the opening. (See Memorandum No. 3 on unsolicited applications.)

APPENDIX 4-13

CODES
(To be used in completing Approval Form - 8577
And Record of Part Time Academic Hire - 8678)

A. Race

1. White, not of Hispanic Origin--origins in any of the original peoples of Europe, North Africa or the Middle East.

2. Black, not of Hispanic Origin--origins in any black racial group.

3. Hispanic--origins of Mexican, Puerto Rican, Cuban, Central or South America or other Spanish culture, regardless of race.

4. Asian or Pacific Islander--origins in any of the original peoples of the Far East, Southeast Asia, the Indian Subcontinent, or Pacific Islands.

5. American Indian or Alaskan Native--origins in any of the original peoples of North America who maintain cultural identification through tribal affiliation or community recognition.

B. Sex

M - Male
F - Female

C. Indicate those applicants on the short list and/or who were interviewed and known to be handicapped.

D. Reasons for non-selection: Full time academic appointments
(Reasons for non-selection for part time appointments are given on page 17).

Candidate's Choice

A- 1 Would not relocate.
A- 2 Accepted another job.
A- 3 Offered the position but declined.
A- 4 Asked not to be considered.
A- 5 Accepted another position within the University.
A- 6 Not available for interview.
A- 7 No job opportunity for spouse.
A- 8 Candidate requires a higher salary than authorized.
A- 9 Not available for full-time employment at the start of the project period or semester.
A-10 Failed to submit transcript/letters of recommendation required.
A-11 Failed to respond to requests for additional information.
A-12 Recommendations (or slides or publications) not submitted in time to be processed and considered for the position.
A-13 Advertised position was at the junior level; this candidate was unavailable for a job except at the senior level.
A-14 See explanation attached.

Degree

B-1 Did not possess a terminal degree.
B-2 Not making satisfactory and timely progress toward a terminal degree.
B-3 Degree in a field not compatible with the needs of the department.
B-4 Dissertation not completed and insufficient evidence that it will be by the end of the year.
B-5 Degree granting institution not as strong in the field as that of the candidate selected. (Strengths of degree granting institutions should be widely disparate if this reason is used. Please use this reason cautiously for female candidates, as a female's choice of schools is sometimes dependent upon her spouse's career; hence she may not have had the luxury of choosing a top ranking school for her work.)
B-6 See explanation attached.

APPENDIX 4-13 (cont'd)

Teaching/Seminar

C-1 Area of specialization of interest overlaps significantly with those of current members of the department and hence does not fit with the needs of the department.
C-2 Area of secondary competence not compatible with the needs of the department as advertised.
C-3 Candidate's teaching (or performing) experience was not suitable for this position.
C-4 Insufficient teaching experience or candidate selected had more teaching experience.
C-5 Interview revealed that this candidate was not interested in the diversity of the teaching assignment required by this position.
C-6 Did not have sufficient technical competence in the primary area.
C-7 Seminar/lecture failed to demonstrate scholarly substance.
C-8 Seminar/lecture demonstrated a communication problem (or a language barrier).
C-9 See explanation attached.

Research, Scholarship, and Publications

D-1 Candidate acceptable but candidate selected has more and/or better publications.
D-2 Insufficient publication (or composition, or exhibition) record.
D-3 Creative artwork (or musical composition) judged inadequate by the research committee on the basis of submitted slides.
D-4 Lack of demonstrated research skills.
D-5 Research/Publications not appropriate to position as advertised.
D-6 Has done insufficient research or has not published adequately considering the length of time.
D-7 Research does not support teaching assignment.
D-8 See explanation attached.

MISCELLANEOUS

E-1 History of difficult inter-personal relationships. (Use only in rare instances when a history truly exists and can be documented. Use cautiously, as racism and sexism are sometimes related to this difficulty).
E-2 Potential conflict of interest with University interests.
E-3 Lacked qualifications for the areas listed in the position description and advertising.
E-4 Candidate well qualified for the position, but quality of teaching and research was higher in the candidate selected. This candidate would be considered for the position if the first choice declines. (This reason should not be used as a "catch-all". It should be used only for unsuccessful candidates on the short list or interview list.)

ACADEMIC ADMINISTRATORS*

F-1 Candidate did not possess the degree(s) specified in the job qualifications.
F-2 Candidate's experience was outside the primary responsibilities of the position as advertised.
F-3 Candidate not interested in the teaching component of the position.
F-4 Candidate well qualified for the position and would be considered for the position if the first choice declined. (Should be used only for the very top 2-3 candidates.)

*Some reasons for non-selection for administrative positions may be similar to those for faculty positions. If so, use the codes that best describe the reason for non-selection. For example:

A-3 offered the position but declined.
A-8 candidate requires a higher salary than authorized.
B-3 degree in a field not compatible with the needs of the department.
D-6 has done insufficient research or has not published adequately considering the length of time.

APPENDIX 4-13 (cont'd)

    F-5 Candidate's contributions in the service area were insufficient. (Includes lack of participation in state or national organizations as well as a lack of participation in departmental or university committees.)

    F-6 Candidate did not have a demonstrated record of obtaining external funding. (Use only when the person selected had such a record and when it is specifically mentioned as a job responsibility.)

    F-7 Candidate had insufficient administrative experience.

    F-8 See explanation attached.

APPENDIX 4-14

UNIVERSITY OF MISSOURI-ST. LOUIS

Affirmative Action Office

8001 Natural Bridge Road
St. Louis, Missouri 63121
Telephone: (314) 453 5695

September 21, 1979

MEMORANDUM NO. 2

FROM LOIS VANDERWAERDT

REASONS FOR NON-SELECTION

The balance between adequate documentation of our hiring process and the expenditure of administrative time and resources is as delicate as reconciling the requirements of various governmental laws and regulations with the realities of academic hiring. The approval form (8577) we have used for the past two years attempts to strike that balance.

The key to documentation is to explain as completely as possible why a person was not selected. This is part of selecting the best qualified person and justifying that selection. Documentation of this nature done at the time of the hire or promotion will preclude having to reconstruct the entire situation during an investigation in the distant future. The soundest reasons, legally, for non-selection of a candidate, for instance, are the most objective - those requiring the least amount of professional judgment. These reasons may be those initiated by the candidate and are indicated on the code sheet as category A. Sound reasons may also be those which cause the candidate to fall below the minimal qualifications set up by the department such as B-1 - did not possess a terminal degree.

The reasons mentioned above are categorized by agencies and the courts as objective reasons. The documentation necessary for candidates not selected for any of these reasons is minimal. Departmental files, for example, should contain either a letter from the candidate stating why s/he no longer wishes to be considered, evidence that the candidate failed to complete the application process (perhaps a letter from the department requesting the information), or a detailed telephone log stating who spoke to the candidate, the date and hour of the conversation, and the content of the conversation.

A second category of reasons are those which require varying degrees of professional judgment: B-2 through E-3 fall into this category. The documentation for candidates not selected for these reasons needs to be more extensive. A written paragraph should be kept in departmental files explaining the rationale for the non-selection of each applicant not selected for reasons requiring the

APPENDIX 4-14 (cont'd)

Memorandum No. 2
September 21, 1979
page 2

the exercise of professional judgment. These reasons are given on the
approval form in abbreviated and coded form. If the reason does not fall
into one of the categories listed on the code sheet, the code for "explanation attached" should be given.

If several persons are not selected for similar reasons, it is acceptable to
categorize them by giving the reason and then listing the persons to whom it
applies. If the reason is that the department or hiring official was unable
to make appropriate adjustments within the department to accommodate the candidate's expertise, for example, the paragraph should explain exactly what
accommodations would have had to have been made and why they were not possible.

A third type of reason is a very difficult one to document because of the
negative connotations of "reasons for non-selection". This reason appears
on the code sheet as E-4. It occurs when a department has one vacancy and
several highly qualified candidates who have survived a lengthy selection
process which may have begun with dozens of applicants. These candidates are
not selected because of any deficiency on their parts; they are not selected
because someone else was deemed by the professional judgment of the department
to be better qualified. Using this as a reason for non-selection is delicate
and must be carefully documented in departmental files so that a defense can
be made that the person selected was truly the best qualified. Obviously
this is less delicate if all the candidates involved are of the same race or
sex. If they are not, we must take great care to ensure and be able to demonstrate, that the vestiges of racism and sexism have not intruded into the
selection of the best qualified candidate.

LV/lo

APPENDIX 4-15

WAIVER REQUEST

Waivers to the search requirements may be requested in the following instances:

A. In emergency situations* where a pool of candidates can be developed immediately by appropriate campus officers. The pool shall include internal as well as outside candidates in existing pools, or, if such a pool does not exist, one may also be generated through local advertising.

B. In situations where a department wishes to secure a visiting faculty person with genuine professional distinction.

C. In situations where a person may be appointed as a temporary administrator to fill a position while a national search is being conducted.

D. In situations where a desirable member of a protected group has applied.

_____

*An emergency situation occurs when there is insufficient time for a national search because someone must be performing the necessary functions within days, and where there are no back-up personnel.

APPENDIX 4-15 (cont'd)

WAIVER REQUEST – (8278)

1. Department_____

2. School/College _____

3. Title _____

4. Person Being Replaced _____

5. Person Being Hired, If Known_____

6. Waiver requested. (See Section IV of Search Guidelines: Determining
   the Scope and Nature of the Search, or see page 8a.)

   A _____ B _____ C _____ D _____   Other (explain)

7. Detailed explanation of reason for request:

                                    Chairperson _____

                                    Dean _____

                                    Date _____

                Recommendation for approval
                (Affirmative Action Officer) _____ Date_____

                Approval of Waiver
                Chancellor or Vice Chancellor _____ Date _____

APPENDIX 4-16

RECORD OF PART TIME ACADEMIC HIRE (8678)

1. Department _____ 2. School/College_____

3. Title_____

4. Offer of $_____ to 5. _____

6. Beginning date_____ 7. Ending date (if known)_____

8. FTE _____

9. Recruiting

10. Number of Applicants Total _____ Female _____ Minority _____

                          Handicap Indicated _____ Race Unknown _____

11. List all applicants in applicant pool. (Include person selected.)

    Name   Race   Sex   Interviewed   Reason for Non-selection

1.
2.
3.
4.
5.
6.
7.
8.
9.
10.

                    Chairperson_____ Date _____

                    Dean _____ Date _____

APPENDIX 4-16 (cont'd)

RECORD OF PART TIME ACADEMIC HIRE (8678a)

1. Department_____ 2. School/College_____

3. Title_____

4. Offer of $ _____ to 5. _____

6. Beginning date _____ 7. Ending date (if known) _____

8. FTE_____

9. Recruiting

10. Number of Applicants Total _____ Female _____ Minority _____

     Handicap Indicated _____ Race Unknown _____

11. Describe the reasons for the selection of the above named person and any factors which make form 8678 inappropriate.

Chairperson_____ Date _____

Dean _____ Date _____

APPENDIX 4-16 (cont'd)

INSTRUCTIONS FOR 8678 and 8678(a)

Numbers one and two - Self explanatory

Number three - Be very specific eg. - Instructor of Music (Voice)

Number four - Amount of offer

Number five - Name of person selected

Number six - eight - Self explanatory

Number nine - Describe recruiting efforts such as newspaper ad-
            vertising and use of previously generated applicant
            pool. Unsolicited applications and letters from
            those who are not qualified should be included.

Number ten - (8678) Indicate numbers as indicated by your records:

                  Total
                  Female
                  Minority
                  Handicapped
                  Race Unknown

Number eleven - As the purpose of this form is documentation, all who
            apply should be considered applicants whether or not
            they have the required degree or speciality. Any of
            the reasons for non-selection for full time academic
            appointments can be used for part time appointments.
            (See page 10) In addition the following reasons can
            be used for part time appointments in numerical code
            on 8678:

            F-1 Time conflict.
            F-2 Previous commitment.
            F-3 Application arrived too late for consideration
                 but has been placed in applicant pool for
                 future consideration.
            F-4 Candidate selected was the only candidate
                 qualified to teach watercolor (or ancient
                 civilization or whatever).

Use of form 8678(a): Although form 8678 will be appropriate for
            keeping a record of many part time academic
            hires, it is not suited for all situations.
            Hence, when appropriate, use 8678(a). An
            explanation which would be an appropriate
            response is that candidate selected was the
            only candidate who has the specific expertise
            for teaching this course.

APPENDIX 5-1

Pre-Employment Inquiry Guide

Reproduced below is a guide to pre-employment inquiries which was issued by the Missouri Commission on Human Rights and published in the July, 1974, issue of the Commission's official newsletter, "Progress."

	It Is Discriminatory to Inquire About:	It Is Not Discriminatory to Inquire About:
1. Name	The maiden name of a married woman applicant. The original name of an applicant whose name has been legally changed	
2. Birthplace and Residence	Birthplace of applicant. Birthplace of applicant's parents. Birth certificate, naturalization or baptismal certificate	Applicant's place of residence. Length of applicant's residence in Missouri and/or city where the employer is located
3. Creed or Religion	Applicant's religious affiliation. Church, parish or religious holidays observed	
4. Race or Color	Applicant's race, or color of applicant's skin, eyes, hair, etc.	General distinguishing characteristics such as scar, etc.
5. Photographs	Photographs with application or after interview but before hiring	
6. Citizenship	Any and all inquiries into whether applicant is now or intends to become a citizen of the U.S., or any other inquiry related to citizenship	Whether the applicant is in the country on a visa which permits him to work
7. National Origin and Ancestry	Applicant's lineage, ancestry, national origin, descent, parentage, or nationality. Nationality of applicant's parents or spouse	
8. Language	Applicant's mother tongue. Language commonly used by applicant at home	Languages applicant speaks and/or writes fluently
9. Relatives	Name and/or address of any relative of applicant	Names of relatives already employed by the company. Name and address of person to be notified in an emergency
10. Military Experience	Applicant's military experience in other than U.S. Armed Forces, National Guard or Reserve units. Applicant's whereabouts in 1914-18, 1941-45, or 1950-53. Dates and conditions of discharge	Military experience in the U.S. Armed Forces
11. Organizations	All clubs, social fraternities, societies, lodges, or organizations to which the applicant belongs, other than professional trade, or service organizations	Applicant's membership in any union, professional or trade organization
12. References	The name of the applicant's pastor or religious leader	Names of persons willing to provide professional and/or character references for applicant
13. Sex and Family Composition	Sex of applicant. Dependents of applicant	
14. Arrest Record	The number and kinds of arrests of an applicant	Numbers and kinds of convictions
15. Height and Weight	Any inquiry into height and weight of applicant, except where it is a bona fide occupational requirement	

APPENDIX 5-2

An Equal Opportunity Employer   **Personnel Services**

APPLICATION FOR EMPLOYMENT

PERSONAL INFORMATION

Print Last Name, First Name, Middle Name As Shown on Social Security	Telephone	Do Not Write in This Box
Street Address	City and State	
Position Desired	☐Full Time ☐Permanent ☐Part Time ☐Temporary	Dates Available (from-to)

EDUCATIONAL INFORMATION

Highest Grade Completed Grade School 1 2 3 4 5 6 7 8 High Sch 9 10 11 12 Other 1 2 College 1 2 3 4 5 6
(Circle)

Name and Address of School	Course or Major	Dates Attended	Date Graduated	Degree Title

Scholastic Honors, Membership in Professional Societies, Etc.

Extracurricular Activities in College and/or Community Activities

SKILLS, SPECIALIZED TRAINING, AND ABILITIES

List all valid occupational licenses held, giving number and expiration dates; list machines you operate; show apprenticeships or types of specialized training. Include nature of course, dates and duration. Include training received while serving in the military.

OTHER QUALIFICATIONS

Show any other pertinent qualifications(published writings, leadership roles, volunteer activities)

APPENDIX 5-2 (cont'd)

EMPLOYMENT RECORD

Show what you have done for at least ten years or from the time you left school. If you have served in the military during this time, please include that information. List present or most recent employment first. Please add supplemental sheets if necessary.

Firm Name	Kind of Business	Salary Starting Leaving
Address of Firm	Dates Employed From To	
Your Title	Supervisor	May we contact for references? Yes No

Describe your duties

Firm Name	Kind of Business	Salary Starting Leaving
Address of Firm	Dates Employed From To	
Your Title	Supervisor	May we contact for references? Yes No

Describe your duties

Firm Name	Kind of Business	Salary Starting Leaving
Address of Firm	Dates Employed From To	
Your Title	Supervisor	May we contact for references? Yes No

Describe your duties

Have you ever been convicted of a felony? ☐ Yes ☐ No   If yes, explain.

Have you ever been employed elsewhere in the university? If yes, give department, supervisor and dates

Have you ever been suspended or forced to resign from a position? If yes, explain.

Have you ever applied for employment elsewhere in the university? If so, where
Ever employed under other than present name? (list below)

Indicate places where you would be willing to accept employment.
Columbia ☐   Kansas City ☐   Rolla ☐   St. Louis ☐   Other(specify)

I certify that the above statements are correct, and if employed, understand that any false information in this application will be sufficient grounds for termination without notice. I further agree that all rules, orders, and regulations of the Board of Curators affecting my employment shall constitute a part of my appointment or employment. I authorize the University to investigate all statements on this application. I understand that six months after date below this application will be placed in the inactive files and that it may be renewed upon my request.

Signature _____ Date_____

pc

APPENDIX 5-3

UNIVERSITY OF MISSOURI

☐ COLUMBIA – ☐ KANSAS CITY – ☐ ROLLA – ☐ ST. LOUIS – ☐ CENTRAL ADMINISTRATION

SUPPLEMENTAL PERSONNEL DATA

NOTE: This supplemental staff information is required to prepare various reports (including Affirmative Action) and to serve Staff Benefits, emergency and public information needs of the University.

NAME (LAST, FIRST, MIDDLE)	SOCIAL SECURITY NUMBER	MARITAL STATUS	PLACE OF BIRTH

DATE OF BIRTH	NAME OF SPOUSE (LAST, FIRST, MIDDLE)	SPOUSE'S OCCUPATION	

LOCAL ADDRESS	LOCAL PHONE NO.	CAMPUS ADDRESS (ROOM, BLDG.)	CAMPUS PHONE NO.

CHECK THE GROUP IN WHICH YOU CLASSIFY YOURSELF: (This information is needed for University Affirmative Action Program.)

1 WHITE (Non-Hispanic. Origins of Europe, North Africa, or Middle East.)

2 BLACK (Non-Hispanic. Origins in any of the Black Racial Groups of Africa.)

3 HISPANIC (Mexican, Puerto Rican, Cuban, Cent. or So. American or other Spanish Cultural origins, regardless of race.)

4 ASIAN OR PACIFIC ISLANDER (Origins in any of original peoples of the Far East, Southeast Asia, the Indian Sub-continent, or the Pacific Islands. Includes China, Japan, Korea, Philippine Islands and Samoa.)

5 AMERICAN INDIAN OR ALASKAN NATIVE (Origins in any of original peoples of No. America and who maintain cultural identification through tribal affiliation or community recognition.)

SEX: ☐ MALE ☐ FEMALE

CHECK ONE: 1 Native U.S.A.   2 Naturalized   3 Non-Citizen U.S.A.

DO YOU HAVE A PHYSICAL OR MENTAL DISABILITY AFFECTING YOUR EMPLOYMENT? (If YES, SPECIFY)

☐ YES   ☐ NO

EDUCATIONAL LEVEL 1 Grammer School Credit 2 Grammer School Graduate 3 High School Credit 4 High School Graduate or G.E.D.

5 Vocational or Business School Credit 6 Vocational or Business School Graduate 7 College or University Credit

COLLEGE GRADUATE: 8 Bachelor's 9 Master's 10 Doctor's

NOTIFY IN CASE OF EMERGENCY (NAME) | TELEPHONE NO. | NAMES AND BIRTHDATES OF CHILDREN

ADDRESS

SIGNATURE OF EMPLOYEE	DATE

UM—UW FORM 202 (REV AUG 77)

APPENDIX 5-4

FLOW CHART FOR STAFF HIRING

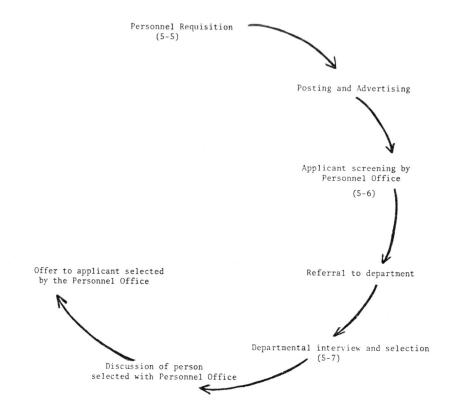

UNIVERSITY OF MISSOURI
COLUMBIA – KANSAS CITY – ROLLA – ST. LOUIS

PERSONNEL REQUISITION – Administrative, Service and Support Positions

1. TITLE OF POSITION TO BE FILLED

2. FULL TIME EQUIVALENCE ___ %

3. POSITION NUMBER

4. REPLACEMENT (NAME AND SALARY OF PERSON REPLACED)

5. WORKING HOURS

6. EMPLOYMENT
☐ PERMANENT
☐ TEMPORARY

7. DATE TO BE FILLED

8. ENDING DATE ☐ INDEFINITE
OTHER _____ (DATE)

9. NEW POSITION (COMPLETE IF NEW POSITION TO BE FILLED)

FUNDS BUDGETED AND APPROVED FOR POSITION $ _____

10. DEPARTMENT

11. NAME OF INTERVIEWER

12. ADDRESS OF INTERVIEWER

13. QUALIFICATIONS OTHER THAN USUAL MINIMUM FOR TITLE

14. SIGNATURE OF ADMINISTRATIVE HEAD

15. DATE

UM-UW FORM 88 (FEB 71)

PERSONNEL

APPENDIX 5-6

Personnel Referral Form

Job Title: _____ Date Posted: _____

Department _____ Class. Verified: _____ B.P. # _____

Person Being Replaced: _____ EEO Category _____

Applicants Interviewed

Name	Race	Sex	Date of Application	Disposition

Name of applicant hired: _____

Date of hire: _____ Starting date: _____ Rate of pay: _____

Type of hire: New_____ Promotion _____ Indefinite _____ Temporary _____

                    Full time _____ Part time _____ Transfer _____ Lateral Transfer _____

R-1-79

APPENDIX 5-7

ADMINISTRATIVE SUPPORT STAFF GOAL ACHIEVEMENT LOG

July 1, 198___ to June 30, 198___

EEO CATEGORY _____

JOB GROUP _____

DEPARTMENT	POSITION TITLE	GOAL[1]	DATE POSTED	PERSON HIRED	RACE/SEX	EFFECTIVE DATE	GOAL MET?

[1] Minority/female

APPENDIX 5-8

U N I V E R S I T Y   O F   M I S S O U R I

☐ COLUMBIA — ☐ KANSAS CITY — ☐ ROLLA — ☐ ST. LOUIS — ☐ CENTRAL ADMINISTRATION

A P P L I C A N T   R E F E R R A L

TO:	DEPARTMENT:

Please interview the applicant named below for the position indicated. Return the original copy of this form to the Personnel Office. If the applicant is not accepted, please return the application along with the completed original copy of this form.

TO BE COMPLETED BY PERSONNEL DEPARTMENT

1. FEDERAL IDENTIFICATION NO.	2. APPLICANT'S NAME (LAST, FIRST, MIDDLE)		
3. JOB TITLE			
4. POSITION NUMBER	5. FTE	6. TYPE OF EMPLOYMENT ☐ 6 — 12 Mo. ☐ Less than 6 months	7. PERQUISITES
8. RECOMMENDED SALARY	9. PERSONNEL COMMENTS		

10. PERSONNEL SIGNATURE	11. DATE

TO BE COMPLETED BY HIRING DEPARTMENT

12. APPLICANT ACCEPTED If "NO" only items 20-22 below need be completed. ☐ YES ☐ NO	13. BEGINNING DATE	14. ENDING DATE
15. SALARY	16. PAYROLL DEPARTMENT AND CODE	
17. PAYMENT DATES	18. ACCOUNTS PAYABLE FROM	19. AMOUNT

20. APPLICANT IS NOT ACCEPTED FOR THE FOLLOWING REASONS (Information required to comply with Federal Law):

21. SIGNATURE OF ADMINISTRATIVE HEAD	22. DATE

THIS FORM COMPLETED, SIGNED AND DATED MUST BE RETURNED TO THE PERSONNEL OFFICE.

UMUW FORM 15 (REV AUG 77)

PERSONNEL

APPENDIX 5-9

Intra Office Monitoring System - Staff

Department _____

Position _____ # _____

Person being replaced _____

Reason for replacement [1] _____

Person hired _____

R/S _____ EEO-6 _____ Starting Date _____

Goal[2] _____

Type of Hire _____ PT OR FT _____ FTE _____

Salary _____

1. _____ Position announcement received.

2. _____ New Employee Forms (116) and Staff Change
           Forms (117) from Budget Office. [3]

3. _____ New employee cards typed from 116's and filed
           alphabetically in the Staff Control boxes and
           by position #.

4. _____ Additions and changes from 117's recorded on
          existing cards in the Staff Control boxes.

5. _____ Personnel Referral Forms received from the
            Personnel Office.

6. ___ Information from the Personnel Referral Forms
       recorded on the Applicant Flow Data Sheet.

7. ____ Personnel Referral Forms filed.

OFFER DECLINED: NAME _____

                R/S _____   DATE _____

[1] Resignation; new position
[2] New hire; promotion; temporary
[3] These forms have a life of their own; for Affirmative
Action purposes, the key is access to them after they
are complete and at a point that does not significantly
disrupt the work flow of another department.(See App 6-2)

APPENDIX 5-10

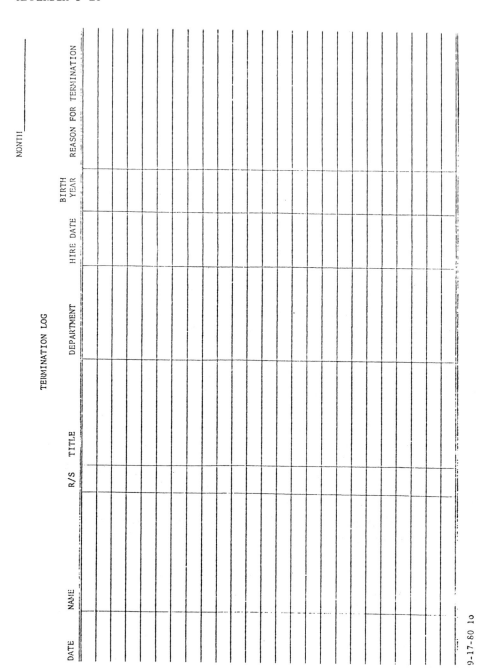

APPENDIX 5-11

Title 29, Code of Federal Regulations, Uniform Guidelines on Employee Selection Procedure

SEC. 4. *Information on impact.*—A. *Records concerning impact.* Each user should maintain and have available for inspection records or other information which will disclose the impact which its tests and other selection procedures have upon employment opportunities of persons by identifiable race, sex, or ethnic group as set forth in subparagraph B below in order to determine compliance with these guidelines. Where there are large numbers of applicants and procedures are administered frequently, such information may be retained on a sample basis, provided that the sample is appropriate in terms of the applicant population and adequate in size.

B. *Applicable race, sex, and ethnic groups for recordkeeping.* The records called for by this section are to be maintained by sex, and the following races and ethnic groups: Blacks (Negroes), American Indians (including Alaskan Natives), Asians (including Pacific Islanders), Hispanic (including persons of Mexican, Puerto Rican, Cuban, Central or South American, or other Spanish origin or culture regardless of race), whites (Caucasians) other than Hispanic, and totals. The race, sex, and ethnic classifications called for by this section are consistent with the Equal Employment Opportunity Standard Form 100, Employer Information Report EEO-1 series of reports. The user should adopt safeguards to insure that the records required by this paragraph are used for appropriate purposes such as determining adverse impact, or (where required) for developing and monitoring affirmative action programs, and that such records are not used improperly. See sections 4E and 17(4), below.

C. *Evaluation of selection rates. The "bottom line."* If the information called for by sections 4A and B above shows that the total selection process for a job has an adverse impact, the individual components of the selection process should be evaluated for adverse impact. If this information shows that the total selection process does not have an adverse impact, the Federal enforcement agencies, in the exercise of their administrative and prosecutorial discretion, in usual circumstances, will not expect a user to evaluate the individual components for adverse impact, or to validate such

individual components, and will not take enforcement action based upon adverse impact of any component of that process, including the separate parts of a multipart selection procedure or any separate procedure that is used as an alternative method of selection. However, in the following circumstances the Federal enforcement agencies will expect a user to evaluate the individual components for adverse impact and may, where appropriate, take enforcement action with respect to the individual components: (1) where the selection procedure is a significant factor in the continuation of patterns of assignments of incumbent employees caused by prior discriminatory employment practices, (2) where the weight of court decisions or administrative interpretations hold that a specific procedure (such as height or weight requirements or no-arrest records) is not job related in the same or similar circumstances. In unusual circumstances, other than those listed in (1) and (2) above, the Federal enforcement agencies may request a user to evaluate the individual components for adverse impact and may, where appropriate, take enforcement action with respect to the individual component.

D. *Adverse impact and the "four-fifths rule."* A selection rate for any race, sex, or ethnic group which is less than four-fifths (⅘) (or eighty percent) of the rate for the group with the highest rate will generally be regarded by the Federal enforcement agencies as evidence of adverse impact, while a greater than four-fifths rate will generally not be regarded by Federal enforcement agencies as evidence of adverse impact. Smaller differences in selection rate may nevertheless constitute adverse impact, where they are significant in both statistical and practical terms or where a user's actions have discouraged applicants disproportionately on grounds of race, sex, or ethnic group. Greater differences in selection rate may not constitute adverse impact where the differences are based on small numbers and are not statistically significant, or where special recruiting or other programs cause the pool of minority or female candidates to be atypical of the normal pool of applicants from that group. Where the user's evidence concerning the

APPENDIX 5-11 (cont'd)

impact of a selection procedure indicates adverse impact but is based upon numbers which are too small to be reliable, evidence concerning the impact of the procedure over a longer period of time and/or evidence concerning the impact which the selection procedure had when used in the same manner in similar circumstances elsewhere may be considered in determining adverse impact. Where the user has not maintained data on adverse impact as required by the documentation section of applicable guidelines, the Federal enforcement agencies may draw an inference of adverse impact of the selection process from the failure of the user to maintain such data, if the user has an underutilization of a group in the job category, as compared to the group's representation in the relevant labor market or, in the case of jobs filled from within. the applicable work force.

E. *Consideration of user's equal employment opportunity posture.* In carrying out their obligations, the Federal enforcement agencies will consider the general posture of the user with respect to equal employment opportunity for the job or group of jobs in question. Where a user has adopted an affirmative action program, the Federal enforcement agencies will consider the provisions of that program, including the goals and timetables which the user has adopted and the progress which the user has made in carrying out that program and in meeting the goals and timetables. While such affirmative action programs may in design and execution be race, color, sex, or ethnic conscious, selection procedures under such programs should be based upon the ability or relative ability to do the work.

APPENDIX 6-1

PERSONNEL INFORMATION CARD - STAFF

NAME   R/S

Social Security No.

BIRTHDATE   CITIZENSHIP   ED. LEVEL

SERVICE DATE:

DATE	TITLE	DEPT.	FTE	POSITION #	SALARY

APPENDIX 6-1 (cont'd)

PERSONNEL INFORMATION CARD - FACULTY

FTE   R/S

NAME   SOCIAL SECURITY #

BIRTHDATE   CITIZENSHIP   ED. LEVEL

SERVICE DATE:

TRACK: YEARS TOWARD TENURE: TENURE DATE:

DATE   TITLE   DEPT   POSITION #   FUND. SOURCE   SALARY

BUDGET POSITION CARD

POSITION #

TITLE:

NAME	SS #	R/S	SERVICE DATE	ACTION	NEW POSITION #	CHANGE DATE

APPENDIX 6-2

UNIVERSITY of MISSOURI
STAFF CHANGE FORM

1. NAME (LAST, FIRST, MIDDLE) 2. FEDERAL I.D. NUMBER 3. CAMPUS

BUDGET
PERSONNEL

PRESENT STATUS

4. POSITION TITLE TITLE CODE

5. BEGINNING-

6. A. FTE- B. [ ] 6-12 MO. [ ] 0-6 MO. [ ] STUDENT C. [ ] 9 MO. [ ] 12 MO.
TERMINAL 1 YR. APPT.?
ENDING- [ ] NON-REGULAR 9. DIFF-

D. [ ] -REGULAR YEARS TOWARD TENURE- 8. TIME BASE-

7. APPOINTMENT SALARY: ANNUAL-

10. PERQUISITE CODE AND VALUE 11. POSITION NUMBER-

12. PAYROLL DEPT. CODE-

13. DATES 14. ACCOUNTS PAYABLE FROM 15. AMOUNT

PROPOSED STATUS

4. POSITION TITLE TITLE CODE

5. BEGINNING-

6. A. FTE- B. [ ] 6-12 MO. [ ] 0-6 MO. [ ] STUDENT C. [ ] 9 MO. [ ] 12 MO.
TERMINAL 1 YR. APPT.?
ENDING- [ ] NON-REGULAR 9. DIFF-

D. [ ] REGULAR YEARS TOWARD TENURE- 8. TIME BASE-

7. APPOINTMENT SALARY: ANNUAL-

10. PERQUISITE CODE AND VALUE 11. POSITION NUMBER-

12. PAYROLL DEPT. CODE-

13. DATES 14. ACCOUNTS PAYABLE FROM 15. AMOUNT

16. COMMENTS - (ATTACH A SEPARATE SHEET IF ADDITIONAL SPACE IS REQUIRED.)

17. [ ] RESIGNATION [ ] -TERMINATION [ ] -EXPIRATION OF APPOINTMENT

LAST DAY OF DUTY- ACC. VACATION- TO BE EFFECTIVE- PORTION OF CONTRACT COMPLETED- ___ %

FORWARDING ADDRESS-

I HEREBY OFFER MY RESIGNATION (SIGNATURE AND DATE)

18. LEAVE OF ABSENCE: [ ] SABBATICAL [ ] MILITARY [ ] OTHER (SPECIFY) 19. [ ] TRANSFER REASON-
BEGINNING- ENDING-

20. RECOMMENDED DATE RECOMMENDED DATE APPROVED-CAMPUS DATE APPROVED-U.WIDE DATE

ACCUMULATED VACATION ___
ACCUMULATED SICK LEAVE ___

DIST: SECRETARY, PAYROLL, PERSONNEL RECORDS, DIVISION, DEPARTMENT, EMPLOYEE

(PERSONNEL USE ONLY) UM-UW 117 (REV SEP 74) **SECRETARY**

TYPE	TRANS CODE	TYPE CODE	DATE	TYPE	TRANS CODE	TYPE CODE	DATE	TYPE	TRANS CODE	TYPE CODE	DATE OR AMOUNT	TYPE	TRANS CODE	TYPE CODE	DATE OR NUMBER
A. NA	2303			SERV. DATE	2501			ANNUAL SAL.	2314			BUD POS #	2319		
APPT OR TIME	2304			SEX	2307			GP CODE	2315			U-WIDE	2340		
BIRTH DATE	2502			STATE RET.	2308			L.O.A.	2316			PERS. ACT	2320		
ELIG. LIFE INS	2301			TITLE CODE	2309			FTE	2317			CITIZEN	2321		
EMP. BASIS	2305			SEC. TITLE	2313			EMP. STA (P.T.S.)	2318			ED. LEVEL	2322		
												END DATE	2503		
												PRI. DEPT	2323		

APPENDIX 6-3

SALARY DISTRIBUTION BY CATEGORY - PART 1   PAGE 80

ST LOUIS   FULL TIME   TECHNICAL   EXCLUDES GRA GTA   AS OF 06/30/80

NAME / TITLE	SEX	R A C E	BIRTH DATE	SERVICE DATE	TITLE DATE	ED LV	FTE	SALARY	SERV BASE	CIT	FUND SOUR TEN
5000 - 7499											
PRE SCHOOL AST	0 F	1	08/13/57	08/15/77	08/15/77	07	1.00	07451	12	1	
PRE SCHOOL AST	0 F	1	01/21/57	12/20/79	12/20/79	08	1.00	07243	12	1	
	F	1						2			
	F							2			
	F							2			
7500 - 9999											
LIBRARY ASSISTANT I	0 F	1	02/07/52	06/14/76	08/23/76	08	1.00	09974	12	1	
COMP TERMINAL OPR	0 F	1	07/13/54	06/08/72	04/01/77	04	1.00	08355	12	1	
PRE SCHOOL AST	0 F	1	05/31/54	12/15/75	02/11/77	07	1.00	08000	12	1	
	F	1						3			
ANIMAL TECHNICIAN	0 F	2	04/17/34	09/01/72	09/01/74	03	1.00	09963	12	1	
LICENSED PRAC NURSE	1 F	2	05/06/23	08/23/76	10/25/79	07	1.00	09130	12	1	
	F	2						2			
LIBRARY ASSISTANT I	0 F	4	11/06/32	05/23/77	07/05/78	07	1.00	09778	12	2	
	F	4						1			
	F							6			
COMP OPERATOR	0 M	1	05/15/57	01/15/79	01/15/79	04	1.00	09334	12	1	
	M	1						1			
	M							1			
								7			
10000 - 12999											
ANNOUNCER	0 F	1	11/04/54	09/21/78	/ /	08	1.00	10969	12	1	
BOOK BUYER	0 F	1	03/05/23	05/15/76	12/01/78	04	1.00	10569	12	1	
LIBRARY ASSISTANT II	1 F	1	04/25/51	08/01/73	12/02/74	08	1.00	11755	12	1	
LIBRARY ASSISTANT II	1 F	1	10/08/46	11/25/68	12/01/76	07	1.00	11955	12	1	
LIBRARY ASSISTANT II	0 F	1	07/15/52	05/22/74	10/01/74	06	1.00	11755	12	1	

APPENDIX 6-4

FACULTY PROFILE 1980-81

COLLEGE/SCHOOL SCHOOL OF OPTOMETRY

DEPARTMENT OPTOMETRY

NAME	RANK	BIRTHDATE	STARTING DATE	TITLE DATE	TENURE DATE	TRACK	LEVEL	SEX	RACE	SALARY

APPENDIX 6-5

NINE YEAR MINORITY FACULTY COMPARISON

ACADEMIC YEAR	1972-73			1973-74			1974-75			1975-76			1976-77		
DEPARTMENT	TOTAL # FACULTY	# MIN	% MIN	TOTAL # FACULTY	# MIN	% MIN	TOTAL # FACULTY	# MIN	% MIN	TOTAL # FACULTY	# MIN	% MIN	TOTAL # FACULTY	# MIN	% MIN
ARTS & SCIENCES															
AOJ	4	0	0%	5	1	20%	7	1	14%	5	1	20%	4	1	25%
BIOLOGY	14	0	0%	14	0	0%	19	1	5%	19	1	5%	21	2	10%
CHEMISTRY	17	0	0%	17	0	0%	17	0	0%	17	0	0%	17	0	0%
ECONOMICS	13	0	0%	13	0	0%	16	0	0%	17	0	0%	17	0	0%
ENGLISH	35	1	3%	41	1	2%	43	1	2%	39	1	3%	38	1	3%
FINE ARTS	10	0	0%	11	0	0%	15	0	0%	16	0	0%	17	1	6%
Art															
Music															
HISTORY	26	1	4%	27	1	4%	28	1	4%	26	1	4%	26	1	4%
MATHEMATICS	23	0	0%	25	0	0%	36	2	6%	32	1	3%	33	1	3%
MODERN LANG.	17	4	24%	20	5	25%	22	5	23%	23	5	22%	21	5	24%
PHILOSOPHY	10	0	0%	10	0	0%	10	0	0%	10	0	0%	11	0	0%
PHYSICS	10	0	0%	11	1	9%	13	1	8%	13	1	8%	13	1	8%
POLITICAL SCI.	17	0	0%	15	0	0%	19	0	0%	20	0	0%	20	0	0%
PSYCHOLOGY	13	0	0%	15	0	0%	18	0	0%	18	0	0%	19	0	0%
SOC/ANTHROPOLOGY	15	1	7%	21	2	10%	24	2	8%	24	1	4%	23	1	4%
SPEECH	----WITH ENGLISH UNTIL 1979-80----														
TOTAL A&S	221	7	3%	245	11	4%	287	14	5%	279	11	4%	280	14	5%

12-1-80 bc

APPENDIX 6-5 (cont'd)

Nine Year Minority Faculty Comparison continued, page 2

DEPARTMENT	1977-78 TOTAL # FACULTY	# MIN	% MIN	1978-79 TOTAL # FACULTY	# MIN	% MIN	1979-80 TOTAL # FACULTY	# MIN	% MIN	1980-81 TOTAL # FACULTY	# MIN	% MIN	1981-82 TOTAL # FACULTY	# MIN	% MIN
ARTS & SCIENCES															
AOJ	8	2	25%	9	2	22%	9	2	22%	10	1	10%			
BIOLOGY	22	1	5%	18	1	6%	19	1	5%	20	1	5%			
CHEMISTRY	17	0	0%	17	0	0%	17	0	0%	17	1	6%			
ECONOMICS	16	0	0%	17	1	6%	20	1	5%	21	1	5%			
ENGLISH	37	1	3%	39	1	3%	30	0	0%	31	0	0%			
FINE ARTS	17	2	12%	18	2	11%									
Art							8	1	13%	10	1	10%			
Music							12	1	8%	13	1	8%			
HISTORY	26	1	4%	27	1	4%	25	1	4%	24	1	4%			
MATHEMATICS	32	0	0%	35	3	9%	28	3	11%	29	2	7%			
MODERN LANG.	23	9	39%	22	7	32%	20	7	35%	18	6	33%			
PHILOSOPHY	12	0	0%	11	0	0%	11	0	0%	11	0	0%			
PHYSICS	13	1	8%	15	1	7%	15	1	7%	16	1	6%			
POLITICAL SCI.	17	0	0%	20	0	0%	19	1	5%	21	1	5%			
PSYCHOLOGY	21	1	5%	21	1	5%	22	0	0%	22	0	0%			
SOC/ANTHROPOLOGY	26	3	12%	25	2	8%	22	2	9%	17	0	0%			
SOCIAL WORK										6	2	33%			
SPEECH							10	0	0%	11	0	0%			
TOTAL A&S	287	21	7%	294	22	7%	287	21	7%	297	19	6%			

—WITH SOC/ANTHRO. UNTIL 1979-80—
—WITH ENGLISH UNTIL 1979-80—

NOTE: Beginning 1980-81, All Faculty appointments are included (Regular and Non-Regular Track, Graduate School or Extension, Research Assistants and Associates).

12-1-80 bc

APPENDIX 6-5 (cont'd)

Nine Year Minority Faculty Comparison continued, page 3

ACADEMIC YEAR	1972-73			1973-74			1974-75			1975-76			1976-77		
DEPARTMENT	TOTAL # FACULTY	# MIN	% MIN	TOTAL # FACULTY	# MIN	% MIN	TOTAL # FACULTY	# MIN	% MIN	TOTAL # FACULTY	# MIN	% MIN	TOTAL # FACULTY	# MIN	% MIN
BUSINESS															
ACCOUNTING	9	0	0%	10	0	0%	11	0	0%	13	1	8%	10	0	0%
FINANCE	7	1	14%	8	2	25%	8	2	25%	10	1	10%	11	1	9%
MGMT, BEHAVIORAL	8	0	0%	8	0	0%	8	0	0%	8	0	0%	10	0	0%
MGMT, QUANT.	5	0	0%	5	0	0%	8	0	0%	11	1	9%	12	1	8%
MARKETING	6	0	0%	6	0	0%	8	0	0%	10	1	10%	9	1	11%
TOTAL BUSINESS	35	1	3%	37	2	5%	43	2	5%	52	4	8%	52	3	6%
EDUCATION															
AFSE	19	2	11%	23	3	13%	26	3	12%	26	3	12%	23	3	13%
BEHAVIORAL ST.	17	0	0%	23	0	0%	26	0	0%	26	0	0%	31	0	0%
CHILDHOOD ED.	12	0	0%	13	0	0%	17	0	0%	16	1	6%	15	1	7%
TOTAL EDUCATION	48	2	4%	59	3	5%	69	3	4%	68	4	6%	69	4	6%
LIBRARY	10	0	0%	12	0	0%	13	0	0%	11	0	0%	13	0	0%
CAD	------WITH ENGLISH AND MATH UNTIL 1979-80------														
TOTAL CAMPUS	314	10	3%	353	16	5%	412	19	5%	410	19	5%	414	21	5%

12-1-80 bc

APPENDIX 6-5 (cont'd)

Nine Year Minority Faculty Comparison continued, page 4

ACADEMIC YEAR	1977-78			1978-79			1979-80			1980-81			1981-82		
DEPARTMENT	TOTAL # FACULTY	# MIN	% MIN	TOTAL # FACULTY	# MIN	% MIN	TOTAL # FACULTY	# MIN	% MIN	TOTAL # FACULTY	# MIN	% MIN	TOTAL # FACULTY	# MIN	% MIN
BUSINESS															
ACCOUNTING	9	0	0%	13	1	8%	15	2	13%	14	1	7%			
FINANCE	13	2	15%	15	2	13%	15	2	13%	14	2	14%			
MGMT, BEHAVIORAL	12	0	0%	14	1	7%	15	0	0%	15	0	0%			
MGMT, QUANT.	12	1	8%	13	1	8%	15	1	7%	16	1	6%			
MARKETING	9	1	11%	8	0	0%	10	0	0%	10	0	0%			
TOTAL BUSINESS	55	4	7%	63	5	8%	70	5	7%	69	4	6%			
EDUCATION															
AFSE	21	3	14%	18	4	22%	19	2	11%	17	2	12%			
BEHAVIORAL ST.	33	1	3%	31	1	3%	27	1	4%	20	1	5%			
CHILDHOOD ED.	15	1	7%	14	0	0%	13	0	0%	12	0	0%			
PHYSICAL EDUCATION										5	0	0%			
TOTAL EDUCATION	69	5	7%	63	5	8%	59	3	5%	54	3	6%			
OPTOMETRY							DEPT. CREATED 79-80			3	0	0%			
LIBRARY	15	1	7%	12	1	8%	14	0	0%	13	0	0%			
ATHLETICS (Non-Regular Faculty)										6	1	17%			
CAD	WITH ENGLISH AND MATH UNTIL 1979-80---						7	4	57%	10	5	50%			
GRADUATE SCHOOL AND COMMUNITY AFFAIRS	(Unclassified Faculty Non-Regular) ----------									6	3	50%			
TOTAL CAMPUS	426	31	7%	432	33	8%	437	33	8%	458	35	8%			

12-1-80 bc   Physical Education reported with Behavioral Studies until 1980-81.

APPENDIX 6-6

APPLICANT FLOW DATA
Faculty

POSITION	SOURCE	SEX			M/RACE						P/RACE						HAND	VETS	#CARDS RET	#APPLT	SEX			CARDS RET	OFFER TO:	R/S	START DATE
		M	F	U	1	2	3	4	5	U	1	2	3	4	5	U					M	F	U				

KEY: M = Male, F = Female, U = Unknown
      1 = White, 2 - Black, 3 = Hispanic, 4 = Asian, 5 = Am. Indian
      HAND = Handicapped, VETS = Veterans, APPLT = Applicants, RET = Returned

9-18-80 lo

APPENDIX 6-7

MONTH _____

EEO Category _____

APPLICANT FLOW DATA
Staff

POSITION	DEPARTMENT	SEX			M/RACE						F/RACE						HAND	VETS	# APPLT	DATE POS. OPEN	OFFER TO:	DATE OF HIRE	TYPE OF HIRE	START DATE	R/S	SALARY
		M	F	U	1	2	3	4	5	U	1	2	3	4	5	U										

KEY: M = Male, F = Female, U = Unknown
       1 = White, 2 = Black, 3 = Hispanic, 4 = Asian, 5 = Am. Indian
       HAND = Handicapped, VETS = Veterans, APPLT = Applicants, R/S = Race/Sex
TYPE OF HIRE = NH - New Hire, PR - Promotion, TR - Transfer

9-18-80 lo

APPENDIX 7-1

PART 60-2—AFFIRMATIVE ACTION PROGRAMS

Subpart A—General

Sec.

Subpart B—Required Contents of Affirmative Action Programs

Subpart C—Methods of Implementing the Requirements of Subpart B

Subpart D—Miscellaneous

Authority: 5 U.S.C. 553(a)(3)(B); 29 CFR 2.7; section 201, E.O. 11246, 30 FR 12319, and E.O. 11375, 32 FR 14303, as amended by E.O. 12086.

Subpart B—Required Contents of Affirmative Action Programs

§ 60-2.10   Purpose of affirmative action program.

An affirmative action program is a set of specific and result-oriented procedures to which a contractor commits itself to apply every good faith effort. The objective of those procedures plus such efforts is equal employment opportunity. Procedures without effort to make them work are meaningless; and effort, undirected by specific and meaningful procedures, is inadequate. An acceptable affirmative action program must include an analysis of areas within which the contractor is deficient in the utilization of minority groups and women, and further, goals and timetables to which the contractor's good faith efforts must be directed to correct the deficiencies and, thus to achieve prompt and full utilization of minorities and women, at all levels and in all segments of its work force where deficiencies exist.

§ 60-2.11   Required utilization analysis.

Based upon the Government's experience with compliance reviews under the Executive Order program and the contractor reporting system, minority groups are most likely to be underutilized in departments and jobs within departments that fall within the following Employer's Information Report (EEO-1) designations: Officials and managers, professionals, technicians, sales workers, office and clerical and craftsmen (skilled). As categorized by the EEO-1 designations, women are likely to be underutilized in departments and jobs within departments as follows: Officials and managers, professionals, technicians, sales workers (except over-the-counter sales in certain retail establishments), craftsmen (skilled and semi-skilled). Therefore, the contractor shall direct special attention to such jobs in its analysis and goal setting for minorities and women. Affirmative action programs must contain the following information:

(a) Workforce analysis which is defined as a listing of each job title as it appears in applicable collective bargaining agreements or payroll records (not job group) ranked from the lowest paid to the highest paid within each department or other similar organizational unit, including departmental or unit supervision. If there are separate work units or lines of progression within a department, a separate list must be provided for each such work unit, or line. including unit supervisors. For lines of progression there must be indicated the order of jobs in the line through which an employee could move to the top of the line. Where there are no formal progression lines or usual promotional sequences. job titles should be listed by department. job families, or disciplines. in order of wage rates or salary ranges. For each job title, the total number of incumbents, the total number of male and female incumbents, and the total number of male and female incumbents in each of the following groups must be given: Blacks, Spanish-

APPENDIX 7-1 (cont'd)

surnamed Americans, American Indians, and Orientals. The wage rate or salary range for each job title must be given. All job titles, including all managerial job titles, must be listed.

(b) An analysis of all major job groups at the facility, with explanation if minorities or women are currently being underutilized in any one or more job groups ("job groups" herein meaning one or a group of jobs having similar content, wage rates and opportunities). "Underutilization" is defined as having fewer minorities or women in a particular job group than would reasonably be expected by their availability. In making the utilization analysis, the contractor shall conduct such analysis separately for minorities and women.

(1) In determining whether minorities are being underutilized in any job group, the contractor will consider at least all of the following factors:

(i) The minority population of the labor area surrounding the facility;

(ii) The size of the minority unemployment force in the labor area surrounding the facility;

(iii) The percentage of the minority work force as compared with the total work force in the immediate labor area;

(iv) The general availability of minorities having requisite skills in the immediate labor area;

(v) The availability of minorities having requisite skills in an area in which the contractor can reasonably recruit;

(vi) The availability of promotable and transferable minorities within the contractor's organization;

(vii) The existence of training institutions capable of training persons in the requisite skills; and

(viii) The degree of training which the contractor is reasonably able to undertake as a means of making all job classes available to minorities.

(2) In determining whether women are being underutilized in any job group, the contractor will consider at least all of the following factors:

(i) The size of the female unemployment force in the labor area surrounding the facility;

(ii) The percentage of the female workforce as compared with the total workforce in the immediate labor area;

(iii) The general availability of women having requisite skills in the immediate labor area;

(iv) The availability of women having requisite skills in an area in which the contractor can reasonably recruit;

(v) The availability of women seeking employment in the labor or recruitment area of the contractor;

(vi) The availability of promotable and transferable female employees within the contractor's organization;

(vii) The existence of training institutions capable of training persons in the requisite skills; and

(viii) The degree of training which the contractor is reasonably able to undertake as a means of making all job classes available to women.

§ 60–2.12 Establishment of goals and timetables.

(a) The goals and timetables developed by the contractor should be attainable in terms of the contractor's analysis of its deficiencies and its entire affirmative action program. Thus, in establishing the size of its goals and the length of its timetables, the contractor should consider the results which could reasonably be expected from its putting forth every good faith effort to make its overall affirmative action program work. In determining levels of goals, the contractor should consider at least the factors listed in § 60–2.11.

(b) Involve personnel relations staff, department and division heads, and local and unit managers in the goal-setting process.

(c) Goals should be significant, measurable, and attainable.

(d) Goals should be specific for planned results, with timetables for completion.

(e) Goals may not be rigid and inflexible quotas which must be met, but must be targets reasonably attainable by means of applying every good faith effort to make all aspects of the entire affirmative action program work.

(f) In establishing timetables to meet goals and commitments, the contractor will consider the anticipated expansion, contraction, and turnover of and in the work force.

(g) Goals, timetables, and affirmative action commitments must be designed to correct any identifiable deficiencies.

(h) Where deficiencies exist and where numbers or percentages are relevant in developing corrective action, the contractor shall establish and set forth specific goals and timetables separately for minorities and women.

(i) Such goals and timetables, with

APPENDIX 7-1 (cont'd)

supporting data and the analysis thereof, shall be a part of the contractor's written affirmative action program and shall be maintained at each establishment of the contractor.

(j) A contractor or subcontractor extending a publicly announced preference for Indians as authorized in 41 CFR 60–1.5(a)(6) may reflect in its goals and timetables the permissive employment preference for Indians living on or near an Indian reservation.

(k) Where the contractor has not established a goal, its written affirmative action program must specifically analyze each of the factors listed in § 60–2.11 and must detail its reason for a lack of a goal.

(l) In the event it comes to the attention of the Office of Federal Contract Compliance Programs that there is a substantial disparity in the utilization of a particular minority group or men or women of a particular minority group, OFCCP may require separate goals and timetables for such minority group and may further require, where appropriate, such goals and timetables by sex for such group for such job classifications and organizational units specified by the OFCCP.

(m) Support data for the required analysis and program shall be compiled and maintained as part of the contractor's affirmative action program. This data will include but not be limited to progression line charts, seniority rosters, applicant flow data, and applicant rejection ratios indicating minority and sex status.

(n) Copies of affirmative action programs and/or copies of support data shall be made available to the Office of Federal Contract Compliance Programs, upon request, for such purposes as may be appropriate to the fulfillment of its responsibilities under Executive Order 11246, as amended.

§ 60–2.13 Additional required ingredients of affirmative action programs.

Effective affirmative action programs shall contain, but not necessarily be limited to, the following ingredients:

(a) Development or reaffirmation of the contractor's equal employment opportunity policy in all personnel actions.

(b) Formal internal and external dissemination of the contractor's policy.

(c) Establishment of responsibilities

for implementation of the contractor's affirmative action program.

(d) Identification of problem areas (deficiencies) by organizational units and job group.

(e) Establishment of goals and objectives by organizational units and job groups, including timetables for completion.

(f) Development and execution of action-oriented programs designed to eliminate problems and further designed to attain established goals and objectives.

(g) Design and implementation of internal audit and reporting systems to measure effectiveness of the total program.

(h) Compliance of personnel policies and practices with the Sex Discrimination Guidelines (41 CFR Part 60–20).

(i) Active support of local and national community action programs and community service programs, designed to improve the employment opportunities of minorities and women.

(j) Consideration of minorities and women not currently in the work force having requisite skills who can be recruited through affirmative action measures.

§ 60–2.14 Program summary.

The affirmative action program shall be summarized and updated annually. The program summary shall be prepared in a format which shall be prescribed by the Director and published in the **Federal Register** as a notice before becoming effective. Contractors shall submit the program summary to OFCCP each year on the anniversary date of the affirmative action program.

§ 60–2.15 Compliance status.

No contractor's compliance status shall be judged alone by whether or not it reaches its goals and meets its timetables. Rather, each contractor's compliance posture shall be reviewed and determined by reviewing the contents of its program, the extent of its adherence to this program, and its good faith efforts to make its program work toward the realization of the program's goals within the timetables set for completion. There follows an outline of examples of procedures that contractors and OFCCP should use as a guideline for establishing, implementing, and judging an acceptable affirmative action program.

APPENDIX 7-1 (cont'd)

Subpart C—Methods of Implementing the Requirements of Subpart B

§ 60-2.20 Development or reaffirmation of the equal employment opportunity policy.

(a) The contractor's policy statement should indicate the chief executive officer's attitude on the subject matter, assign overall responsibility and provide for a reporting and monitoring procedure. Specific items to be mentioned should include, but not be limited to:

(1) Recruit, hire, train, and promote persons in all job titles, without regard to race, color, religion, sex, or national origin, except where sex is a bona fide occupational qualification. (The term "bona fide occupational qualification" has been construed very narrowly under the Civil Rights Act of 1964. Under Executive Order 11246, as amended, and this part, this term will be construed in the same manner.)

(2) Base decisions on employment so as to further the principle of equal employment opportunity.

(3) Ensure that promotion decisions are in accord with principles of equal employment opportunity by imposing only valid requirements for promotional opportunities.

(4) Ensure that all personnel actions such as compensation, benefits, transfers, layoffs, return from layoff, company sponsored training, education, tuition assistance, social and recreation programs, will be administered without regard to race, color, religion, sex, or national origin.

§ 60-2.21 Dissemination of the policy.

(a) The contractor should disseminate its policy internally as follows:

(1) Include it in contractor's policy manual.

(2) Publicize it in company newspaper, magazine, annual report, and other media.

(3) Conduct special meetings with executive, management, and supervisory personnel to explain intent of policy and individual responsibility for effective implementation, making clear the chief executive officer's attitude.

· (4) Schedule special meetings with all other employees to discuss policy and explain individual employee responsibilities.

(5) Discuss the policy thoroughly in both employee orientation and management training programs.

(6) Meet with union officials to inform them of policy, and request their cooperation.

(7) Include nondiscrimination clauses in all union agreements, and review all contractual provisions to insure they are nondiscriminatory.

(8) Publish articles covering EEO programs, progress reports, promotions, etc., of minority and female employees, in company publications.

(9) Post the policy on company bulletin boards.

(10) When employees are featured in product or consumer advertising, employee handbooks or similar publications both minority and nonminority, men and women should be pictured.

(11) Communicate to employees the existence of the contractor's affirmative action program and make available such elements of its program as will enable such employees to know of and avail themselves of its benefits.

(b) The contractor should disseminate its policy externally as follows:

(1) Inform all recruiting sources verbally and in writing of company policy, stipulating that these sources actively recruit and refer minorities and women for all positions listed.

(2) Incorporate the equal opportunity clause in all purchase orders, leases, contracts, etc., covered by Executive Order 11246, as amended, and its implementing regulations.

(3) Notify minority and women's organizations, community agencies, community leaders, secondary schools, and colleges, of company policy, preferably in writing.

(4) Communicate to prospective employees the existence of the contractor's affirmative action program and make available such elements of its program as will enable such prospective employees to know of and avail themselves of its benefits.

(5) When employees are pictured in consumer or help wanted advertising, both minority and nonminority men and women should be shown.

(6) Send written notification of company policy to all subcontractors, vendors, and suppliers requesting appropriate action on their part.

§ 60-2.22 Responsibility for implementation.

(a) An executive of the contractor

APPENDIX 7-1 (cont'd)

should be appointed as director or manager of company equal opportunity programs. Depending upon the size and geographical alignment of the company, this may be his or her sole responsibility. He or she should be given the necessary top management support and staffing to execute the assignment. His or her identity should appear on all internal and external communications on the company's equal opportunity programs. His or her responsibilities should include, but not necessarily be limited to:

(1) Developing policy statements, affirmative action programs, internal and external communication techniques.

(2) Assisting in the identification of problem areas.

(3) Assisting line management in arriving at solutions to problems.

(4) Designing and implementing audit and reporting systems that will:

(i) Measure effectiveness of the contractor's programs.

(ii) Indicate need for remedial action.

(iii) Determine the degree to which the contractor's goals and objectives have been attained.

(5) Serve as liaison between the contractor and enforcement agencies.

(6) Serve as liaison between the contractor and minority organizations, women's organizations and community action groups concerned with employment opportunities of minorities and women.

(7) Keep management informed of latest developments in the entire equal opportunity area.

(b) Line responsibilities should include, but not be limited to the following:

(1) Assistance in the identification of problem areas and establishment of local and unit goals and objectives.

(2) Active involvement with local minority organizations, women's organizations, community action groups and community service programs.

(3) Periodic audit of training programs, hiring and promotion patterns to remove impediments to the attainment of goals and objectives.

(4) Regular discussions with local managers, supervisors, and employees to be certain the contractor's policies are being followed.

(5) Review of the qualifications of all employees to insure that minorities and women are given full opportunities for transfers and promotions.

(6) Career counseling for all employees.

(7) Periodic audit to insure that each location is in compliance in areas such as:

(i) Posters are properly displayed.

(ii) All facilities, including company housing, which the contractor maintains for the use and benefit of its employees, are in fact desegregated, both in policy and use. If the contractor provides facilities such as dormitories, locker rooms and rest rooms, they must be comparable for both sexes.

(iii) Minority and female employees are afforded a full opportunity and are encouraged to participate in all company sponsored educational, training, recreational, and social activities.

(8) Supervisors should be made to understand that their work performance is being evaluated on the basis of their equal employment opportunity efforts and results, as well as other criteria.

(9) It shall be a responsibility of supervisors to take actions to prevent harassment of employees placed through affirmative action efforts.

§ 60-2.23 Identification of problem areas by organizational units and job groups.

(a) An in-depth analysis of the following should be made, paying particular attention to trainees and those categories listed in § 60-2.11(b).

(1) Composition of the work force by minority group status and sex.

(2) Composition of applicant flow by minority group status and sex.

(3) The total selection process including position descriptions, position titles, worker specifications, application forms, interview procedures, test administration, test validity, referral procedures, final selection process, and similar factors.

(4) Transfer and promotion practices.

(5) Facilities, company sponsored recreation and social events, and special programs such as educational assistance.

(6) Seniority practices and seniority provisions of union contracts.

(7) Apprenticeship programs.

(8) All company training programs, formal and informal.

(9) Work force attitude.

(10) Technical phases of compliance, such as poster and notification to labor unions, retention of applications, notification to subcontractors, etc.

(b) If any of the following items are

APPENDIX 7-1 (cont'd)

found in the analysis, special corrective action should be appropriate.

(1) An "underutilization" of minorities or women in specific job groups.

(2) Lateral and/or vertical movement of minority or female employees occurring at a lesser rate (compared to work force mix) than that of nonminority or male employees.

(3) The selection process eliminates a significantly higher percentage of minorities or women than nonminorities or men.

(4) Application and related preemployment forms not in compliance with Federal legislation.

(5) Position descriptions inaccurate in relation to actual functions and duties.

(6) Formal or scored selection procedures not validated as required by the OFCCP Uniform Guidelines on Employee Selection Procedures (see 41 CFR Part 60-3).

(7) Test forms not validated by location, work performance and inclusion of minorities and women in sample.

(8) Referral ratio of minorities or women to the hiring supervisor or manager indicates a significantly higher percentage are being rejected as compared to nonminority and male applicants.

(9) Minorities or women are excluded from or are not participating in company sponsored activities or programs.

(10) De facto segregation still exists at some facilities.

(11) Seniority provisions contribute to overt or inadvertent discrimination, i.e., a disparity by minority group status or sex exists between length of service and types of job held.

(12) Nonsupport of company policy by managers, supervisors or employees.

(13) Minorities or women underutilized or significantly underrepresented in training or career improvement programs.

(14) No formal techniques established for evaluating effectiveness of EEO programs.

(15) Lack of access to suitable housing inhibits recruitment efforts and employment of qualified minorities.

(16) Lack of suitable transportation (public or private) to the work place inhibits minority employment.

(17) Labor unions and subcontractors not notified of their responsibilities.

(18) Purchase orders do not contain EEO clause.

(19) Posters not on display.

§ 60-2.24 Development and execution of programs.

(a) The contractor should conduct detailed analyses of position descriptions to insure that they accurately reflect position functions, and are consistent for the same position from one location to another.

(b) The contractor should validate worker specifications by division, department location or other organizational unit and by job title using job performance criteria. Special attention should be given to academic, experience and skill requirements to insure that the requirements in themselves do not constitute inadvertent discrimination. Specifications should be consistent for the same job title in all locations and should be free from bias as regards to race, color, religion, sex (except where sex is a bona fide occupational qualification) or national origin. Where requirements screen out a disproportionate number of minorities or women, such requirements should be professionally validated to job performance.

(c) Approved position descriptions and worker specifications, when used by the contractor, should be made available to all members of management involved in the recruiting, screening, selection, and promotion process. Copies should also be distributed to all recruiting sources.

(d) The contractor should evaluate the total selection process to insure freedom from bias and, thus, aid the attainment of goals and objectives.

(1) All personnel involved in the recruiting, screening, selection, promotion, disciplinary, and related processes should be carefully selected and trained to insure elimination of bias in all personnel actions.

(2) The contractor shall observe the requirements of the OFCCP Uniform Guidelines on Employee Selection Procedures.

(3) Selection techniques other than tests may also be improperly used so as to have the effect of discriminating against minority groups and women. Such techniques include but are not restricted to, unscored interviews, unscored or casual application forms,

APPENDIX 7-1 (cont'd)

arrest records, credit checks, considerations of marital status or dependency or minor children. Where there exist data suggesting that such unfair discrimination or exclusion of minorities or women exists, the contractor should analyze its unscored procedures and eliminate them if they are not objectively valid.

(e) Suggested techniques to improve recruitment and increase the flow of minority or female applicants follow:

(1) Certain organizations such as the Urban League, Job Corps, Equal Opportunity Programs, Inc., Concentrated Employment programs, Neighborhood Youth Corps, Secondary Schools, Colleges, and City Colleges with high minority enrollment, the State Employment Service, specialized employment agencies, Aspira, LULAC, SER, the G.I. Forum, the Commonwealth of Puerto Rico are normally prepared to refer minority applicants. Organizations prepared to refer women with specific skills are: National Organization for Women, Welfare Rights organizations, Women's Equity Action League, Talent Bank from Business and Professional Women (including 26 women's organizations), Professional Women's Caucus, Intercollegiate Association of University Women, Negro Women's sororities and service groups such as Delta Sigma Theta, Alpha Kappa Alpha, and Zera Phi Beta; National Council of Negro Women, American Association of University Women, YWCA, and sectarian groups such as Jewish Women's Groups, Catholic Women's Groups and Protestant Women's Groups, and women's colleges. In addition, community leaders as individuals shall be added to recruiting sources.

(2) Formal briefing sessions should be held, preferably on company premises, with representatives from these recruiting sources. Plant tours, presentations by minority and female employees, clear and concise explanations of current and future job openings, position descriptions, worker specifications, explanations of the company's selection process, and recruiting literature should be an integral part of the briefings. Formal arrangements should be made for referral of applicants, followup with

sources, and feedback on disposition of applicants.

(3) Minority and female employees, using procedures similar to subparagraph (2) of this paragraph, should be actively encouraged to refer applicants.

(4) A special effort should be made to include minorities and women on the Personnel Relations staff.

(5) Minority and female employees should be made available for participation in Career Days, Youth Motivation Programs, and related activities in their communities.

(6) Active participation in "Job Fairs" is desirable. Company representatives so participating should be given authority to make on-the-spot commitments.

(7) Active recruiting programs should be carried out at secondary schools, junior colleges, and colleges with predominant minority or female enrollments.

(8) Recruiting efforts at all schools should incorporate special efforts to reach minorities and women.

(9) Special employment programs should be undertaken whenever possible. Some possible programs are:

(i) Technical and nontechnical co-op programs with predominately Negro and women's colleges.

(ii) "After school" and/or work-study jobs for minority youths, male and female.

(iii) Summer jobs for underprivileged youth, male and female.

(iv) Summer work-study programs for male and female faculty members of the predominantly minority schools and colleges.

(v) Motivation, training and employment programs for the hardcore unemployed, male and female.

(10) When recruiting brochures pictorially present work situations, the minority and female members of the work force should be included, especially when such brochures are used in school and career programs.

(11) Help wanted advertising should be expanded to include the minority news media and women's interest media on a regular basis.

(f) The contractor should insure that minority and female employees are given equal opportunity for promotion. Suggestions for achieving this result include:

(1) Post or otherwise announce promotional opportunities.

(2) Make an inventory of current minority and female employees to determine academic, skill and experience level of individual employees.

(3) Initiate necessary remedial, job training and workstudy programs.

(4) Develop and implement formal employee evaluation programs.

(5) Make certain "worker specifications" have been validated on job performance related criteria. (Neither minority nor female employees should be required to possess higher qualifications than those of the lowest qualified incumbent.)

(6) When apparently qualified minority or female employees are passed over for upgrading, require supervisory personnel to submit written justification.

(7) Establish formal career counseling programs to include attitude development, education aid, job rotation, buddy system and similar programs.

(8) Review seniority practices and seniority clauses in union contracts to ensure that such practices or clauses are nondiscriminatory and do not have a discriminatory effect.

(g) Make certain facilities and company-sponsored social and recreation activities are desegregated. Actively encourage all employees to participate.

(h) Encourage child care, housing and tranportation programs appropriately designed to improve the employment opportunities for minorities and women.

§ 60-2.25 Internal audit and reporting systems.

(a) The contractor should monitor records of referrals, placements, transfers, promotions and terminations at all levels to ensure that nondiscriminatory policy is carried out.

(b) The contractor should require formal reports form unit managers on a schedule scheduled basis as to the degree to which corporate or unit goals are attained and timetables met.

(c) The contractor should review report results with all levels of management.

(d) The contractor should advise top management of program effectiveness and submit recommendations to improve unsatisfactory performance.

§ 60-2.26 Support of action programs.

(a) The contractor should appoint key members of management to serve on merit employment councils, community relations boards and similar organizations.

(b) The contractor should encourage minority and female employees to participate actively in National Alliance of Businessmen programs for youth motivation.

(c) The contractor should support vocational guidance institutes, vestibule training programs and similar activities.

(d) The contractor should assist secondary schools and colleges in programs designed to enable minority and female graduates of these institutions to compete in the open employment market on a more equitable basis.

(e) The contractor should publicize achievements of minority and female employees in local and minority news media.

(f) The contractor should support programs developed by such organizations as National Alliance of Businessmen, the Urban Coalition and other organizations concerned with employment opportunities for minorities or women.

Subpart D—Miscellaneous

§ 60-2.30 Use of goals.

The purpose of a contractor's establishment and use of goals is to insure that it meet its affirmative action obligation. It is not intended and should not be used to discriminate against any applicant or employee because of race, color, religion, sex, or national origin.

§ 60-2.31 Preemption.

To the extent that any state or local laws, regulations or ordinances, including those which grant special benefits to persons on account of sex, are in conflict with Executive Order 11246, as amended, or with the requirements of this part, OFCCP will

APPENDIX 7-1 (cont'd)

regard them as preempted under the Executive order.

§ 60-2.32   Supersedure.

All orders, instructions, regulations, and memorandums of the Secretary of Labor, other officials of the Department of Labor and contracting agencies are hereby superseded to the extent that they are inconsistent herewith, including a previous "Order No. 4" from this office dated January 30, 1970. Nothing in this part is intended to amend 41 CFR Part 60–3 or 41 CFR Part 60–20.

PART 60–20—SEX DISCRIMINATION GUIDELINES

Sec.
60–20.1   Title and purpose.
60–20.2   Recruitment and advertisement.
60–20.3   Job policies and practices.
60–20.4 · Seniority systems.
60–20.5   Discriminatory wages and
    placements.
60–20.6   Affirmative action.
60–20.7   Pregnancy, childbirth and related
    medical conditions.
60–20.8   Sexual advances and favors.

Authority: Sec. 201, E. O. 11246, 30 FR 12319, and E. O. 11375, 32 FR 14303, as amended by E. O. 12086.

§ 60-20.1   Title and purpose.

The purpose of the provisions in this part is to set forth the interpretations and guidelines of the Office of Federal Contract Compliance Programs regarding the implementation of Executive Order 11246, as amended, for the promotion and ensuring of equal opportunities for all persons employed or seeking employment with Government contractors or with contractors performing under federally assisted construction contracts, without regard to sex. Experience has indicated that special problems related to the implementation of the Executive Order require a definitive treatment beyond the terms of the Order itself. These interpretations are to be read in connection with existing regulations, set forth in Parts 60–1 and 60–2 of this chapter.

§ 60-20.2   Recruitment and advertisement.

(a) Contractors engaged in recruiting activity shall recruit employees of both sexes for all jobs unless sex is a bona fide occupational qualification.

(b) Advertisements in newspapers and other media for employment sponsored by or on behalf of contractors shall not depict, express a preference, or indicate that a particular sex is sought, desired or better suited for a particular job unless sex is a bona fide occupational qualification for the job. The placement of an advertisement in columns headed "Male" or "Female", or similar wording, will be considered an expression of a preference, limitation, specification, or discrimination based on sex.

§ 60-20.3   Job policies and practices.

(a) Written personnel policies relating to this subject area must expressly indicate that there shall be no discrimination against employees on account of sex. If the contractor deals with a bargaining representative for its employees and there is a written agreement on conditions of employment, such agreement shall not be inconsistent with these guidelines.

(b) Employees of both sexes shall have an equal opportunity to any available job that he or she is qualified to perform, unless sex is a bona fide occupational qualification.

Note.—In most Government contract work there are only limited instances where valid reasons can be expected to exist which would justify the exclusion of all men or all women from any given job.

(c)(1) The contractor must not make any distinction based upon sex in employment opportunities, wages, hours or other conditions of employment, including fringe benefits. As the Supreme Court held in *Los Angeles Department of Water and Power* v. *Manhart*, 435 U.S. 702 (1978), fringe benefits for similarly situated men and women must be equal, notwithstanding that the contractor's contributions for men and women are unequal.

(2) [Reserved.]

(d) Any distinction between married and unmarried persons of one sex that is not made between married and unmarried persons of the opposite sex will be considered to be a distinction made on the basis of sex. Similarly, a contractor must not deny employment to women with young children unless it has the same exclusionary policies for men; or terminate an employee of one sex in a particular job classification upon reaching a certain age unless the same rule is applicable to members of the opposite sex.

(e) The contractor's policies and practices must assure appropriate physical facilities to both sexes. The contractor may not refuse to hire men or women, or deny men or women a particular job because there are no restroom or associated facilities, unless the contractor is able to show that providing the facilities would be unreasonable for such reasons as excessive expense or lack of space.

(f)(1) A contractor must not deny a female employee the right to any job that she is qualified to perform in reliance upon a state "protective" law. For example, such laws include those which prohibit women from performing in certain types of occupations (e.g., a bartender or a core-maker); from working at jobs requiring more than a certain number of hours; and from working at jobs that require lifting or carrying more than designated weights.

(2) Such legislation was intended to be beneficial, but, instead, has been found to result in restricting employment opportunities for men and/or women. Accordingly, it cannot be used as a basis for denying employment or for establishing sex as a bona fide occupational qualification for the job.

(g) The contractor must not specify any differences for male and female employees on the basis of sex in either mandatory or optional retirement age.

(h) Nothing in these guidelines shall be interpreted to mean that differences in capabilities for job assignments do not exist among individuals and that such distinctions may not be recognized by the contractor in making specific assignments. The purpose of these guidelines is to ensure that such distinctions are not based upon sex.

§ 60-20.4 Seniority systems.

When they exist, seniority lines and lists must not be based upon sex. Where such a separation has existed, the contractor must eliminate this distinction and provide appropriate relief.

§ 60-20.5 Discriminatory wages and placements.

(a) *Wages.* The contractor's wage schedules must not be related to or based on the sex of the employees.

While the more obvious cases of discrimination exist where employees of different sexes are paid different wages on jobs which require substantially equal skill, effort and responsibility and are performed under similar working conditions, compensation practices with respect to any jobs where males or females are concentrated will be scrutinized closely to assure that sex has played no role in the setting of levels of pay.

(b) *Placements.* The Contractor may not discriminatorily restrict one sex to certain jobs. In such a situation, the contractor shall provide appropriate relief and shall ensure that all jobs are made available to all qualified employees without regard to sex. (Example: An electrical manufacturing company may have a production division with three functional units: One (assembly) all female; another (wiring), all male; and a third (circuit boards), also all male. The highest wage attainable in the assembly unit is considerably less than that in the circuit board and wiring units. In such a case the contractor must take steps to provide qualified female employees opportunity for placement in job openings in the other two units with red circling of wages, where appropriate, and without loss of seniority.)

§ 60-20.6 Affirmative action.

(a) Women typically have not been found in significant numbers in management. In many companies management trainee programs are one of the ladders to management positions. Traditionally, few if any, women have been admitted into these programs. An important element of affirmative action shall be a commitment to include female candidates in such programs.

(b) Distinctions based on sex may not be made in other training programs. Both sexes should have equal access to all training programs and affirmative action programs should demonstrate that such access has been provided.

(c) The contractor shall take affirmative action to recruit women for jobs in which they previously have been excluded or are underrepresented. The contractor also shall take affirmative action to encourage the participation of women in training programs for jobs in which they have been previously excluded or are underrepresented.

Note.—This can be done by various methods. Examples include, but are not limited to (1) Including in itineraries of recruiting trips, (i) women's colleges where graduates with skills desired by the contractor can be found, and (ii) female

APPENDIX 7-1 (cont'd)

students of coeducational institutions and (2) stating in advertisements that women will be considered equally with men for jobs.

§ 60-20.7 Pregnancy, childbirth and related medical conditions.

(a) Employees or applicants for employment shall not be denied employment because of pregnancy, childbirth or related medical conditions.

(b) Disabilities caused or contributed to by pregnancy, childbirth, or related medical conditions, for all job-related purposes, shall be treated the same as disabilities caused or contributed to by other medical conditions, under any health or disability insurance or sick leave plan available in connection with employment. Written or unwritten employment policies and practices involving matters such as the commencement and duration of leave, the availability of extensions, the accrual of seniority and other benefits and privileges, reinstatement, and payment under any health or disability insurance or sick leave plan, formal or informal, shall be applied to disability due to pregnancy, childbirth or related medical conditions on the same terms and conditions as they are applied to other disabilities. Health insurance benefits for abortion, except where the life of the mother would be endangered if the fetus were carried to term or where medical complications have arisen from an abortion, are not required to be paid by the contractor; nothing herein, however, precludes the contractor from providing abortion benefits or otherwise affects bargaining agreements in regard to abortion.

(c) Where the termination of an employee who is temporarily disabled is caused by an employment policy under which insufficient or no leave is available, such a termination violates the Order if it has a disparate impact on employees of one sex and is not justified by business necessity.

(d)(1) Any fringe benefit program, or fund, or insurance program which is in effect on October 31, 1978, which does not treat women affected by pregnancy, childbirth, or related medical conditions the same as other persons not so affected but similar in their ability or inability to work, must be in compliance with the provisions of § 60-20.7(b) by April 29, 1979. In order to come into compliance with the provisions of § 60-

20.7(b) there can be no reduction of benefits or compensation which were in effect on October 31, 1978, before October 31, 1979, or the expiration of a collective bargaining agreement in effect on October 31, 1978, whichever is later.

(2) Any fringe benefit program implemented after October 31, 1978, must comply with the provisions of § 60-20.7(b) upon implementation.

§ 60-20.8 Sexual harassment and favors.

(a) Unwelcome sexual advances, requests for sexual favors, and other verbal or physical conduct of a sexual nature are violations of the Order when (1) submission to such conduct is made either explicitly or implicitly a term or condition of an individual's employment, (2) submission to or rejection of such conduct by an individual is used as the basis for employment decisions affecting such individual, or (3) such conduct has the purpose or effect of "unreasonably" interfering with an individual's work performance or creating an intimidating, hostile or offensive work environment.

(b) A contractor is liable under the Order for the acts of its officials, managers and supervisors when these individuals engage in the activities described in paragraph (a) of this section, regardless of whether their specific acts were authorized or forbidden by the contractor and regardless of whether the contractor knew or should have known of their occurrence.

(c) With respect to conduct between fellow employees, a contractor is responsible for acts of sexual harassment in the workplace where the contractor (or its officials, managers and supervisors) knows or should have known of the conduct and fails to take immediate and appropriate action.

(d) A contractor also may be responsible for the acts of nonemployees, with respect to sexual harassment of employees in the workplace, where the contractor (or its officials, managers and supervisors) knows or should have known of the conduct and fails to take immediate and appropriate corrective action. In reviewing these cases, OFCCP will consider the extent of the contractor's control and any other legal responsibility which the contractor may

APPENDIX 7-1 (cont'd)

have with respect to the conduct of such nonemployees.

(e) Where employment opportunity or benefits are granted because of an individual's submission to the contractor's sexual advances or requests for sexual favors, the contractor may be held liable under the Order for unlawful sex discrimination against other persons who were qualified for but denied that employment opportunity or benefit.

PART 60–50—GUIDELINES ON DISCRIMINATION BECAUSE OF RELIGION OR NATIONAL ORIGIN

Sec.
60–50.1 Purpose and scope.
60–50.2 Equal employment policy.
60–50.3 Accommodations to religious observance and practice.
60–50.4 Enforcement.
60–50.5 Nondiscrimination.

§ 60–50.1 Purpose and scope.

(a) The purpose of the provisions in this part is to set forth the interpretations and guidelines of the Office of Federal Contract Compliance Programs regarding the implementation of Executive Order 11246, as amended, for promoting and ensuring equal employment opportunities for all persons employed or seeking employment with Government contractors or with contractors performing under federally assisted construction contracts, without regard to religious or national origin.

(b) Members of various religious and ethnic groups continue to be excluded from executive, middle-management, and other job levels because of discrimination based upon their religion and/or national origin. These guidelines are intended to remedy such unfair treatment.

(c) These guidelines also are intended to clarify the obligations of contractors with respect to accommodating to the religious observances and practices of employees and prospective employees.

(d) The employment problems of blacks, Hispanics, Asians or Pacific Islanders, American Indians or Alaskan natives are treated under Part 60–2 of this chapter and under other regulations and procedures implementing the requirements of Executive Order 11246, as amended. Accordingly, the remedial provisions of § 60–50.2(b) shall not be applicable to the employment problems of these groups.

(e) Nothing contained in this Part 60–50 is intended to supersede or otherwise limit the exemption set forth in § 60–1.5(a)(5) of this chapter for contractors with certain educational institutions.

§ 60–50.2 Equal employment policy.

(a) *General requirements.* Under the equal opportunity clause contained in section 202 of Executive Order 11246, as amended, contractors are prohibited from discriminating against employees or applicants for employment because of religion or national origin, and must take affirmative action to ensure that applicants are employed, and that employees are treated during employment, without regard to their religion or national origin. Such action includes, but is not limited to the following: Employment, upgrading, demotion, or transfer; recruitment or recruitment advertising; layoff or termination; rates of pay or other forms of compensation; and selection for training, including apprenticeship.

(b) *Outreach and positive recruitment.* Contractors shall review their employment practices to determine whether members of the various religious and/or ethnic groups are receiving fair consideration for job opportunities. Special attention shall be directed toward executive and middle-management levels, where employment problems relating to religion and national origin are most likely to occur. Based upon the findings of such reviews, contractors shall undertake appropriate outreach and positive recruitment activities, such as those listed below, in order to remedy existing deficiencies. It is not contemplated that contractors necessarily will undertake all the listed activities. The scope of the contractor's efforts shall depend upon all the circumstances, including the nature and extent of the contractor's deficiencies and the contractor's size and resources.

(1) Internal communication of the contractor's obligation to provide equal employment opportunity without regard to religion or national origin in such a manner as to foster understanding, acceptance, and support among the contractor's executive, management, supervisory, and all other employees and to encourage such persons to take

APPENDIX 7-1 (cont'd)

the necessary action to aid the contractor in meeting this obligation.

(2) Development of reasonable internal procedures to ensure that the . contractor's obligation to provide equal employment opportunity without regard to religion or national origin is being fully implemented.

(3) Periodically informing all employees of the contractor's commitment to equal employment opportunity for all persons, without regard to religion or national origin.

(4) Enlisting the assistance and support of all recruitment sources (including employment agencies, college placement directors, and business associates) for the contractor's commitment to provide equal employment opportunity without regard to religion or national origin.

(5) Reviewing employment records to determine the availability of promotable and transferable members of various religious and ethnic groups.

(6) Establishment of meaningful contacts with religious and ethnic organizations and leaders for such purposes as advice, education, technical assistance, and referral of potential employees.

(7) Engaging in significant recruitment activities at educational institutions with substantial enrollents of students from various religious and ethnic groups.

(8) Use of religious and ethnic media for institutional and employment advertising.

§ 60–50.3 Accommodations to religious observance and practice.

A contractor must accommodate to the religious observances and practices of an employee or prospective employee unless the contractor demonstrates that it is unable to reasonably accommodate to an employee's or prospective employee's religious observance or practice without undue hardship on the conduct of the contractor's business. As part of this obligation, a contractor must make reasonable accommodations to the religious observances and practices of an employee or prospective employee who regularly observes Friday evening and Saturday, or some other day of the week, as the Sabbath and/or who observes certain religious holidays during the year and who is conscientiously opposed to performing

work or engaging in similar activity on such days, when such accommodations can be made without undue hardship on the conduct of the contractor's business. In determing the extent of the contractor's obligations under this section, at least the following factors shall be considered; (a) Business necessity, (b) financial costs and expenses, and (c) resulting personnel problems.

60–50.4 Enforcement.

The provisions of this part are subject to the general enforcement, compliance review, and complaint procedures set forth in Part 60–1 of this chapter.

§ 60–50.5 Nondiscrimination.

The provisions of this part are not intended and shall not be used to discriminate against any qualified employee or applicant for employment because of race, color, religion, sex, or national origin.

PART 60–60—CONTRACTOR EVALUATION PROCEDURES FOR CONTRACTORS FOR SUPPLIES AND SERVICES [REMOVED]

PART 60–250—AFFIRMATIVE ACTION OBLIGATIONS OF CONTRACTORS AND SUBCONTRACTORS FOR DISABLED VETERANS AND VETERANS OF THE VIETNAM ERA

Subpart A—Preliminary Matters, Affirmative Action Clause, Compliance

Subpart B—General Enforcement and Complaint Procedures

Subpart C—Ancillary Matters

APPENDIX 7-1 (cont'd)

60–250.31 Recordkeeping.
Appendix A
Appendix B

Authority: Sec. 503(a), Pub. L. 92–540, 86 Stat. 1097 (38 U.S.C. 2012), as amended by Sec. 402, Pub. L 93–508, 88 Stat. 1593 (38 U.S.C. 2012).

Appendix B

The following is a set of procedures which contractors may use to meet the requirements of § 60–250.5(b).

(1) The application or personnel form of each known protected veteran should be annotated to identify each vacancy for which he or she was considered, and the form should be quickly retrievable for review by the agency, the Department of Labor and the contractor's personnel officials for use in investigations and internal compliance activities.

(2) The personnel or application records of each known protected veteran should include (i) the identification of each promotion for which he or she was considered, and (ii) the identification of each training program for which he or she was considered.

(3) In each case where a protected veteran is rejected for employment, promotion or training, a statement of the reasons should be appended to the personnel file or application form. This statement should include a comparison of the qualifications of the protected veteran and the person(s) selected, as well as a description of the accommodations considered. This statement should be available to the applicant or employee concerned upon request.

(4) Where applicants or employees are selected for hire, promotion or training and the contractor undertakes any accommodation which makes it possible for the contractor to place a protected veteran on the job, the application form or personnel record should contain a description of that accommodation.

PART 60-741—AFFIRMATIVE ACTION OBLIGATIONS OF CONTRACTORS AND SUBCONTRACTORS FOR HANDICAPPED WORKERS

Subpart A—Preliminary Matters, Affirmative Action Clause, Compliance

Sec.
60–741.1 Purpose and application.
60–741.2 Coverage and waivers.
60–741.3 Affirmative action clause.
60–741.4 Applicability of the affirmative action program requirement.
60–741.5 Affirmative action policy, practices and procedures.
60–741.6 Determination of handicap.
60–741.7 Listing of employment openings.

Subpart B—General Enforcement and Complaint Procedure

60–741.20 Subcontracts.
60–741.21 Duties of agencies.
60–741.22 Evaluations by the OFCCP Assistant Regional Administrator.
60–741.23 Complaint procedures.

Subpart C—Ancillary Matters

60–741.30 Recordkeeping.
Appendix A
Appendix B
Appendix C

Authority: Sec. 503, Pub. L. 93–1112, 87 Stat. 393 (20 U.S.C. 793), as amended by sec. 111, Pub. L. 93–516, 88 Stat. 1619 (29 U.S.C. 706) and Executive Order 11758.

Appendix C

The following is a set of procedures which contractors may use to meet the requirement of § 60–741.5(b).

(1) The application or personnel form of each known handicapped applicant should be annotated to identify each vacancy for which the applicant was condsidered, and the form should be quickly retrievable for review by the Department of Labor and the contractor's personnel officials for use in investigations and internal compliance activities.

(2) The personnel or application records of each known handicapped employee should include (i) the identification of each promotion for which the handicapped employee was considered, and (ii) the identification of each training program for which the handicapped employee was considered.

(3) In each case where a handicapped employee or applicant is rejected for employment, promotion or training, a statement of the reason should be appended to the personnel file or application form. This statement should include a comparison of the qualifications of the handicapped appliance or employee and the person(s) selected, as well as a description of the accommodations considered. This statement should be available to the applicant or employee concerned upon request.

(4) Where applicants or employees are selected for hire, promotion or training and the contractor undertakes any accommodation which makes it possible for the contractor to place a handicapped individual on the job, the application form or personnel record should contain a description of that accommodation.

APPENDIX 7-2

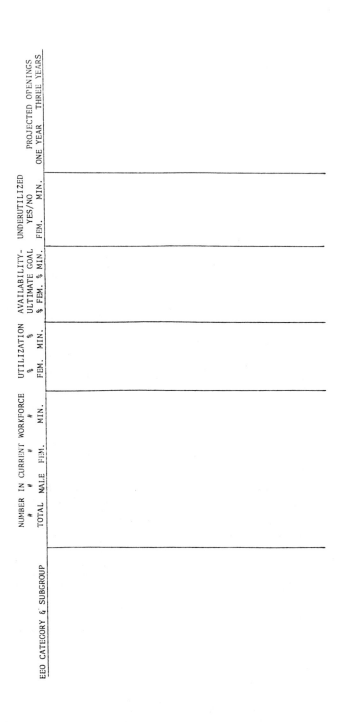

APPENDIX 7-2 (cont'd)

WORKFORCE ANALYSIS
1979-1980

EEO CATEGORY & SUBGROUP	NUMBER IN CURRENT WORKFORCE				UTILIZATION %		AVAILABILITY ULTIMATE GOAL		UNDERUTILIZED YES/NO		GOALS - 1 YEAR - # OF NEW HIRES - % PLACEMENT RATE			
	# TOTAL	# MALE	# FEM.	# MIN.	% FEM.	% MIN.	% FEM.	%MIN.	FEM.	MIN.	FEMALE #	%	MINORITY #	%
1 - ADMIN/EXEC/MANAGERIAL	82	64	18	4	22.0	4.9	32.2	9.3	yes	yes	4	50.0	2	25.0
2 - FACULTY, TOTAL	402	290	112	31	27.9	7.7	28.8	12.1	yes	yes	20	33.3	11	18.3
Humanities	116	79	37	10	31.9	8.6	36.3	9.3	yes	yes	5	38.4	1	7.7
Social Sciences	92	71	21	7	22.8	7.6	30.7	11.1	yes	yes	7	27.4	3	17.6
Phys.& Biol. Sci. & Math	79	62	18	5	22.8	6.3	18.8	15.7	no	no	2	22.2	3	22.2
Education	59	43	16	3	27.0	5.0	31.9	14.8	yes	yes	2	50.0	1	25.0
Business	70	59	11	6	15.7	8.6	8.8	11.4	no	yes	2	16.7	2	16.7
Library	14	5	9	0	64.0	0.0	45.1	18.4	no	yes	2	40.0	2	40.0
3 - PROF. NON-FACULTY	58	25	33	8	56.9	13.8	51.6	16.8	no	yes	7	53.8	3	23.1
4 - CLERICAL, TOTAL	225	1	224	41	99.6	18.2	67.5	17.7	no	no	51	100.0	13	25.4
Entry Level	80	1	79	15	98.7	18.7	65.0	18.1	no	no	19	100.0	6	18.7
Trained	87	0	87	15	100.0	17.2	74.1	18.1	no	yes	25	100.0	5	20.0
Skilled	58	0	58	11	100.0	18.9	82.5	17.7	no	no	7	100.0	2	28.6
5 - TECHNICAL	36	19	17	5	47.2	13.9	53.4	15.6	yes	yes	4	50.0	2	25.0
6 - SKILLED CRAFT	58	56	2	6	3.4	10.3	8.6	10.8	yes	yes	2	16.7	2	16.7
7 - SERVICE/MAINT., TOTAL	170	113	57	104	33.5	61.2	47.5	29.2	yes	no	15	48.3	13	42.0
No High School Degree Required	119	73	46	85	38.6	71.4	48.2	30.6	yes	no	10	50.0	10	50.0
High School Degree	51	40	11	19	22.0	38.0	45.5	26.4	yes	no	5	45.4	3	27.3

3-1-80

APPENDIX 7-3

AVAILABILITY FACTOR COMPUTATION

EEO CATEGORY _____

JOB GROUP _____

	Raw Statistics		Value Weight		Weighted Factor	
	Min.	Fem.	Min.	Fem.	Min.	Fem.
1. Percentage of population in the specified labor or recruitment area.						
2. Percentage of unemployment in the specified labor or recruitment area.						
3. Percentage of minorities or females in total work force in the specific labor area.						
4. Percentage of availability of minorities or females with the requisite skills in the specified labor area.						
5. The availability of minorities or females having requisite skills in an area in which the contractor can reasonably recruit.						
6. Percentage of minorities or females promotable and transferable within the contractor's organization in the specified labor area.						
7. Estimate of existence of training institutions for the requisite skills required for minorities or females.						
8. Estimate of training efforts the contractor is reasonably able to undertake to make the job group available to minorities or females.						

FINAL AVAILABILITY FACTOR _____

APPENDIX 7-3 (cont'd)

Administrative, Managerial, Executive EEO Category

Availability: Source and Reason

Factor

1,2,3   Source: SMSA Planning Data published annually by the State
         Department of Employment Security.

         Weight: Low weight given to these because of the specialized
         nature of the job - usually requires advanced degree and/or
         extensive experience.

   4   Source: Annual report of SMSA by State Division of Employment
         Security.

         Weight: Analysis of recent hires indicated weight given to
         those hired from local area.

   5   Source: U.S. Household data from the State Department of
         Employment Security.

         Weight: Analysis of recent hires indicated weight given to
         hires from national area.

   6   Source: Percentage minority and female in previous year's faculty
         and professional non-faculty categories; one-hald weight given
         to each.

         Weight: Analysis of recent hires.

   7   Source: Summary of enrollments at area graduate schools.

         Weight: Low weight given because experience in addition to a
         graduate degree generally needed for this category.

   8   Source: No training program for this category per se. Educa-
         tional assistance information not available by race and sex.

APPENDIX 7-3 (cont'd)

Faculty

Availability: Source and Reason

Factor

1,2,3   Source: SMSA Annual Planning Information by the State Division
           of Employment Security.

           Weight: Low weight given to these factors for faculty
           availability because of the specialized nature of the job
           requirements. All new regular faculty hires require a Ph.D.
           which has no relation to general population, general unem-
           ployment, or general work force.

4   Source: Survey made by institutional Affirmative Action Office
           of area universities regarding faculty composition.

           Weight: Low weight given in overall category because only a
           out of 26 (3.8%) of regular faculty openings were filled by
           persons formerly employed from the three local institutions
           above. The availability from these institutions is not pro-
           vided by department, hence is inadequate for measuring indivi-
           dual department needs.

5   Source: National Research Council - Doctoral Recipients.
           Summary of the Ph.D. graduates for three most recent years.

           Weight: The best estimate available, providing availability
           of Ph.D. degree holders by discipline. The three average
           gives a measure of a larger pool than just one year.

6   Source: The percentage of the institution's faculty at the
           assistant professor level, as of the beginning of the previous
           academic year.

           Weight: Low weight given to promotable pool because advancement
           is dependent on the tenure/promotion process which considers years
           of service, teaching, and research quality.

7   Source: Survey by institutional Affirmative Action Office enroll-
           ments at local higher education institutions for the previous year.

           Weight: Low weight given because this percent does not reflect
           specific disciplines.

8   Source: Not available.

APPENDIX 7-3 (cont'd)

Clerical

Availability: Source and Reason

Factor

1,2,3   Source: SMSA Annual Planning Information by the State Division
of Employment Security.

Weight: Higher weight given to these factors for entry level
and lower weights given for trained and skilled levels. As
more specialized skills are required, the general population
and work force become less indicative of availability.

4   Source: SMSA Annual Planning Information by the State
Division of Employment Security.

Weight: Because this measure includes all clerical employees,
the weight for categories 4 and 5 combined was reduced as the
job group level changed from lower to higher skilled. More
employees at higher levels would be hired through promotions
rather than outside hires.

5   Source: The recruiting area is the SMSA. SMSA Annual Planning
Information by the State Division of Employment Security.

Weight: Same as factor 4 above.

6   Source: Percent of females and minorities is current entry
level group for trained level percent in trained level group
for skilled level.

Weight: Weights for trained level and for skilled level were
determined by an estimate for the percentage of trained and
skilled positions filled by promotions.

7   Source: High school graduates and enrollment data not available
by race and sex. Percentages for factor 3 were used as a substitute.

Weight: Low weight given because of the unavailability of the
data. No weight given for skilled level because experience
required.

8   The institution has in-house clerical training programs, but
enrollment data not available by race and sex.

APPENDIX 7-4

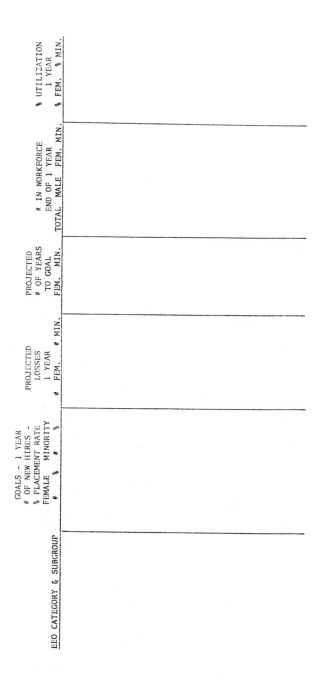

APPENDIX 7-4 (cont'd)

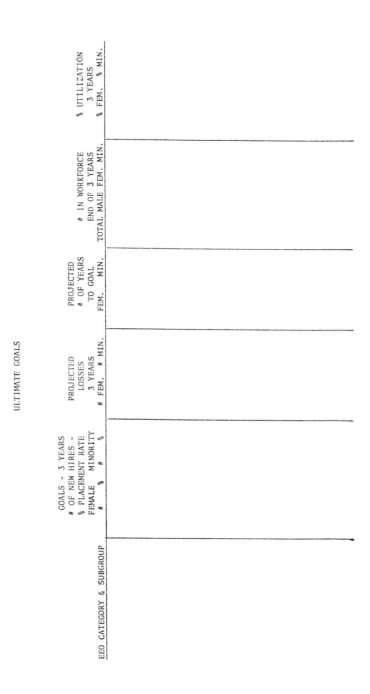

APPENDIX 7-5

GOAL ACHIEVEMENT SUMMARY
198___ - 8___

EEO Category/ Subgroup	No. of Positions	Avail- ability Fem. Min.	Utili- zation Fem. Min.	Projected Vacancies	Goals Fem. Min.	Adj. Util. Fem. Min.	Actual Vacan.	Actual Hires W/Male Fem. Min.	Position Reclassif. W/Male Fem. Min.	Open Pos. 6-30*	Actual Adj. Util. Fem. Min.

*End of fiscal year for staff.

APPENDIX 7-6

IMPACT RATIO ANALYSIS (IRA)
See also FCCM 2-A-12 ff

Job Group:

APPLICANTS

Step 1	Step 2	Impact Ratio
TS ÷ AW = HAR/OAR	HAR ÷ OAR =	
TS ÷ AF_1 = HAR/OAR	HAR ÷ OAR =	
TS ÷ AM^1 = HAR/OAR		

HIRES

Step 1	Step 2	Impact Ratio
TA ÷ HW = HAR/OAR	HAR ÷ OAR =	
TA ÷ HF_1 = HAR/OAR	HAR ÷ OAR =	
TA ÷ HM^1 = HAR/OAR		

PROMOTIONS[2]

Step 1	Step 2	Impact Ratio
TW ÷ PW = HAR/OAR	HAR ÷ OAR =	
TW ÷ PF_1 = HAR/OAR	HAR ÷ OAR =	
TW ÷ PM^1 = HAR/OAR		

TERMINATIONS[3]

Step 1	Step 2	Impact Ratio
TW ÷ XW = LRT/ORT	LTR ÷ OTR =	
TW ÷ XF_1 = LRT/ORT	LTR ÷ OTR =	
TW ÷ XM^1 = LRT/ORT		

[1] Separate analysis for racial minorities is required under certain conditions.
[2] Same analysis for trainees
[3] Same analysis for any adverse personnel action (disciplinary actions, layoffs, etc)

LEGEND

Applicants

   TS = total SMSA
   AW = white applicants
   AF = female applicants
   AM = minority applicants

Hires

   TA = total applicants
   HW = white hires
   HF = female hires
   HM = minority hires

Promotions

   TW = total workforce
   PW = whites promoted
   PF = females promoted
   PM = minority promoted

Terminations

   TW = total workforce
   XW = whites terminated
   XF = females terminated
   XM = minority terminated

HAR = highest acceptance rate (selected from results of step 1; the other rates
     (OAR) becomes the numbers to be divided)
LTR = lowest term. rate
OTR = other term. rate

APPENDIX 7-7

FOCUS JOB ANALYSIS

JOB AREAS IN WHICH FEM./MIN. ARE CONCENTRATED OR UNDERREPRESENTED	JAAR[1]	UNDERREPRESENTATION		CONCENTRATION		SALARY	COMPARISON OF JOB AREAS TO DETERMINE DISPARITIES
		Min.	Female	Min.	Female		

[1] See FCCM 2-A-46 through 2-A-85
[2] Compared wage rates, working conditions, upward mobility potential, etc.

pc

APPENDIX 7-8

ADMINISTRATIVE SERVICE AND SUPPORT STAFF PERSONNEL ACTIVITY REPORT

July, 198___ through June, 198___

JOB GROUP	TOTAL, # EMPLOYEES	ALL EMPLOYEES		RACIAL DISTRIBUTION														
		MALE	FEMALE	MALE						FEMALE								
				Wh	Bl	His	As	A.I.	Wh	Bl	His	As	A.I.	RACE UNKNOWN

Racial Code: Wh - White, Bl - Black, His - Hispanic,
As - Asian, A.I. - American Indian

pc

APPENDIX 7-8 (cont'd)

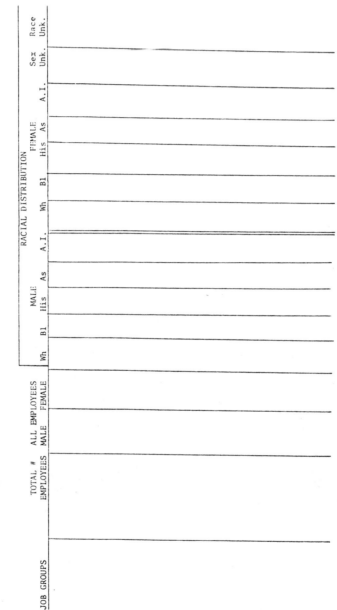

ACADEMIC YEAR 198___-8
FACULTY AND ADMINISTRATORS WITH ACADEMIC APPOINTMENTS
PERSONNEL ACTIVITY REPORT

Racial Code: Wh- White, Bl- Black, His- Hispanic,
As- Asian, A.I.- American Indian

pc

APPENDIX 7-9

DISABLED EMPLOYEE ACCOMMODATION LOG

Date	Name	Position Title	Personnel Action[*]	Reason for Rejection (if applicable)[**]	Type of Disability	Accommodation Made or Considered

[*] Includes hire, transfer, promotion, consideration for a training program.

[**] When a rejection occurs, the file should contain a comparison of the qualifications of the person(s) selected with those of the veteran or the disabled person as well as a detailed description of the accommodation considered.

pc

APPENDIX 7-10

Information Card

for

Disabled Employees and Vietnam Veterans*

As part of our Affirmative Action Plan, we are asking disabled employees and
employees who are Vietnam Era Veterans to identify themselves. This
information is voluntary but will be kept confidential. Please indicate
the nature of your disability and the nature of the accommodations we could
make to enable you to perform the job safely and properly, including special
equipment, changes in the physical layout of the job, elimination of certain
duties relating to the job, or other accommodations. If you are not
handicapped/disabled, a Vietnam Era Veteran or a disabled Veteran, do not
return this card.

NAME _____   SS # _____

VIETNAM ERA VETERAN _____

DISABLED VETERAN _____

HANDICAPPED/DISABLED _____

Mobility impaired _____   Learning disability _____
Visually impaired _____   Wheelchair _____
Hearing impaired _____   Other (describe) _____

Describe necessary accommodations: _____

                                   _____

                                   _____

*This card, sent to all employees annually with a pay check, is returned to the
Affirmative Action Office.

APPENDIX 7-10 (cont'd)

DISABLED STUDENT INFORMATION CARD*

The University of Missouri-St. Louis is working to become more accessible to
our disabled students. Because disabled students have special needs, we
would like to know how many of you are students on our campus and what your
needs are. We also would like to encourage you to participate in campus
activities of all kinds, as well as in the Disabled Students Organization.
If you have a disabling condition, would you please complete this form?

Your providing this information is voluntary, and all information will be
kept confidential. If you need special services, contact the Coordinator of
Special Services at 553-5211, 301 Woods Hall.

Types of disability   If you wish to participate in the
                                             Disabled Students Organization
    Mobility impaired _____   and/or utilize special services,
    Visually impaired _____   please provide the following:
    Hearing impaired _____
    Learning disabled _____   NAME _____
    Wheelchair _____
    Other (specify) _____   ADDRESS _____ ZIP_____

                                             PHONE _____

*This card can be part of the registration packet or the orientation materials
 for new students. It can also be published in the student newspaper.

APPENDIX 8-1

AFFIRMATIVE ACTION OFFICE RECORD OF GRIEVANCE

I.   Name_____ Date_____

     Address_____ Phone_____

     Student_____   Employee_____   Academic_____   Non-Academic_____

     Department_____

     Immediate Supervisor_____

II. Discrimination based on: Race_____   Sex_____   Religion_____   National Origin_____

     Age_____   Handicap_____   Other (Specify)_____

     Individual_____   Class_____   (If others are affected by this possible violation,

     give their names and/or positions)_____

     Nature of Charge:

     _____ Advertising   _____ Layoff/Recall   _____ Admission
     _____ Benefits   _____ Promotion   _____ Financial Aid
     _____ Demotion   _____ Qualifications   _____ Athletics
     _____ Discharge   _____ Referral   _____ Student Programs
     _____ Equal Pay   _____ Seniority
     _____ Exclusion   _____ Terms and Conditions
     _____ Hiring   _____ Training/Apprenticeship
     _____ Intimidation/Reprisal   _____ Union Representation
     _____ Job Classification   _____ Wages/Salary

III. What corrective action would you like to see taken regarding this grievance?_____

     _____

     _____

IV. Narrative (attach extra sheets if needed)

     Signatures: _____   Grievant_____

                 _____   Person receiving grievance

7/77 PC

APPENDIX 8-2

ANNUAL EVALUATION   May 4, 1978
                                  IV.4.1.4
Department of _____

May 1980-May 1981

NAME_____   RANK_____

                                           FTE in Department_____

Salary, 1976-77_____

Salary, 1977-78_____   Increment, percent_____

Salary, 1978-79_____   Increment, percent_____

Salary, 1979-80_____   Increment, percent_____

Salary, 1980-81_____   Increment, percent_____

TEACHING:

   Teaching Load Credit: Fall_____; Winter_____

   Teaching Evaluation Date (Summary):

RESEARCH:

   Publications (Published and in press during period):

SERVICE:

SUMMARY EVALUATION:

APPENDIX 8-3

DEPARTMENT SALARY ANALYSIS SUMMARY

NAME

SEX

RANK

SALARY INCREMENT
AND PERCENT RAISE

I.   Teaching

      A.   Student
           evaluations
           Dept. avg: ____

      B.   Teaching load
           Normal: ____ hrs.

II.   Research

      Articles
      Books
      Performance
      Exhibits

III. Service

      Departmental
      College
      Campus
      Community

* Grievant

APPENDIX 8-4a

<u>SUGGESTIONS FOR RESOLVING SEXUAL HARASSMENT PROBLEMS</u>

1. Arrange for a student to drop a course or to alter future courses
    of study to avoid contact with the offending professor.

2. Transfer   an employee to another department or perhaps to another
    shift to avoid having to work under the offending employee/supervisor.

3. In some cases a verbal warning, a promise not to commit such abuses
    again and adequate compensation for the aggrieved party may be an
    appropriate resolution. A goal of counselling and mediating sexual
    harassment problems is to sensitize the harasser to the effects of
    such behavior, to be constructive and not unduly punitive in the
    disciplinary action. If the harasser does not follow through with
    the agreed upon resolution or commits subsequent acts of sexual
    harassment, a formal grievance and sterner sanctions are appropriate.

4. Sanctions will depend on the severity of the incident and may range
    from an informal discussion with the harasser to termination from
    employment with the university. Sanctions may include a letter of
    reprimand placed in the harasser's personnel file, involuntary demo-
    tion of the harasser, transfer of the harasser to another depart-
    ment or position, counselling or enrollment in training designed
    to sensitize the harasser to the effects of such behavior. Pro-
    gressive discipline is recommended especially for grievances reach-
    ing the formal grievance procedures.

    1st stage -- a letter of reprimand will be written and placed in
    the harasser's personnel file, with a terminal life of two years
    (usually); action will be taken to compensate the aggrieved party
    for any loss or injustice.

    2nd stage -- a letter of reprimand for the harasser's file and sus-
    pension without pay for a period of time (to be determined); again,
    the aggrieved party will be adequately compensated for loss or
    injustice.

    3rd stage -- termination of employment of the harasser, aggrieved
    party to be reinstated, restored, adequately compensated, etc.

APPENDIX 8-4*b*

POLICY AND PROCEDURE ON SEXUAL HARASSMENT

POLICY

Faculty, staff and students are responsible for maintaining a working and
educational environment that is harmonious with the university's mission
of teaching, research, and service. Sexual harassment is anathema to that
harmony and such misconduct is a violation of university policy.

DEFINITION

Sexual harassment may be defined as unsolicited nonreciprocal behavior
involving a person who is in a position to control or affect another university employee's job or student's status as a student and who is using
that authority and power to coerce that employee or student to submit to
sexual activity or to punish their refusal to submit and/or who is using
that authority and power to sexually harass the employee or student. Sexual
harassment includes conduct unreasonably interfering with an employee's work
performance or with a student's status as a student or creating an intimidating, hostile, or offensive working or educational environment. Sexual
harassment may consist of a variety of behaviors directed to employees or
students, including but not limited to, subtle pressure for sexual activity,
inappropriate touching, inappropriate language, demands for sexual favors
and physical assault.

WHAT TO DO

Students or employees who believe they have been sexually harassed should
contact the Affirmative Action Office and make an appointment to discuss
the problem with the Director. Prior to that discussion, they should
organize their thoughts about the problem, citing examples, dates and identifying other individuals who may have observed the incident. They should
decide what would be an acceptable resolution to the problem.

Students and employees should contact the Affirmative Action Office even if
they do not intend to file a formal grievance because informal options are
available to deal with problems of harassment. These options are discussed
during informal consultation and anyone affected by problems of sexual
harassment is encouraged to discuss them informally.

Students may also wish to discuss the problem with a faculty or staff member
known to them and with whom they are comfortable, with the Dean of Student
Affairs, or with the Coordinator of the Women's Center.

PROCEDURE

Most issues of this nature will be resolved through informal consultation.
Employees or students who believe they may have been victims of sexual
harassment should contact the Affirmative Action Office. That office will

1. counsel and provide information for the employee or student
2. attempt informal resolution of the complaint
3. inform the employee or student of the appropriate formal
    grievance procedures.

The following grievance procedures are available on campus

1. Students: Senate Welfare & Grievance Committee
2. Faculty: Faculty Grievance Procedures
3. Staff: Staff Grievance Procedures

APPENDIX 8–5*a*

Title VII Sexual Harassment Guidelines And Educational Employment

Introduction

On November 10, 1980 the Equal Employment Opportunity Commission (EEOC) issued final interpretive guidelines* on sexual harassment[1] under Title VII of the Civil Rights Act of 1964[2] which state that:

- Title VII prohibits sexual harassment of employees;
- employers are responsible for the actions of their agents and supervisors; and
- employers are responsible for the actions of all other employees if the employer knew or should have known about the sexual harassment.

What is Title VII?

Title VII of the Civil Rights Act of 1964 prohibits employment discrimination on the basis of race, color, religion, national origin, and sex.

Who is covered by Title VII?

Title VII covers all employers who employ 15 or more employees. Title VII covers all educational institutions, and the guidelines cover all of their employees.

Who enforces the guidelines?

The Equal Employment Opportunity Commisson which issued the guidelines is the enforcement agency for Title VII.

Why were the guidelines issued?

Sexual harassment in the workplace is a continuing and widespread problem. EEOC has stated, "Sexual harassment like harassment on the basis of color, race, religion, or national origin has long been recognized by the EEOC as a violation of . . . Title VII of the Civil Rights Act of 1964 . . . However, despite the position taken by the Commission, sexual harassment continues to be especially widespread . . . Therefore, EEOC (amends) its Guidelines on Discrimination because of Sex."

An example of the breadth of this problem is shown by a 1975 study conducted by Working Women's Institute in which 70 percent of the respondents reported that they had experienced sexual harassment on the job. In another study, conducted by *Redbook Magazine*, almost one half of employed women surveyed said that they—or a woman they knew—had quit a position or been fired because of sexual harassment on the job.[4]

Do the guidelines have the force of law?

Strictly speaking, no. The guidelines are advisory and courts take them into account. Moreover, the guidelines closely parallel already existing court decisions in which the courts have held that sexual harassment violates Title VII and that employers are responsible for the actions of their employees. Thus, the guidelines are consistent with current case law.

Do the guidelines prohibit personal relationships between employees?

No. The guidelines address themselves to unwelcome conduct and clearly distinguish sexual harassment from a "particular action or incident (which is) a purely personal, social relationship without a discriminating employment effect.[5] In determining whether conduct constitutes sexual harassment, the commission "will look at the record as a whole and at the totality of the circumstances, such as the nature of the sexual advances and the context in which the alleged incidents occurred. The determination of the legality of a particular action will be made from the facts, on a case by case basis."[6]

What is sexual harassment?

The guidelines define sexual harassment as unwelcome sexual advances, requests for sexual favors, and other verbal or physical conduct of a nature which constitute harassment when:

- submission to the conduct is either explicitly or implicitly a term or condition of an individual's employment;
- submission to or rejection of such conduct by an individual is used as the basis for employment decisions affecting that individual; and/or
- such conduct has the purpose or effect of unreasonably interfering with an individual's work performance or creating an intimidating, hostile, or offensive working environment.[7]

Do the guidelines give specific examples of activities that constitute sexual harassment?

No. The guidelines simply offer a flexible and very broad definition of sexual harassment with no specific examples.

Specific examples, however, that *may* constitute sexual harassment under the guidelines are:

- subtle pressure for sexual activity;
- unnecessary patting or pinching;
- constant brushing against another employee's body;
- "friendly" arms around the shoulder;
- "accidental" brushes or touches;
- deliberate assaults or molestations;
- demanding sexual favors accompanied by implied threats concerning an individual's employment status;
- demanding sexual favors accompanied by implied or overt promises of preferential treatment with regard to an individual's employment status; and
- explicit offers of money for sex.[8]

Are sexual jokes, slurs, and insults directed at members of one sex prohibited by the guidelines?

The answer to this question is unclear. Though the guidelines state that sexual harassment can be "physical" or "verbal," the guidelines also state that the conduct must be "of a sexual nature." Thus, it is unclear whether derogatory and degrading comments or jokes directed at members of one sex constitute sexual harassment.

The Circuit Court of the District of Columbia, however, has found that activity need not have a sexual content in order to constitute sexual harassment. Though the cases involved activity that

Guidelines are reprinted on back page.

[1] This paper was primarily written by Susan Howard of Suffolk University Law, who was an intern with the Project on the Status and Education of Women

THE PROJECT ON THE STATUS AND EDUCATION OF WOMEN of the Association of American Colleges provides information concerning women in education, and works with institutions, government agencies and other associations and programs affecting women in higher education. The Project is funded by Carnegie Corporation of New York and The Ford Foundation. Publication of these materials does not necessarily constitute endorsement by AAC, Carnegie Corporation of New York, of The Ford Foundation, or any of its sponsoring organizations. This publication may be reproduced in whole or part without permission, provided credit is given to the Project on the Status and Education of Women, Association of American Colleges 1818 R Street, NW, Washington, DC 20009. All requests for copies should be accompanied by a self-addressed, stamped envelope

APPENDIX 8-5*a* (cont'd)

was sexual in content, the court said that the content of the activity was "immaterial." The activity need only to be directed at members of one sex.

> ". . . (R)etention of her job was conditioned upon submission to sexual relations—an extraction which the supervisor would not have sought from any male."

> ". . . The vitiating sex factor thus stemmed not from the fact that what appellant's supervisor demanded was sexual activity—*which of itself is immaterial*—but from the fact that he imposed upon her tenure in her then position a condition which he would not have fastened upon a male employee." (italics added) [*Williams v. Saxbe*, 413 F. Supp. 654 (D.D.C. 1972)].

In a later case the same court said:

> "It was and is sufficient to allege a violation of Title VII to claim that the rule creating an artificial barrier to employment has been applied to one gender and not to the other." *Barnes v. Costle*, 561 F. 2d. 983 (1977).

The National Advisory Council on Women's Educational Programs[¹] has urged that the guidelines be expanded or interpreted by EEOC so as to prohibit activity of a "gender-charged" nature. In a letter to EEOC, the Council stated:

> "An atmosphere charged with such anti-woman (or anti-man) bias is as potentially harmful to employees as is an atmosphere charged with racist sentiment, and constitutes 'sexual' harassment in a very real manner."

The "atmosphere" that the council refers to is created by "behavior (which) may include denigration of women (or men) through sexist humor, remarks, or other activities which create an 'intimidating, hostile, or offensive working climate,' but which do so without any suggestion that sexual activity take place between the principals.""[¹º]

EEOC and, ultimately, the courts will settle this question.

What must institutions do to comply with the guidelines?

The guidelines state that an employer *should* take all necessary steps to prevent sexual harassment such as:

- affirmatively raising the subject;
- expressing strong disapproval;
- developing appropriate sanctions;
- informing employees of their right to raise and how to raise the issue of harassment under Title VII; and
- developing methods to sensitize all concerned."[¹¹]

Is an employer responsible for the actions of its agents and supervisors?

Yes, the guidelines hold employers fully responsible for the actions of their agents and supervisors "*regardless* of whether the specific acts complained of were authorized or even forbidden by the employer and regardless of whether the employer knew or should have known of their occurrence.""[¹²] (italics added)

Is an institution responsible for the actions of its employees?

Yes. The guidelines, however, impose a less strict standard by which to measure the employer's responsibility if the harasser is simply an employee and not an agent or a supervisory employee. The employer is responsible for the actions of such employees *only* if the employer (or its agents or supervisory employees) "knows or should have known of the conduct and fails to take immediate and appropriate corrective action."[¹³]

In addition, an employer may also be responsible for the actions of *non-employees* who sexually, harass employees in the workplace where the employer (or its agents or supervisory employees) "knows or should have known of the conduct and fails to take immediate and appropriate corrective action."[¹⁴]

Why should institutions be interested in prohibiting sexual harassment?

As a booklet published by AFSCME[¹⁵] argues, "Probably the majority of offenders are supervisors, so sexual harassment should be considered a problem for management to resolve. Work environments in which sexual harassment is sanctioned are not the most productive, and personnel decisions may be made without regard to the job performance.""[¹⁶] The booklet notes "sexual harassment undermines the integrity of the 'workplace.'"[¹⁷] and therefore, "it is good management practice to have a strong policy against sexual harassment."[¹⁸]

In addition, employers will also want to avoid charges of sexual harassment. In such cases, EEOC can ask for an award of front pay, back pay, reinstatement, promotion, or any other type of relief that will rectify the situation. Both EEOC and the courts have wide discretion in correcting situations where sexual harassment has or is occurring. If an employer refuses to settle a complaint through the conciliation process, EEOC can file suit and ask a federal judge for relief.

Do the guidelines prohibit sexual harassment of students?

The guidelines apply only to employees. Students who are employees, however, are covered by the guidelines in the same manner as other employees.

Is there any other law that protects students from sexual harassment?

Title IX of the Education Amendments of 1972[¹⁹] may prohibit sexual harassment of students.[²⁰] In the case of *Alexander et al v. Yale* [631 Fed. 2d. 178 (2nd Cir. 1980)] a federal magistrate said, in a preliminary hearing which permitted the case to go to trial, ". . . academic advancement conditioned upon submission to sexual demands constitutes sex discrimination in education." The case involved a claim by a former Yale College student that her political science professor had offered her an "A" for sex. (The case lost on appeal because of failure to prove that an improper advance was made or that the student was adversely affected as a consequence.)[²¹]

The Office for Civil Rights (OCR) at the Department of Education is the primary enforcement agency for Title IX, and has not yet issued any guidelines about whether Title IX covers sexual harassment. The National Advisory Council on Women's Educational Programs, however, has submitted to OCR a legal memorandum which concluded that Title IX prohibits sexual harassment of students, faculty and staff.[²²]

Will institutions be informed if a sexual harassment complaint is filed against them?

Yes. EEOC notifies institutions of complaints within 10 days.

Who can file a complaint against an institution?

Individuals and/or organizations on behalf of aggrieved employee(s) or applicant(s). Organizations also may file class or pattern complaints without identification of individuals. Members of the Commission may also file charges.

Is there a time limit for filing complaints?

Yes. A complaint must be filed within 180 days of the alleged incident.

How is a complaint made?

By a sworn complaint form, obtainable from the Equal Employment Opportunity Commission, 2401 E St., NW, Washington, DC 20508, or the District area EEOC office.

Are the names of complainants kept confidential?

The complainant's name is divulged to the institution when an investigation is made. Charges, however, are not made public by EEOC, nor can any of its efforts during the conciliation process be

APPENDIX 8-5*a* (cont'd)

made public by EEOC or its employees. The aggrieved party, however, and the respondent are not bound by the confidentiality requirement. If court action becomes necessary, the identity of the parties becomes a matter of public record.

Can investigations be made without complaints?

No. EEOC can conduct investigations *only* if charges have been filed.

Are there recordkeeping requirements? Does the government have access to records?

No specific recordkeeping requirements have been promulgated. EEOC, however, has the power to require that specified records be kept relevant to the determination of whether or not violations under Title VII have occurred. EEOC also is empowered to review all relevant records, such as records of grievance procedures relating to sexual harassment.

Are grievance procedures required?

Grievance procedures are not required under Title VII, nor is EEOC required to give weight to findings under such procedures. Thus, individuals are not required to file complaints with the institution before filing with EEOC.[13]

Do the guidelines apply to labor organizations?

Yes. Labor organizations are subject to the same requirements and sanctions as employers.

Is retaliation for filing complaints illegal?

Yes. Employers are prohibited from discharging or discriminating against any employee or applicant for employment because he or she has made a complaint, assisted with an investigation, or instituted proceedings.

What can an institution do?

An institution can make people more aware about the problem of sexual harassment by the following activities:

- developing a specific policy against sexual harassment;
- disseminating the policy in memos, posters, flyers, radio spots, etc.;
- developing a procedure to inform new employees;
- surveying the workplace to find out the extent of the problem at the institution;
- developing and disseminating information about grievance procedures to handle sexual harassment complaints. (The grievance procedure may or may not be the same as other existing grievance procedures. Sexual harassment complaints are often initially handled more appropriately by informal procedures followed by more formal procedures if the complaint is not resolved. Individuals who wish to pursue a grievance are likely to go to court if the institution has no procedure for them to use.);
- developing a union grievance procedure, where appropriate; and
- developing a code of conduct for all employees.

These guidelines add strength to the growing commitment among institutions and the academic community that sexual harassment will no longer be tolerated.

. . . .

FOOTNOTES

[1] 29 C.F.R. Chapter XIV, Section 1604.11, Federal Register, Vol. 45, No. 219, p 74676-74677. (See guidelines reprinted on back page.)

[2] 42 U.S.C. Sections 2000e *et seq.* (1964).

[3] Memo to public interest groups from Eleanor Holmes Norton, chair, EEOC, 3/11/80.

[4] *Redbook* Magazine, November 1976.

[5] Memo to public interest groups from Eleanor Holmes Norton, Chair, EEOC, 3/11/80.

[6] 29 C.F.R. Section 1604.11(b)

[7] 29 C.F.R. Section 1604.11(a).

[8] See, for example, the order issued by the Mayor of the District of Columbia concerning sexual harassment, and the list compiled by the American Federation of State, County and Municipal employees in *Sexual Harassment, On the Job: What the Union Can Do,* available from AFSCME Research Department, 1625 L St., NW Washington, DC 20036

[9] The Council is a federally mandated body whose members are appointed by the President.

[10] Letter to EEOC from National Advisory Council on Women's Educational Programs 6/10/80.

[11] 29 C.F.R. Section 1604.11(f).

[12] 29 C.F.R. Section 1604.11(c)

[13] 29 C.F.R. Section 1604.11(d).

[14] 29 C.F.R. Section 1604.11(e).

[15] *Sexual Harassment, On the Job: What the Union Can Do,* American Federation of State, County, and Municipal Employees, 1625 L St., NW, Washington, DC 20036.

[16] Ibid, p. 11.

[17] Ibid., p. 32.

[18] Ibid., p. 11.

[19] 20 U.S.C. Sections (68) *et seq.* (1972).

[20] Title IX prohibits sex discrimination in any educational program or activity that receives federal financial assistance. Almost all educational institutions receive federal assistance and are therefore covered by Title IX.

[21] In addition, several institutions have used university procedures, without the use of Title IX, to discipline faculty members for sexual harassment of students.

At San Jose State University (CA), a tenured associate professor of philosophy was fired for fondling and propositioning five of his female students.

At the University of California at Berkley, a professor was suspended without pay for one quarter for fondling and propositioning 13 students, offering a good grade for sex, and writing an unfavorable letter of recommendation for one student who refused his sexual advances.

At Harvard University, (MA), a government professor was formally reprimanded after a student contended that he had tried to kiss her.

[22] The issue of whether Title IX protects employees, as well as students, is currently being litigated in the courts. The U.S. Supreme Court will probably soon rule on this question. If the Court finds that Title IX covers employment discrimination it is likely that Title IX will incorporate the Title VII sexual harassment guidelines or that the courts will find the guidelines incorporated implicitly. See Romeo and North Haven.

[23] Title IX, on the other hand, requires grievance procedures, although individuals may bypass them and file charges directly with OCR.

APPENDIX 8-5a (cont'd)

Reprinted from:
Federal Register / Vol. 45. No. 219 / Monday, November 10, 1980 / Rules and Regulations   74676-74677

EQUAL EMPLOYMENT OPPORTUNITY COMMISSION

29 CFR Part 1604

Discrimination Because of Sex Under Title VII of the Civil Rights Act of 1964, as Amended; Adoption of Final Interpretive Guidelines

AGENCY: Equal Employment Opportunity Commission.

ACTION: Final Amendment to Guidelines on Discrimination Because of Sex.

SUMMARY: On April 11, 1980, the Equal Employment Opportunity Commission published the Interim Guidelines on sexual harassment as an amendment to the Guidelines on Discrimination Because of Sex, 29 CFR part 1604.11. 45 FR 25024. This amendment will re-affirm that sexual harassment is an unlawful employment practice. The EEOC received public comments for 60 days subsequent to the date of publication of the Interim Guidelines. As a result of the comments and the analysis of them, these Final Guidelines were drafted.

EFFECTIVE DATE: November 10, 1980.

FOR FURTHER INFORMATION CONTACT: Karen Danart, Acting Director, Office of Policy Implementation, Equal Employment Opportunity Commission, 2401 E Street, NW., Washington, D.C. 20506, (202) 634-7060.

[*Supplementary Information* concerning comments received on the interim guidelines, and relevant case law is omitted.]

Accordingly, 29 CFR Chapter XIV, Part 1604 is amended by adding § 1604.11 to read as follows:

PART 1604—GUIDELINES ON DISCRIMINATION BECAUSE OF SEX

§ 1604.11 Sexual harassment.

(a) Harassment on the basis of sex is a violation of Sec. 703 of Title VII.[1] Unwelcome sexual advances, requests for sexual favors, and other verbal or physical conduct of a sexual nature constitute sexual harassment when (1) submission to such conduct is made either explicitly or implicitly a term or condition of an individual's employment (2) submission to or rejection of such conduct by an individual is used as the basis for employment decisions affecting such individual, or (3) such conduct has the pur-

___
[1] The principles involved here continue to apply to race, color, religion or other origin.

pose or effect of unreasonably interfering with an individual's work performance or creating an intimidating, hostile, or offensive working environment

(b) In determining whether alleged conduct constitutes sexual harassment, the Commission will look at the record as a whole and at the totality of the circumstances, such as the nature of the sexual advances and the context in which the alleged incidents occurred. The determination of the legality of a particular action will be made from the facts, on a case by case basis.

(c) Applying general Title VII principles, an employer, employment agency, joint apprenticeship committee or labor organization (hereinafter collectively referred to as "employer") is responsible for its acts and those of its agents and supervisory employees with respect to sexual harassment regardless of whether the specific acts complained of were authorized or even forbidden by the employer and regardless of whether the employer knew or should have known of their occurrence. The Commission will examine the circumstances of the particular employment relationship and the job junctions performed by the individual in determining whether an individual acts in either a supervisory or agency capacity.

(d) With respect to conduct between fellow employees, an employer is responsible for acts of sexual harassment in the workplace where the employer (or its agents or supervisory employees) knows or should have known of the conduct, unless it can show that it took immediate and appropriate corrective action.

(e) An employer may also be responsible for the acts of non-employees, with respect to sexual harassment of employees in the workplace, where the employer (or its agents or supervisory employees) knows or should have known of the conduct and fails to take immediate and appropriate corrective action. In reviewing these cases the Commission will consider the extent of the employer's control and any other legal responsibility which the employer may have with respect to the conduct of such non-employees.

(f) Prevention is the best tool for the elimination of sexual harassment. An employer should take all steps necessary to prevent sexual harassment from occurring, such as affirmatively raising the subject, expressing strong disapproval, developing appropriate sanctions, informing employees of their right to raise and how to raise the issue of harassment under Title VII, and developing methods to sensitize all concerned.

(g) Other related practices: Where employment opportunities or benefits

are granted because of an individual's submission to the employer's sexual advances or requests for sexual favors, the employer may be held liable for unlawful sex discrimination against other persons who were qualified for but denied that employment opportunity or benefit.

(Title VII, Pub. L. 88-352, 78 Stat. 253 (42 U.S.C. 2000e et sez.))
(FR Doc. 80-34981 Filed 11-7-80, 8.45 am)
BILLING CODE 6570-06-M

APPENDIX 8-5*b*

This hand-out, prepared and distributed by the Utah State University Committee on the Status of Women, may be useful as a model for other institutions developing ways to inform students about discrimination and sexual harassment on campus.

What Can Students Do About Sex Discrimination?

What can you as a student do when you believe that . . .
* course material ignores or depreciates you because of your sex?
* an adviser does not take your career and educational goals seriously because she/he appears to believe them inappropriate for members of your sex?
* you are denied resources, such as financial aid, teaching assistantships, or admission to a program for sexist reasons?
* you are pressured by a professor or staff person to participate with him/her in social and/or sexual activities?

Students often feel powerless in such situations, but there are people on the USU campus who are willing to talk to them about those problems without any obligation on the part of either party. Such situations as those described above are not condoned by Utah State University nor the teaching profession. In some instances they occur out of ignorance or misunderstanding and need only to be brought to the attention of the professor. In other instances they can be considered unethical and subject to professional reprimand.

Marilynne Glatfelter, USU Counseling Center, (ext. 7591)
#*Janice Pearce,* HPER Department (ext. 7379)
Glen Maw, USU Counseling Center, Help Line (ext. 7591)
#*Karen Morse,* Chemistry Department (ext. 7160)
Jane Lott, HECE Department (ext. 7263)
Anne Hatch, USU Women's Center (ext. 7528)
Judith Gappa or Archie Savage, Affirmative Action Office (ext. 8222)

*These people are members of the USU Committee on the Status of Women, currently chaired by Dr. Pearce.

#These people are members of the Professional Relationships and Faculty Welfare Committee.

Actions You Can Take

(In suggested order)

1. Talk to the professor or staff person. Carefully explain why you view the particular comment, joke, course reading, action taken, etc. as sexist. Regard the meeting as a kind of consciousness-raising session where you help him/her understand how you feel. Sometimes people aren't aware of how their remarks or actions affect someone else, and communicating your feelings to the professor might be most helpful to him/her in avoiding such actions in the future. Be sure to prepare for the meeting ahead of time with documentation (e.g. class notes, tapes, specific comments he/she made) and a logical presentation. (Sometimes people don't understand how sexist remarks can hurt; it might help you to draw the analogy of racist or anti-ethnic remarks—''Would you make fun of a person's skin color or ethnic background? Then why do so with sex?'')

To get support for yourself, consider going to see the professor with several other people from the class. If you can't find others in the class (and discussing the issues with other students in itself may help raise consciousness), take friends along who aren't in the class. You might also seek help from the list of names below.

2. Contact University people and groups who are concerned about sexual discrimination. These people are willing to listen to you, discuss specific incidents, and provide help and advice if you want them:

3. If you have talked to the professor or staff person and sexual discrimination continues, write a letter to him/her documenting the incidents and explaining why they are offensive to you. State that you have not obtained results from previous discussion(s) and note the date(s) of the discussion(s). Send a carbon copy to the head of his/her department or unit and perhaps to one of the above-listed people. If you fail to receive a satisfactory answer from the staff members and/or head, request a meeting with the two of them and take along an objective third party (another professor or one of the people in the above list).

4. Don't enroll in classes which are sexually discriminatory, and let the professor know why you haven't enrolled. In filling out course evaluation forms, make it known why such discriminatory comments or actions have offended you. If the professor has responded to your earlier complaints and has made efforts to change, support those efforts in your evaluation. Remember to always give full support to professors who are fair and who treat students as human beings regardless of their sex.

5. It may be necessary to file a formal grievance or complaint. This is a very serious step and should not be undertaken without discussion and counsel with a member of the teaching profession who understands established grievance procedures at USU. Once again consult with one of the people on the above list.

THE PROJECT ON THE STATUS AND EDUCATION OF WOMEN of the Association of American Colleges provides information concerning women in education, and works with institutions, government agencies and other associations and programs affecting women in higher education. The Project is funded by Carnegie Corporation of New York and The Ford Foundation. Publication of these materials does not necessarily constitute endorsement by AAC, Carnegie Corporation of New York or The Ford Foundation, or any of the Project's sponsoring organizations. This publication may be reproduced in whole or part without permission, provided credit is given to the Project on the Status and Education of Women, Association of American Colleges, 1818 R Street, NW, Washington, DC 20009, and the Utah State University Committee on the Status of Women.

February 1981

APPENDIX 8-5c

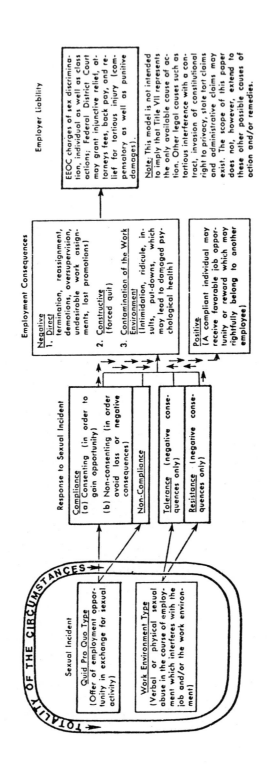

MODEL OF EMPLOYER LIABILITY

*from "The EEOC's Bold Foray into Sexual Harassment on the Job: New Implications for Employer Liability"
by Donna E. Ledgerwood and Sue Johnson-Dietz in the Proceedings of the 33rd Annual IRRA Meeting,
1980, p. 56.

APPENDIX 8-6

EQUAL EMPLOYMENT OPPORTUNITY COMMISSION	PERSON FILING CHARGE

TO:

THIS PERSON *(Check one)*

CLAIMS TO BE AGGRIEVED

IS FILING ON BEHALF OF A PERSON CLAIMING TO BE AGGRIEVED

DATE(s) OF ALLEGED VIOLATION

PLACE OF ALLEGED VIOLATION

CHARGE NUMBER

NOTICE OF CHARGE OF EMPLOYMENT DISCRIMINATION

(See Notice of Non-Retaliation on reverse)

You are hereby notified that a charge of employment discrimination under Title VII of the Civil Rights Act of 1964, as amended, 42 U.S.C. Section 2000e et. seq., has been filed against you. Information relating to the date, place, and circumstances of the alleged unlawful employment practice or practices is provided herein.

If you wish to submit any information in writing, it will be made a part of the file and will be considered when this charge is investigated. Telephone communications cannot be made a part of the record. Section 1602.14 of the Commission's Regulations *(See attachment)* requires the preservation of all personnel records relevant to this charge, as described below, until it is resolved.

You will be contacted when investigation commences.

BASIS OF DISCRIMINATION

☐ RACE OR COLOR ☐ SEX ☐ RETALIATION ☐ RELIGION ☐ NATIONAL ORIGIN

NATURE OF CHARGE

HIRING	DISCHARGE	LAYOFF	RECALL
WAGES	PROMOTION	DEMOTION	SENIORITY
JOB CLASSIFICATION	TRAINING/ APPRENTICESHIP	EXCLUSION	UNION REPRESENTATION
SEGREGATED LOCALS	REFERRAL	QUALIFICATION/ TESTING	ADVERTISING
BENEFITS	SEGREGATED FACILITIES	INTIMIDATION/ REPRISAL	TENURE
TERMS AND CONDITIONS	OTHER/EXPLAIN		

DATE	TYPED NAME/TITLE OF AUTHORIZED EEOC OFFICIAL	SIGNATURE

EEOC FORM 131
SEP 77

RESPONDENT'S COPY

I hereby certify that I mailed the original of this Notice to the addressee herein above.
DATE	EEOC EMPLOYEE *(Signature)*

EEOC FORM 131
SEP 77

FILE COPY

APPENDIX 8-6 (cont'd)

EQUAL EMPLOYMENT OPPORTUNITY COMMISSION

TO:		EEOC CHARGE NUMBER

NOTICE OF CHARGE OF DISCRIMINATION WITH COPY OF CHARGE

(See Section 1602.14, EEOC Rules and Regulations, and Section 704(a), Notice of Non-Retaliation on reverse)

You are hereby notified that the attached charge of employment discrimination under Title VII of the Civil Rights Act of 1964. as amended, 42 U.S.C. Section 2000e et. seq., has been filed against you.

No action is required on your part at this time. However, your attention is directed to:

(1) Section 1601.15 of the Commission's Procedural Regulations which provides that persons charged with employment discrimination. such as yourself. may submit a statement of position or evidence with respect to the allegations contained in this charge. If you wish to submit such information in writing it will be made a part of the file and will be considered at the time we investigate this charge. Telephone communication cannot be made a part of the record:

(2) Section 1602.14 of the Commission's Regulations which requires the preservation of all personnel records relevant to this charge until a final disposition of this charge is made: and

(3) Section 704(a) of the Civil Rights Act which prohibits retaliation.

For future correspondence on this matter. please use the charge number shown above.

Enclosure: Copy of charge

DATE	TYPED NAME OF DISTRICT DIRECTOR	SIGNATURE

EEOC FORM SEP 77 131-A   RESPONDENT'S COPY

CERTIFICATION. *I hereby certify that I mailed the original of this notice to the addressee herein and attached a copy of the charge reference herein.*

DATE	EEOC EMPLOYEE SIGNATURE

EEOC FORM SEP 77 131-A   FILE COPY

APPENDIX 8-6 (cont'd)

EQUAL EMPLOYMENT OPPORTUNITY COMMISSION

TO: ⌐   ¬ | EEOC CHARGE NUMBER

　

└   ┘

NOTICE OF CHARGE OF DISCRIMINATION AND NOTICE OF FACT FINDING CONFERENCE

(See Section 1602.14, EEOC Procedural Regulations, and Section 704(a), Notice of Non-Retaliation on reverse)

TO: RESPONDENT — You are hereby notified that the attached charge of employment discrimination under Title VII of the Civil Rights Act of 1964, as amended (42 U.S.C. Section 2000e, et. seq.), has been filed against you.

TO: RESPONDENT and CHARGING PARTY — You are hereby requested to appear and participate in a Fact Finding Conference scheduled for .... at .... o'clock at ....

The Conference will be conducted by the Commission representative named below.

The Fact Finding Conference is an investigative forum intended to define the issues, to determine which elements are undisputed, to clarify issues, to obtain evidence, and to ascertain whether there is a basis for a Negotiated Settlement of the Charge. Although it is not necessary, you may bring a lawyer with you to the Conference. However, you may not send a substitute for yourself or bring persons not requested without permission from the Commission representative in this charge.

The Commission encourages the parties to settle this charge on terms which are mutually agreeable by means of a Negotiated Settlement prior to the making of a determination by the Commission as to whether the allegations made in this charge are true. The Commission will work with the parties to attain such Negotiated Settlement and if a settlement is made between the parties, the Commission will not issue a finding on the merits of this charge and will agree not to process this charge further.

Preliminary to and as a necessary part of the Fact Finding Conference, you are requested to answer fully any questionnaire which may be attached to this notice and return it to the Commission's representative 7 days before the Conference. You may, in addition, submit, in writing, a statement of position or evidence with respect to this charge, including a proposal for settling this charge by Negotiated Settlement, or you may call the Commission representative. Such information will be made a part of the file and will be considered by the Commission during the course of this investigation, except that settlement proposals will not be made public by the Commission or used as evidence in this or subsequent proceedings without the written consent of the parties concerned.

Respondents who refuse to attend a Fact Finding Conference may be required by subpoena to appear at the District Office and testify about disputed factual matters.

Charging party failure to attend a scheduled Conference or to cooperate in the scheduling of a Conference can result in dismissal of the charge.

In further correspondence on this matter, please use the charge number shown above. Inquiries should be directed to:

	Commission Representative
	Telephone Number
Enclosure: Copy of Charge / Questionnaire	

DATE	TYPED NAME OF DISTRICT DIRECTOR	SIGNATURE

EEOC FORM SEP 77 131-B   **RESPONDENT'S COPY**

DATE	TYPED NAME OF DISTRICT DIRECTOR	SIGNATURE

EEOC FORM SEP 77 131-B   **CHARGING PARTY COPY**

DATE	TYPED NAME OF DISTRICT DIRECTOR	SIGNATURE

EEOC FORM SEP 77 131-B   **FILE COPY**

APPENDIX 8-6 (cont'd)

EQUAL EMPLOYMENT OPPORTUNITY COMMISSION

	EEOC CHARGE NUMBER
TO:	

NOTICE OF CHARGE OF DISCRIMINATION AND REQUEST FOR INFORMATION

(See Section 1602.14, E.E.O.C. Rules and Regulations, and Section 704(a), Notice of Non-Retaliation on reverse)

You are hereby notified that the attached charge of employment discrimination under Title VII of the Civil Rights Act of 1964, as amended, 42 U.S.C. Section 2000e et. seq., has been filed against you.

You are requested to cooperate in the investigation of this charge by complying fully with the attached request for information which pertains to the allegations contained in this charge. You may, in addition, submit in writing a statement of position or other evidence with respect to the allegations. Such information will be made a part of the file and will be considered by the Commission during the course of this investigation. Telephone communications cannot be made a part of the record.

In addition to complying with the request for information mentioned above, your attention is directed to Section 1602.14 of the Commission's Regulations which requires the preservation of all personnel records relevant to this charge until a final disposition of this charge is made and to the non-retaliation requirements under Section 704(a) of the Civil Rights Act.

For future correspondence on this matter, please use the charge number shown above

DATE	TYPED NAME OF DISTRICT DIRECTOR	SIGNATURE

EEOC FORM 131–C
SEP 77   **RESPONDENT'S COPY**

CERTIFICATION. *I hereby certify that I mailed the original of this Notice, a copy of the charge and request for information referenced herein to the addressee herein.*

DATE	EEOC EMPLOYEE SIGNATURE

EEOC FORM 131–C
SEP 77   **FILE COPY**

APPENDIX 8-7

SECTION 14
FACT FINDING CONFERENCE

14.1 <u>Authority for Fact Finding Conference</u> — Section 1601.15(c) of the Commission's Procedural Regulations provides:

> The Commission may require a fact finding conference with the parties prior to a determination on a charge of discrimination. The conference is primarily an investigative forum intended to define the issues, to determine which elements are undisputed, to resolve those issues that can be resolved and to ascertain where there is a basis for negotiated settlement of the charge.

14.2 <u>Purpose of the Fact Finding Conference</u> — The purpose of the Fact Finding Conference is to accelerate the investigation of a charge to the point that a finding on its merits can be made or to bring the charge to an equitable resolution through a written settlement agreement.

14.3 <u>Determining Appropriateness of Fact Finding Conference Procedures</u>

(a) <u>Narrowly Defined Charges</u> — The Fact Finding Conference procedure is designed to ensure rapid processing of charges in which the allegations to be fully processed are primarily narrowly defined allegations of differential treatment. The Commission anticipates that a majority of charges filed can be processed under these procedures. In general, all other new charges will be processed by the Systemic and Continued Investigation/Conciliation units.

(b) <u>Reviewing Charges Prior to Assignment to Fact Finding Conference</u> — When a jurisdictional defense or a claimed exemption from Title VII is asserted, it is more efficient for the Commission to make an initial determination on the Commission's jurisdiction or the validity of a respondent claim to exemption.

(c) <u>Charges Generally Excluded</u>

(1) Commissioner Charges, including systemic charges

(2) Charges filed on behalf of an aggrieved person, where the aggrieved person requests that his or her identify remain confidential.

(3) Charges being processed under expedited procedures for local or national settlement agreements or consent decrees unless those procedures are compatible with rapid charge processing procedures.

(4) Charges which have been selected by the Top Management Committee for handling in the ELI Program (See Section 12.).

(5) Charges where the alleged discrimination derives from an acknowledged policy and other charges where there is no factual dispute.

APPENDIX 8-7 (cont'd)

      (6) Charges where the parties' geographic locations preclude a conference.

14.4 <u>Preparation of Investigative Plan</u> – Charges determined appropriate for processing under this procedure will be assigned to an EOS in the Fact Finding Unit. The EOS will immediately prepare an investigative plan. If the EEOC Form 155 indicates that there is an ongoing Systemic Investigation of the respondent in the District Office, the EOS will consult with the appropriate Systemic Unit EOS in preparing the plan. The plan and Request for Information will be prepared by the EOS and reviewed by the supervisor within six days of receipt of the charge by the District Office or by the 706 Agency where there is a dual filing agreement.

      (a) <u>Identify the Basis(es) and Issue(s)</u> – Identify the basis(es) and the issue(s) by careful analysis of the Intake EOS's notes of the interview of charging party and of any other interviews or documents in the file.

      (b) <u>Determine Appropriate Comparative Data and Other Evidence Required</u> – Since virtually all charges to be processed through a Fact Finding Conference will be allegations of differential treatment, determine what would constitute the best comparative data. Also identify additional evidence needed (e.g., job bids or pay records).

      (c) <u>Determine If Charging Party Witness Contact Required</u> – Determine whether or not statements from witnesses identified by charging party are required to present a balanced evidentiary record of the comparative data needed in the case. Such statements are required when, for example, comparative data is not amenable to objective measurement.

      (d) <u>Determine Respondent Witnesses To Be Invited to the Conference</u> – The EOS will determine what witnesses should be invited to the Fact Finding Conference to serve as respondent witnesses. These will ordinarily include, but need not be limited to, at least the person alleged by charging party to have made or enforced the decision which discriminated against charging party and someone at management level to explain policy involved in the adverse action. If the EOS cannot determine with sufficient specificity from the charging party interview notes or other material in the file who such witnesses would be, in order to invite them to the conference, the EOS will call respondent to determine the identity of appropriate respondent witnesses.

      (e) <u>Prepare Request for Information</u> – The EOS will prepare a respondent Request for Information using EEOC Order 901, Appendix A, Document Assembly System for the Compliance Process, augmented as necessary by hand-drafted questions on matters unique to the charge. The questionnaire should seek factual statements and documents and should generally avoid complicated compilations on the part of the respondent. List names and titles of respondent witnesses requested to appear at the Fact Finding Conference and what information each witness is expected to provide. Set the due date for respondent's answers bearing in mind

APPENDIX 8-7 (cont'd)

the nature and extent of the questions posed. Do not set a due date which is
so short that it engenders requests for extensions.

14.5 Providing Notice of the Charge and Scheduling the Fact Finding
      Conference with the Parties

      (a)   Notifying Respondent of the Charge - Attach the Request for
            Information, a copy of this section of the EEOC Compliance Manual
and a copy of EEOC Form S-4 (see Exhibit 82-A) to a copy of the charge and
the original of EEOC Form 131-B, Notice of Charge and Notice of Fact Finding
Conference (see Exhibit 14-A). Enter the place and time of the conference in
accordance with the guidance at (c) and (e), below. Use the original of
EEOC Form 131-B as the transmittal and, within ten days of receipt, mail the
entire package to respondent's representative, i.e., the persons empowered
to negotiate a settlement. Sign the certificate of service portion of the
file copy of EEOC Form 131-B and place in the charge file.

      (b)   Notifying the Charging Party - Simultaneously with the notice
            to respondent, the EOS will mail a copy of EEOC Form 131-B
(see Exhibit 14-A) and a copy of EEOC Form S-5 (see Exhibit 82-B) to the
charging party. If charging party requests that he/she be accompanied at
the Fact Finding Conference either by a translator or by a union representative, attach a letter to charging party granting permission. (See Exhibit
14-B.) Where charging party has an attorney, charging party's attorney
should also attend. Counsel who does not attend a Fact Finding Conference
cannot be consulted on the spot. Usefulness of the conference would be
undermined if settlement were offered, tentatively accepted and only later,
after consultation with the attorney who was not present at the conference,
refused by the charging party or respondent. Therefore, every effort should
be made to secure the attendance of counsel. However, if a charging party's
attorney does not attend the conference, the charging party must be counseled
that he/she should consult with counsel before deciding whether to sign a
settlement agreement.

      (c)   Scheduling the Conference - A date approximately three weeks
            after respondent and charging party can be reasonably expected
to have received the notices should be selected as the Conference date.
Providing this latitude will (1) enable respondents to provide responses to
requested documentation and information sufficiently in advance to analyze
the submissions prior to the Conference and (2) minimize the need for
rescheduling by providing the parties ample time to arrange their schedules
to accommodate the Conference date.

      (d)   Rescheduling Conferences - When requests for rescheduling by
            respondent or charging party are reasonable and timely, comply
with the request. Charging parties, however, are to be cautioned that
failure to cooperate in the scheduling of Conferences or to attend scheduled
Conferences can result in dismissal of their charge. Respondents who refuse
to attend a Fact Finding Conference may be required by subpoena to appear
and testify about disputed factual matters (see Section 24). Requests for
rescheduling will often be made by telephone and must therefore by carefully
logged and the new date confirmed by letter.

APPENDIX 8-7 (cont'd)

    (e) <u>Place of Conference</u> - Normally, Fact Finding Conferences will be held in District or Area Offices. Where this is not feasible because of the geographic location of the parties, effort should be made to hold the Conference in another federal office or other government space in a location more convenient to the parties.

14.6 <u>Pre-conference Interviews</u> - The EOS will hold some or all of the following interviews prior to the Fact Finding Conference.

    (a) <u>Respondent</u> - If review of respondent's response to the Request for Information indicates a need for clarification or amplification of evidence submitted, contact the respondent representative.

    (b) <u>Charging Party Witnesses</u> - If called for in the EOS's investigative plan, contact witnesses named by charging party.

    (c) <u>Charging Party</u> - The EOS will call the charging party and ask him or her to come to the field office early for the Fact Finding Conference so that the EOS can explain, again, the conference format, indicate who will be attending, and determine the charging party's posture toward settlement.

14.7 <u>Conference Format</u> - The Fact Finding Conference is an informal investigative technique, not an adversary proceeding. So that the conference can accomplish its purpose of establishing the facts and enabling the parties to assess the substance of the allegations, the EOS will firmly control and direct the proceedings. Witnesses will not be present during the Fact Finding Conference except when serving as a witness. The EOS will ask them to sit outside the conference room to wait until they are called upon to state what happened or to explain a given policy or otherwise present relevant material. If appropriate, an EOS from the Systemic Unit will be a non-participating observer.

    (a) <u>Preliminaries</u> - The EOS will first introduce himself/herself and the note-taker and then charging party and respondent attendees. All persons present will be asked to sign their names, titles, and day telephones on the sign-in sheet (see Exhibit 14-C).

A pre-prepared list of evidence submitted prior to the conference will be presented to the parties at the table. If respondent has brought evidence to the conference, it will be received by the EOS who will give a brief descriptive title to each type of document presented, so that the charging party is aware of the type of evidence presented to the Commission by the respondent.

    (b) <u>Opening Statement</u> - After concluding the preliminaries, the EOS will read the Fact Finding Conference Opening Statement (see Exhibit 14-D) to ensure that all parties understand that:

        (1) A full record of the conference is being made by a staff note-taker and that when and if the Fact Finding Conference is recessed and a settlement offer is proposed, all discussions of such offers and responses will be recorded in a separate set of notes.

APPENDIX 8-7 (cont'd)

      (2) If counsel for respondent and/or charging party is present, they will be limited to an advisory role and will not be permitted to speak for their client or to cross-examine.

      (3) Each allegation of the charge will be closely examined and fully discussed; the charging party will be allowed ample time to explain and support each allegation; the respondent to present and defend its position.

    (c) Statement and Attempted Resolution of Facts in Dispute - The charge will be read by the EOS with a section-by-section assent by charging party and assent or denial by respondent. Should the charging party wish to amend the charge and the change is minor, the change will be made on the charge form, initialed by the charging party and copies made of the amended charge and given to both parties. Should the change be major, a new charge from incorporating the amendments will be typed up, signed by the charging party, copied and given to the parties prior to their leaving the office.

    Charging party's case is then elicited by the EOS, followed by respondent's position. Matters of factual dispute will be stated by the EOS as they become apparent; every attempt will be made to resolve these factual disputes or to agree what evidence would resolve the disputed matters.

    (d) Settlement Discussions - It is appropriate at any time for one or the other party to suggest a recess to discuss settlement of the charge. Upon such a request, the recess will be called by the EOS and a settlement attempt made. The EOS may also suggest a recess to consider settlement. Should the attempt fail, the EOS will re-convene the conference and continue the investigation.

    When all immediately available information has been gathered and it is apparent that more information will have to be obtained before a finding can be made, the EOS should ask the parties once again before closing the Fact Finding Conference to consider settling the charge.

    (e) Closing the Conference - If the charge is not settled and all available information has been obtained, the EOS will bring the conference to a close by informing the parties that the conference is at an end and what the next step in processing will be.

14.8 Post-conference Follow-up - If a settlement has been reached, have the agreement typed and signed prior to the departure of the parties, where possible, and close the charge in accordance with the provisions of 15.6. If the case is ready for a no cause determination, the the EOS will prepare an Investigator's Memorandum (see Section 29), hold pre-determination interviews with the parties, and recommend dismissal of the charge in accordance with Section 4. If the case is ready for a cause determination, the EOS will prepare appropriate sections of the conference report described below and submit the case for legal review for sufficiency of evidence to make a cause finding. When a settlement has not been reached and the record of the Fact Finding Conference warrants a more comprehensive

APPENDIX 8-7 (cont'd)

investigation, the note-taker will go over the notes taken with the EOS to explain them and to be sure that both agree on key points of the conference proceedings. The EOS, using the notes, will write a conference report using the following format:

 (a) <u>Charging Party's Case</u> - a presentation of all evidence in support of charging party's allegation(s), indicating the source of the evidence, e.g., whether it was a statement made at the conference (and by whom), or contained in charging party documentation or other source;

 (b) <u>Respondent's Defense</u> - a presentation of all evidence in support of respondent's position, indicating the source of the evidence;

 (c) <u>Evidence, If Any, of Pretext</u> - a presentation of any evidence that respondent's stated reason for taking the adverse action against charging party was merely a pretext for discriminating against charging party;

 (d) <u>Further Information Needed</u> - a statement of precisely what further information is needed to come to a determination on the merits of the charge, indicating where possible the documentation, witness statements or other evidence which should be obtained.

14.9 <u>Dismissal When Charging Party Fails or Refuses to Appear or be Available for Fact Finding Conferences</u>

 (a) <u>General</u> - Although this section requires that a Fact Finding Conference be held in most instances (see 14.3 for exceptions), District and Area Directors may determine during the course of attempting to arrange a Conference that specific circumstances presented by the parties or which otherwise come to the Director's attention, such as the unplanned hospitalization of charging party or where appearing would be an economic hardship to charging party, dictate that other investigative techniques, such as mail questionnaires or interviews be used.

 (b) <u>Reasonable Accommodation of Charging Party</u> - Attempt to accommodate charging party requests for rescheduling a Fact Finding Conference if the request is made in a timely manner (i.e., shortly after receiving the notice) and the request is reasonable in light of the particular circumstances, such as the necessity to accommodate the schedule of charging party's attorney, translator, union representative or the necessity of arranging in advance for absence from work. Unexplained failure to attend, however, or untimely requests for postponements (i.e., requests made on the day of the Fact Finding Conference) will be followed by a notice that failure to cooperate will result in the dismissal of the charge in 30 days.

 (c) <u>Charging Party Must Have Effective Notice of the Consequences of Failure or Refusal to Appear</u> - In general the notice sent to charging party (see Exhibit 14-A) is adequate and effective notice of the consequences of failure to cooperate. If the failure to appear is occasioned by charging party's inability to read or write, however, or

APPENDIX 8-7 (cont'd)

inability to read or write English and the Director has knowledge of such inability, this should be taken into account and supplemental notice provided, such as a telephone call or personal interview.

(d) Final Request for Cooperation Must Precede the Dismissal – When it becomes apparent that the charging party's failures/refusals to attend are willful and with knowledge of the consequences, the charge will be dismissed.

(e) Use EEOC Form 161, Notice of Right to Sue, as Notice of Dismissal– Upon expiration of 30 days from the date shown on the return receipt signed by charging party, send EEOC Form 161 to charging party and respondent. Enter the name and address of the person claiming to be aggrieved in the the "to" block, the issuing office name and address in the "from" block, and the name and telephone number of the Commission employee designated by the issuing official to provide the advice required by EEOC Form 161. Check the block next to "you failed to provide requested necessary information, or failed or refused to appear or to be available for interviews or conferences or otherwise refused to cooperate to the extent that the Commission has been unable to resolve your charge."

APPENDIX 8-7 (cont'd)

FACT FINDING CONFERENCE OPENING STATEMENT

This is a fact finding conference held as part of the Commission's investigation pursuant to the Procedural Regulations of the Equal Employment Opportunity Commission, Section 1601.15(c) and the Commission's Compliance Manual, Section 14. The purpose of this conference is to assist the Commission in its investigation of the charge and is thus part of the Commission's investigatory process. It is not a formal hearing, and no determination will be made today as to the merits of the charge. The statements made here are not made under oath; however, all participants are expected to tell the truth.   Investigatory notes will be taken by a member of the Commission's staff and statements made here which pertain to the merits of the allegation which has been raised will be used by the Commission as evidence when it makes its determination.

After certain preliminaries, the agenda is as follows: first the charge will be read section-by-section to ascertain from the charging party that this is what he/she alleges and to learn whether respondent agrees or disagrees with the statements read. Then the charging party will be allowed to present his/her perception of the events leading to the filing of this charge, without interruption by the respondent. Respondent will then be allowed to answer the charge and to present its explanation of the same events, without interruption by the charging party.

All questions and statements are to be addressed to me. There will be no cross conversation or cross examination. If anyone wishes to respond to what another has said, please wait until that person is through. If you want to have a particular question asked, you may ask me to ask it.   If the question is appropriate, I shall ask it.

(This statement is to be read only if charging party or respondent is accompanied by an attorney:

(Respondent)(Charging Party) is accompanied by an attorney at this conference.   I remind you that your role here today is limited to that of an advisor to your client; your client will at all times be asked to speak for him/herself. You may not cross-examine witnesses or the other party.

The Commission strongly urges both parties to consider amicable settlement of this charge of discrimination. A discussion of settlement is appropriate here today.   Therefore, if at any time during the conference any party has a proposal to resolve the dispute, we will discuss the suggestions, if mutually agreed, in the hope of settling the matter. In that event, the Fact Finding Conference will be recessed and the content of discussion of settlement will not be made a part of the record of evidence to be used by the Commission in any formal determination of the merits of the charge, but a separate record will be made.

APPENDIX 8-8

<u>SETTLEMENT AGREEMENT</u>

1. In exchange for the promises made by_____,
   hereinafter referred to as the "respondent", contained in paragraph (8) of the
   Agreement,_____, hereinafter referred to as
   the "person claiming to be aggrieved", agrees not to institute a law suit under
   Title VII of the Civil Rights Act of 1964, as amended, based on Charge
   Number_____filed with the Equal Employment Opportunity Commission,
   and the Equal Employment Opportunity Commission agrees not to use this charge as
   the jurisdictional basis for a civil action under Section 706(f)(1) of Title VII.

2. It is understood that this agreement does not constitute an admission by the
   Respondent of any violation of Title VII of Civil Rights Act of 1964, as amended.

3. This agreement constitutes the complete understanding between the Respondent,
   Charging Party and the Equal Employment Opportunity Commission. No other promises
   or agreements shall be binding unless signed by these parties.

4. The Respondent agrees to provide written notice to the Director of the
   District Office within ten (10) days of satisfying each obligation contained in
   this agreement.

5. The person claiming to be aggrieved agrees to withdraw any charge(s) filed with a
   state or local fair employment agency covering the same matters alleged in the
   EEOC charge resolved by the present agreement.

6. The person claiming to be aggrieved and Respondent agree that this agreement may
   be used as evidence in a subsequent proceeding in which any of the parties allege
   a breach of this agreement.

7. The Equal Employment Opportunity Commission's participation in this agreement
   does not reflect any judgment by the Commission on the merits of the charge.
   Furthermore, the Equal Employment Opportunity Commission does not waive or in any
   manner limit its right to process or seek relief in any other charge, including
   but not limited to a charge filed by a member of the Commission against Respondent.

8. In exchange for the promises of the person claiming to be aggrieved and the Equal
   Employment Opportunity Commission contained in this agreement, the Respondent agrees

_____

_____

_____

_____   _____
Charging Party   Date

_____   _____
Respondent   Date

APPROVED ON BEHALF OF THE COMMISSION:

_____   _____
District Director   Date

APPENDIX 8-9

<u>Equal Employment Opportunity Commission</u>

Major Steps in Resolution of an Individual Charge

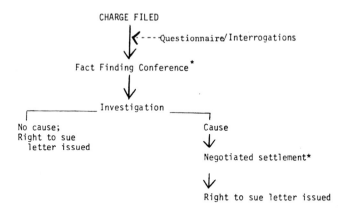

*Key points of potential settlement

APPENDIX 8-10

Office for Civil Rights

Major Steps in Resolution of an Individual Charge

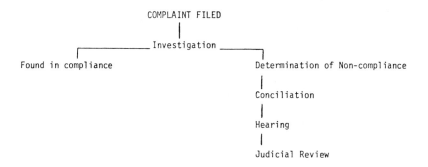

APPENDIX 8-11

REQUIREMENTS OF TITLE VII FOR COMMON VIOLATIONS

HIRING OR DISCHARGE. Hiring or discharge may not be based on qualifications which affect either minorities or females disproportionately unless essential to the operation of the business (See *Qualifications, Testing* below). Similarly, females may not ordinarily be refused employment because of pregnancy or terminated therefor at a particular stage of pregnancy where not physically disabled. Further, an employer may not refuse to hire or discharge a person who because of religious beliefs refuses to work on Sabbaths, for example, without showing that reasonable accommodations would cause an undue hardship on the employer's business.

LAYOFF AND RECALL. Where a seniority system carries forward the present effects of past discrimination (See *Job Classifications or Seniority* below), layoffs or members of the class discriminated against are unlawful. In such a situation layoffs and recalls to vacated positions must be based on company seniority in order to erase the taint of past discrimination, even where recall in such a manner may affect the expectations of the former incumbents.

While a layoff may be a single act, the failure to recall may constitute a continuing violation so that the Commission may accept a charge filed at any time up to 180 days (300 days in some circumstances) after an aggrieved person is properly recalled on a nondiscriminatory basis.

WAGES. Classes of individuals (by race, color, religion, sex or national origin) performing substantially equal work in the same establishment must be paid wages regardless of the fact that their jobs may be classified differently.

In order to compensate an aggrieved person for financial harm caused by discriminatory practices, including unequal wages, back pay may be required for a period commencing two years prior to the filing of a charge with the Commission.

PROMOTION OR DEMOTION. Where promotions are denied because of requirements which carry forward the effects of past discrimination, such as departmental seniority or unnecessary residency in a prior qualifying job, or because of requirements which are invalid (See *Qualification, Testing* below), such failure to promote is unlawful.

Since a failure to promote is a continuing violation, the Commission may accept a charge 180 days (300 days in some circumstances) after the aggrieved person is promoted to the proper job.

JOB CLASSIFICATIONS OR SENIORITY. Job classifications may not be segregated on the basis of race, color, religion, sex, or national origin. For example, a job classification with a weight-lifting requirement which is used to exclude women as a class, where individual women are able to qualify, is unlawful.

Furthermore, a seniority system may not carry into the present the effects of formerly segregated job classifications. This results, for instance, where departmental seniority causes classes of formerly excluded employees to lose their accumulated company seniority upon transferring to the job from which they had been excluded. At least for the victims of the past discrimination, the system must be changed to a company-seniority one.

TRAINING OR APPRENTICESHIP. Where a union has engaged in a program resulting in a predominately white or male membership, affirmative efforts must be made to establish nondiscriminatory apprenticeship or on-the-job training programs, which include minorities and women. The program must be publicized generally and in the minority community in such a way as to overcome the union's reputation for exclusiveness and ensure participation of minorities and

women. Any unjustified qualifications (see below) required for the program, including a high school diploma, passing unvalidated tests, or the absence of arrest records, must be eliminated. The same applies to training programs of employers.

EXCLUSION. A union which is predominately white or male may not require as a basis for membership a minority applicant to be a family relation of a present member of require a minority of female applicant to receive the endorsement of a present member or the majority vote of the membership. Such a union which has kept its membership artificially small in relation to the demand in the area for the skills of its members may be required to increase its size in order to include more minority and female members.

UNION REPRESENTATION. A union is required to represent minorities and females fairly with respect to processing grievances (including assisting in the filing of a discrimination charge with the EEOC), bargaining for the elimination of unlawful employment practices, and otherwise opposing the existence of unlawful employment practices with or without specific contract authority or instructions from its international union to do so.

SEGREGATED LOCALS. Locals which are segregated along the lines of race, color religion, sex or national origin are inherently discriminatory and must be merged even where the members of each local favor separation. Protective transitional arrangements are to be included, where necessary, in any merger agreement for the benefit of the "minority" union.

REFERRAL. A local union which has maintained a predominately white or male membership and has effectively excluded minorities and females from its hiring hall may not continue a system under which only persons who meet artificial standards of experience which are in excess of that required to perform the job are given priority in referral under the collective bargaining contract. The system must be modified to refer also on a priority basis minorities and females who are able to perform the required work.

QUALIFICATIONS, TESTING. Qualifications, including a high school diploma, passing a written test or demonstrating speaking or writing ability, may have a disparate effect in screening out minorities from employment opportunities in comparison with others in an employer's applicant flow or workforce. Unless they can be shown to be essential to the safe and efficient operation of the business, or otherwise justified by business necessity, such qualifications are unlawful.

Business necessity may be shown for a qualification through a validation study in which a positive relationship is established between the qualification and the successful performance of the job sought. Where a qualification (e.g., a test score) is used to select employees for a training program for a job or promotion, the qualification must show a positive relationship not only between the qualification and success in training but also between such training and the successful performance of the job sought.

ADVERTISING. Advertisements, including help-wanted advertisements, may not contain material which indicates a preference for an individual on the basis of race, color, religion, sex or national origin except where religion, sex, or national origin is essential to successful performance of the job. (In addition, religious institutions are entitled to prefer members of a particular faith in employment and advertisements therefor.) For example, advertisements may not be placed or requested to be placed under columns headed "Male" or Female".

APPENDIX 8-11 (cont'd)

BENEFITS. All fringe benefits including medical, hospital, retirement, disability, and leave benefits must be provided to men and women equally regardless of the fact that the cost of such benefits may be greater with respect to one sex than for the other. A pregnant employee is entitled to the same disability benefits during the period she is unable to work because of pregnancy as a male would receive during a period of disability.

SEGREGATED FACILITIES. Employers must take care that all company facilities are available to all employees on a nondiscriminatory basis. Thus, an employer cannot lawfully maintain racially segregated restroom or locker facilities, lunchrooms snackbars, drinking fountains, payrolls lines, or badge-number identification systems, etc. Further, the fact that an employer may have to provide separate company facilities for employees of each sex under state law will not justify discrimination as to hiring, promotion or job classification on the basis of sex.

INTIMIDATION. Employers, unions or employment agencies have a responsibility to maintain an environment free of harassment, intimidation, insults, or ridicule based on race, color, religion, sex or national origin.

REPRISAL. Any discrimination or adverse action taken against an individual because he or she filed a charge with EEOC, cooperated in any EEOC investigation, or opposed an unlawful employment practice, is itself a violation of the law. Section 704(a) of the Civil Rights Act of 1964, as amended, prohibits such reprisal. It is intended to provide exceptionally broad coverage for protestors of discrimination.

OTHER TERMS AND CONDITIONS. With respect to all other terms and conditions of employment, employers, unions or employment agencies must treat individuals without regard to race, color, religion, sex or national origin.

PRESERVATION OF RECORDS

EEOC RULES AND REGULATIONS

§ 1602.14 Preservation of records made or kept.

(a) Any personnel or employment record made or kept by an employer (including but not necessarily limited to application forms submitted by applicants and other records having to do with hiring, promotion, demotion, transfer, lay-off, or termination, rates of pay or other terms of compensation, and selection for training or apprenticeship) shall be preserved by the employer for a period of 6 months from the date of the making of the record or the personnel action involved, whichever occurs later. In the case of involuntary termination of an employee, the personnel records of the individual terminated shall be kept for a period of 6 months from the date of termination. Where a charge of discrimination has been filed, or an action brought by the Commission or the Attorney General, against an employer under Title VII, the respondent employer shall preserve all personnel records relevant to the charge or action until final disposition of the charge or the action. The term "personnel records relevant to the charge," for example, would include personnel or employment records relating to the aggrieved person and to all other employees holding positions similar to that held or sought by the aggrieved person and application forms or test papers completed by an unsuccessful applicant and by all other candidates for the same position as that for which the aggrieved person applied and was rejected. The date of "final disposition of the charge or the action" means the date of expiration of the statutory period within which the aggrieved person may bring an action in a U.S. District Court or, where an action is brought against an employer either by the aggrieved person, the Commission, or by the Attorney General, the date on which such litigation is terminated.

(b) The requirements of this section shall not apply to application forms and other preemployment records of applicants for positions known to applicants to be of a temporary or seasonal nature.

APPENDIX 10-1

Summary Evaluation of <u>Boomerang</u>

Fall - 1978

1. The initial presentation of <u>Boomerang</u> was made to the Chancellor, Vice
    Chancellors, Deans, and Academic Directors--about twenty persons in all.
    The participation of this group was a key factor in the success of the
    program, as they liked the program, and hence, encouraged their sub-
    ordinates to attend. The other groups (20-25 people each) were a mixture
    of academic administrators and professional staff. Mixed groups rather
    than academic administrators separated from staff supervisors are
    advantageous because 1) faculty and staff of administrators both have
    the responsibility to manage their departments properly, and the appro-
    priate procedures and attitudes are essentially the same for both groups.
    2) The professional staff often feels isolated from much that goes on in
    the institution and the combining the groups emphasizes our "oneness" as a
    university. 3) A better mix of women and minorities was possible when the
    faculty and staff were combined.

    Only a couple of academics suggested in their evaluations that academics
    should be treated separately/differently. In general, when academics
    comprised at least six members of a group, they were dominant; but as they
    were generally articulate and usually not overbearing, that is not
    necessarily a minus.

    If academics were only sparsely represented (less than five), they tend
    to be significantly less vocal. The sophistication of the program was
    also lower when the number of academics was lower.

    Both academic administrators and professional staff rated the program as
    excellent. Virtually no negative evaluations were received; the most
    negative comment was that if the films were set in academia rather than in
    industry, they would be more relevant to the uniqueness of higher education.

2. <u>Boomerang</u> was presented most successfully in two four-hour segments, as
    opposed to one eight-hour or four two-hour segments. The best times were
    8:30 - 12:30 and 1:00 - 5:00. Participants arrived a little ahead of
    those starting times, visited, ate donuts, and generally got settled.

3. The best means of organizing the sessions was to send individual invitations
    to eligible supervisors and administrators and to place a notice regarding
    the program in the campus newsletter. Both the invitations and the notice
    explained the purpose and contents of the program. A list of times the
    program will be offered provides participants with an opportunity to choose
    times most convenient for their schedules. Trying to control the composition
    of the groups so that administrators and subordinates were not in the same
    groups is very difficult.

4. Subsequent to presentation of <u>Boomerang</u>, the number of people coming to the
    Affirmative Action Office to discuss Affirmative Action problems increased
    markedly. Both academic and professional staff have come; they have been
    participants in the program or have heard about the Affirmative Action
    Office from a participant. The program proved to be excellent campus
    relations for the Affirmative Action Office, but more importantly, people
    began coming to the Affirmative Action Office before they created problems
    by making decisions that might be discriminatory. Supervisors and admin-
    istrators seem to be doing a better job of managing because grievances
    and charges of discrimination dropped significantly subsequent to presenta-
    tion of <u>Boomerang</u>.

5. The program will be repeated twice annually so that new supervisors and
    administrators will have an opportunity to participate.

APPENDIX 10-2

Problems I-IV were developed by Professor Robert Carothers of Edinboro State College, Edinboro, Pennsylvania. They were used as discussion mechanisms at a series of conferences sponsored by the AAUP on faculty responsibilities for classroom accessibility.

PROBLEM I

This fall you are teaching a section of World Geography, an introductory course in the Geography Department usually taken for general education (i.e., core) credit. When the class meets for the first session, you learn that Joseph Marcello, a blind student, has enrolled in your section. This is a matter of some concern to you, since when you taught the course before, you made extensive use of the large wall maps which have been installed in the classroom. This term you planned on using these maps again, as well as several sets of slides of Europe which you prepared following your summer vacation in Germany, France and Italy. Your first reaction is to suggest another elective to Joseph, one which is not so dependent upon visually apprehended teaching devices. On second thought, however, you decide to see if you can develop a strategy which will allow Joseph to take your course and have a reasonable chance of success.

DIRECTIONS: Please try to solve this problem through discussion in your group. The directions which follow are designed to assist you in identifying the issues in this problem and in developing a plan to make your course accessible to Joe Marcello. As much as possible, follow the directions in sequence.

1. Just what is the problem here? Try to frame several statements of the problem, each beginning with "The problem is, how to ... " Keep asking yourself "Why? What is my basic purpose here?" until you arrive at a "How to ... " definition the group can generally agree upon.

2. Once you have defined the problem, you should begin thinking of alternatives which might be solutions to the problem. Make a list of these (at least five or six), trying not to be judgmental about the ideas suggested. The goal is to generate a range of possible responses to the problem. For example, what modifications in the learning environment could be made by you as the teacher? What alterations in teaching technique (i.e., presentation of material) might be appropriate? What outside resources could be recruited? Can (should) the system of student evaluation in the course be modified in Joe's case to compensate for Joe's inability to acquire knowledge through sight? And so forth.

3. From the list of possibilities you have generated, move toward the selection of a plan, evaluating each possibility in terms of criteria you decide are appropriate (e.g., time, money, morality, acceptability, effectiveness, etc.).

4. When you decide upon a strategy for solving this problem, turn to matters of implementation. Who bears the responsibility for making your plan happen? Who bears the cost? Identify the sources of "attack" or opposition to your plan. How will you protect your plan from these opponents?

5. Finally, as individuals, try to adapt and concretize the plan for use on your own campus. To the degree possible, list the actual steps you would take, including, if a part of your plan, the office and people you would use.

APPENDIX 10-2 (cont'd)

PROBLEM II

You are teaching a section of General Psychology, a course required of all freshman education students and elected by many other freshmen and sophomores. In your class is Helen Prynne, a young woman with cerebral palsy. The disorder has left Helen with severe motor skill disability, as well as speech impairment. She is wheelchair-bound and comes to class with an aide who takes notes for her. After the third week of class, Helen's attendance becomes more and more sporadic. She has called your office on each occasion of an absence, however, to explain why she was not in class. These explanations include failure of her transportation to arrive on time, failure of medical equipment on which she is dependent, failure of her aide to show up for the class, and simple illness. You are becoming more and more concerned about this problem as midterm approaches; your class book indicates that Helen has now missed more than half of the meetings of her section.

Again, please consider this problem in your group.

1. You may want to begin this discussion by asking whose problem this is. Do you, as a classroom teacher, have any responsibility for solving this problem? How much?

2. At least part of this problem would seem to stem from poor management of support services. Should you intervene? If so, with whom?

3. Mid-term exams are on the horizon. Should you make special arrangements for Helen to take your test (assume that the test is a combination of objective and essay questions)? Should you make up a different test for Helen because of her absences? Should you exempt her from the exam?

4. Assume that you come to believe that not all of Helen's absences are for the reasons she gives you, that she is avoiding the class because of fear of failure, or because she is enjoying (too much?) the social contacts college life has given her. Should you confront her with your belief? Would you do so with a non-handicapped student? Is there anything which makes this situation different from usual instances of student irresponsibility?

5. As a conclusion to your discussion of this problem, try to formulate a statement in your group of what you believe is the special responsibility (if any) of a professor to a handicapped student. Write it down and keep the statement for later discussions.

APPENDIX 10-2 (cont'd)

PROBLEM III

Your chairman finally scheduled you for the seminar in the Victorian Novel. Your dissertation was on Dickens, and you have published two articles recently, in reputable journals, exploring the nuances of his social criticisms. In short, you have been looking forward to teaching this class for some time, and you have limited enrollment to twelve students, all of them to be English majors. Among them is Mary Ann Perowski, a hearing-impaired student who is skillful at lip-reading but whose speech is badly garbled and extremely difficult to understand. While it is quickly apparent to you from her written work that Mary Ann is both bright and conscientious, her attempts to participate in the seminars are less than successful. She wants very much to speak to the points raised by you and the other students, but expressing herself is slow and arduous. Often she must repeat herself several times before she is understood. You find this process painful and, you must admit, you resent this interruption in the flow of class discussion. Yesterday, one of the brightest students in the seminar came to your office and, with considerable embarrassment, told you that Mary Ann's participation in the class is making him so nervous he is ready to drop the course. You convinced him to stay, but are beginning to feel that you must do <u>something</u>.

Please consider this problem in your group.

1. Again, let's begin by trying to define the problem. Let's assume, for the moment, that something should be done to resolve the forces in tension. State your definition in "how to ..." terms.

2. Think of some strategies to effect a solution. Remember that the goal here is generating alternatives. Give yourself several options to choose from. List at least three.

3. Considering all the parties involved, which of your alternatives (or what combination of alternatives) seems most likely to work?

4. Assume that this problem arises not in your class but in the class of a colleague and that you learn of it from a student enrolled in that class. How can you assist your colleague? What are the dangers to be anticipated?

APPENDIX 10-2 (cont'd)

PROBLEM IV

For the past three years you have known Bill Benning as a student and, subsequently, as a friend. He first enrolled into your section of Education in American Society as a freshman. At that time he had recently come out of a veterans hospital after extensive rehabilitation for the effects of shrapnel damage to the spinal area incurred in the last weeks of Vietnam. He knew then that he would probably be paralyzed from the neck down for the rest of his life. He had overcome much of the bitterness he felt during his long hospitalization, and he had decided to become an elementary teacher. While at first you were somewhat dismayed at his chances for success, after sensing his determination and seeing his imagination and creativity in performing in your classes, you began to believe in Bill and to share his ambition.

Now, however, both you and Bill have encountered a major obstancle. Bill needs a semester of student-teaching in order to complete his program. Your university places its student-teachers in neighboring school districts under the direct supervision of cooperating classroom teachers who are paid a nominal sum for their efforts. Accepting a student teacher is entirely optional with the school district, and depends upon the willingness of the cooperative teacher. Your colleague in the placement office called you yesterday to report that no school district is willing to place Bill in one of its classrooms. In each case, the building principal has pleaded the lack of facilities, the inexperience of his staff with handicapped persons, the trauma which Bill's appearance might cause small children, and, in general, the "hassle" this situation would cause him.

Your reaction was anger. But with some time to recover you accept the problem as a challenge. You get permission from your friend in placement to attempt to intervene for Bill and to act as his advocate with several of the building principals you have come to know over the past years.

DIRECTIONS: One person in your group should take on the role of the reluctant building principal. Then, role-play an encounter between one of you acting as advocate and this principal. Let each person in the group try his or her hand at being the advocate, trying out different approaches to the problem of gaining cooperation. Take some time between each attempt to discuss and evaluate that approach. Try to decide, individually, which approaches might be best in situations on your own campus.

While the fact patterns may diverge, this situation is a model for a dilemma which you, as an advocate of handicapped persons, will have to face many times. The exercise is intended as rehearsal.

APPENDIX 10-2 (cont'd)

PROBLEM V

Sally Jacobson is majoring in Business Administration. She is an excellent student and aspires to enter the field of sales. You teach a marketing class and invited a stock broker to speak to the class about careers in that field. The speaker openly discouraged women in the class from becoming stock brokers, noting that the few women who had attempted a career in that area had been unsuccessful because they could not stand up to the male competition and because clients are not comfortable dealing with women in financial matters. He suggested that women desiring careers in sales consider advertising or careers as buyers for department stores.

Sally later comes to you to complain about the sexist views of the guest speaker. You know that women who are token in traditionally male fields often have a difficult time but also that women have a proven track record of success as stock brokers and that women are entering the field in increasing numbers.

How will you advise Sally? What should you do to correct any misimpressions the guest speaker has left with the rest of the class? What information can you provide the class about successful women stock brokers? Should you discuss his anti-female approach with the guest speaker? Does the answer to that question differ if you intend to invite him to speak to future classes? Should you discuss the issue of sexism with future guest speakers before they address your class? What should you do about textbooks and visual aids that are sexist or present a stereotyped view of women?

APPENDIX 10-2 (cont'd)

PROBLEM VI

You have just been informed that you will be teaching a
survey course in modern American literature in the fall semester. You decide that the emphasis will be on the works of
authors whose literary merit is well established. Because your
department offers courses in both Afro-American literature and
Womens Studies, you select authors whose works are not represented in those courses.

The result of applying this criteria is that virtually
all the authors selected are white males. You have been sensitized to the issues of sexism and racism in the classroom and
classroom materials and are anxious to demonstrate that sensitivity. How can you include minority and female authors without infringing on the "territory" of the more specialized courses
mentioned above?

Should you continue with your selection of traditional
authors and suggest to students that they enroll in the specialized courses if they have an interest in those areas? Should
you include minority and female authors even if they are covered
in the specialized courses to provide students with an introduction to these works? Have you eliminated authors whose
works are treated in other specialized courses as well as in
Afro-American literature and Womens Studies? What students are
most likely to miss reading the works of female and minority
writers if you eliminate those works from your class? What
discrimination have you perpetuated if you eliminate these authors
from your syllabus?

APPENDIX 10-2 (cont'd)

PROBLEM VII

Joan Riley is in her last semester of school, has come to you as chairperson of the French Department and related the following story:

Joan was enrolled in an independent study course under a professor in the department. During the semester, the professor repeatedly asked for dates until she reluctantly accepted. Although she rebuffed his attempted kisses as gracefully as she could, the day before the final examination he assigned another book for her to read. Joan had received A's on all previous assignments. She felt this additional assignment was unreasonable but nevertheless attempted to purchase the book. The book was out of print and unavailable. When she returned to his office, he renewed his offer to take her out, a request she declined. She received a perfect score on the first three pages of the examination. The fourth page consisted of an essay on the book he had assigned the previous day. He called her at home that evening to tell her that she had failed the examination since the last page was weighted heavily. When she flirted with him and agreed to go out with him, he said he knew she was a capable student and would turn in a "B" grade for the course.

What is your responsibility as department chairperson? Does your institution have grievance procedures students may utilize for grievances based on grades or on sexual harassment? Should your response differ if Joan is an attractive divorceé in her mid 30's rather than a 20 year-old single woman? Should your response differ if you previously have had students come to you with similar complaints about the same professor? Should you communicate her complaint to the professor? What is the institution's legal responsibility regarding sexual harassment of students?

This problem was adapted from an actual incident recounted in Till, F., Sexual Harassment. Washington, D.C.: National Advisory Council on Women's Educational Programs, 1980.

APPENDIX 10-2 (cont'd)

PROBLEM VIII

A black student in your course on Sociology of
the Family wants to do his research paper on one aspect
of black family structure. He comes to you and asks for
some guidance on where to begin his research. He points
out that the textbook cites many studies on the problems
of single parent black families. He would like to focus
his research on the strengths of the matriarchial system.

Because you have had a number of black students in
your classes, you are sensitive to the imbalance presented
in many textbooks (e.g. Jensen's theories on racial inferiority are presented but credence is not given to contrary
arguments and opposing studies are frequently not cited;
the biases of standard personality tests is well known but
tests that simulate and identify these biases are often
not presented). You have become more multi-cultural in
your approach because of the black students in your classes
and are able to suggest several journals to the student
which are likely to contain articles on matriarchial black
families.

What else can you do to provide a broader basis of
knowledge for all of your students? Could students
assist you by locating sources for inclusion in your class
bibliography? Can other faculty members provide information and resources you may not be aware of? How can you
through classroom lecture and discussion balance the biases
all too frequently present in available textbooks and resources?

This problem was developed with the assistance of
Dr. Frederick Spencer, Assistant Professor of Sociology,
UMSL.

APPENDIX 10-2 (cont'd)

EXERCISES

1. Prepare two sets of cards. Half should say D. A. Barring-
    ton, Educator, owns a townhouse; the other half should say
    Dorothy Barrington, Educator, owns a townhouse. Have the
    participants estimate the position, age, and salary of
    Barrington on the other side of the card. Collect the cards
    and discuss the responses. Generally Dorothy will be older,
    earn less money, and have a less prestigious position. D.A.
    will be assumed to be male, younger, have a higher salary
    and a more prestigious position. Discuss why the partici-
    pants made the above described assumptions. *

    * from A Handbook for Workshops on Sex Equity in Education,
      written by Mary-Ellen Verheyden-Hilliard under a contract
      from HEW's Office of Education.

2. Have participants recast the following sentences to eliminate
    sexist terminology. For other illustrations, see the excel-
    lent book by Casey & Swift, The Handbook of Non Sexist Writing.

    A. Biased: Man works to utilize his skills to the fullest
                  extent. He takes pride in accomplishment.

        Recast: People work to utilize their skills to the
                  fullest extent. They take pride in their
                  accomplishments.

    B. Biased: The sooner a flaw has been discovered in the
                  work of a new performer, the sooner the assis-
                  tant can help her with corrective measures.

        Recast: The sooner a flaw has been discovered in the
                  work of a new performer, the sooner the assis-
                  tant can help this person with corrective
                  measures.

    C. Biased: The division head is well liked, a man of fine
                  character and long experience.

        Recast: The division head is well liked, an individual
                  of fine character and long experience.

3. Have participants draw their concept of Neanderthal man.
    Dr. Elizabeth Nelson of California State University, who
    has used this exercise, found that, over a 5 year period,
    there have never been more than two female Neanderthals per
    class of 50 students - and they were often being dragged off
    by the hair. This exercise illustrates the fallacy of using
    the generic "man" to include all human beings.

APPENDIX 10-2 (cont'd)

STAFF

Director	Bernice Resnick Sandler	*Staff Asst.*	Carolyn Fontaine
Assoc. Director	Grace L. Mastalli	*Staff Asst.*	Julie Kuhn
Admin. Assoc.	Mary De Mouy	*Staff Asst.*	Joann Detwyler
Research Asst.	Ursula Barrett Paquette	*Staff Asst.*	Suzanne Jones

Women's Re-Entry Project

Staff Assoc.	Reneé Creange	*Project Assoc.*	Jeanne Fisher-Thompson
Admin. Assoc.	Jean O'Gorman	*Project Assoc.*	Loribeth Weinstein

project on the status and education of **women**

Sexist Biases in Sociological Research: Problems and Issues[1]

Prepared by the Committee on the Status of Women in Sociology[2]
American Sociological Association

Sexist bias in sociological research is a topic of current concern. This document identifies five aspects of the research process where bias frequently occurs: research problems selection and formulation, review of previous research, selection of population and sample, validity issues, and interpretation of research results. The various problems are closely linked and reinforcing; and studies frequently have major shortcomings in several areas at the same time. Many of the issues discussed here could also be generalized to race and class bias.

The A.S.A. Committee on the Status of Women in Sociology prepared this document to encourage all members of the profession, whether teacher, researcher, grant officer, research consumer, or publication editor, to recognize and solve the problems described. Several of the most serious types of problems in each area are identified, and, where appropriate, examples of the general problems are provided. The issues are clearly not exhaustive, and readers are invited to identify and share additional problems and to recommend solutions. Any comments and suggestions should be sent to the Committee on the Status of Women in Sociology, ASA, 1722 N St., NW, Washington, DC 20036.

I. Research Problem Selection and Formulation

GENERAL PROBLEM

1. Gender-blind social theory

Gender may be a significant variable in a social setting, institution, or society, but the gender variable is not explored or incorporated into a theory, interpretation, or analysis of the system.

EXAMPLE

Analysis of social inequality in a society without reference to gender inequality.

2. Significant topics ignored

Topics of particular significance for women are ignored.

Insufficient research on the organization of housework and sex discrimination in the U.S.

3. Selective treatment of topics

Aspects of a topic of special salience for men are defined as covering the entire topic while aspects of special salience for women are under-researched.

Primarily male-victim crimes receiving far greater attention than primarily female-victim crimes (e.g., sexual assault, sexual harassment, family violence).

4. Inadequate specification of research problem

a. A research problem is formulated for men or women only, but this limitation is not explicitly noted.

Research questions posed about the work place implicitly referring to men only; questions posed about the home place referring to women only.

b. A research model is improperly assumed to apply to men or to women only.

c. Inadequate exploration of topics which transcend sex-stereotyped divisions.

Assumption that the adjustment of women to work depends on the household situation while the adjustment of men is largely unaffected by the family.

Insufficient attention to the relationship between employment experience and child-rearing.

5. Pejorative labeling or conceptualization

Situations in which men or women act outside of prescribed sex roles are defined as areas for the study of deviant behavior or "problems"; situations in which they conform to prescribed roles are assumed to be non-problematic.

Emphasis on the problems of female-headed households and single-parent families; absence of studies of the problems associated with two-parent families. Unpaid housework and child-rearing are not considered "work" and women involved in such activity are considered to be outside the labor force.[3]

(Continued on back)

Reference Notes

[1] Reprinted from American Sociological Association *Footnotes,* January 1980.

[2] This document was developed by Michael Useem with the assistance of: Joan Huber, Council Liaison ('78), Essie Rutledge; Pepper Schwartz; Joan Stelling, Chair ('77-'78); Barrie Thorne, Chair ('78-'80); and Gaye Tuchman. Input was also received from Lewis Coser, Helen Hughes, Council Liaison ('79) Joyce Ladner; and Doris Wilkinson, Staff Liaison to the Committee. The document was approved by the ASA Council at its June 1979 meeting.

[3] The U.S. Department of Labor, Bureau of Labor Statistics, defines the *civilian labor force* as the sum of the unemployed and the civilian employed. The *total labor force* includes those in the armed forces.

APPENDIX 10-2 (cont'd)

II. Review of Previous Research

GENERAL PROBLEM

1. Failure to mention that samples are single-sex or have highly imbalanced sex ratios.

The results of a study are cited but no reference is made to the gender composition of the sample upon which the results are based.

2. Failure to note that samples are single-sex or have highly imbalanced sex ratios when reviewing a body of literature.

3. Methodological weaknesses of previous research ignored

Previous studies are cited which purport to reach conclusions casting women in an inferior light; the studies suffer from serious methodological weaknesses, but the reviewer fails to warn the reader about these problems and how they may invalidate the results.

EXAMPLE

Citation of a study demonstrating a positive association between position in the job hierarchy and work satisfaction; failure to mention that the study sampled men only.

Summary of results of previous research on occupational mobility, without indication that nearly all studies cited are of men only.

Uncritical citation of studies purporting to find sex differences in fear of success, field dependence, and industrial productivity.

III. Selection of Population and Sample

GENERAL PROBLEM

1. Women or men are arbitrarily excluded from sample

A research problem applies to a population with both men and women but only a single sex is sampled for study.

2. Inadequate justification for exclusion of men or women from sample

Men or women are arbitrarily excluded from a study because of financial constraints, convenience, lack of familiarity, or personal preference of the investigator; it is presumed that the topic is only relevant for men or women.

EXAMPLE

Studies of language acquisition which focus on the interaction of mother and child, neglecting the role of the father.

Studies of occupational mobility or work roles which include men only on the untested assumption that the male experience is the most important aspect.

IV Validity Issues

GENERAL PROBLEM

1. Biased question wording in surveys

Numerous problems associated with question wording yield conclusions which are invalid.

2. Scales validated on a single sex

A scale is validated on a sample of men or women only but is then applied to samples of both men and women.

3. Cross-sex interviewing

On highly sensitive gender-related questions, efforts are not made to ensure that interviewers are of the sex that will yield the least bias in eliciting responses.

EXAMPLE

A respondent is asked to designate a single person as "head of household".

An instrument for the measurement of the need for achievement is developed on male samples but is then used for measurement with both men and women.

V. Interpretation of Research Results

GENERAL PROBLEM

1. Over generalization of single-sex studies

Discussion of the results of a study based on a single-sex sample fail to qualify conclusions; implicit or explicit assertions are made of the generalizability of the findings of both sexes.

2. Improper entitlement of single-sex study reports

Publication titles of single-sex studies make no reference to this limitation.

3. Inferences unwarranted by the data

a. Conclusions with adverse implications for women are improperly drawn from the data.

b. Observed differences between men and women are attributed to individual-level biological and psychological gender differences; no effort is made to investigate whether social factors correlated with gender in the U.S. may account for the observed sex differences.

EXAMPLE

Results of a study of the correlates of job satisfaction among men generalized to both men and women.

Female-based study entitled "The American Family System"; male-based study entitled "The American Stratification System."

Rape victims held partially responsible for the assault; women in bureaucratically organized professions held partially responsible for the limits on their professional autonomy.

Lower aspirations for bureaucratic promotion and advancement among women attributed to general sex differences, ignoring differences in opportunity structures.

Spring 1980

ASSOCIATION OF AMERICAN COLLEGES • 1818 R Street, NW, Washington, DC 20009 • (202) 387-1300

APPENDIX 10-2 (cont'd)

A BASIC LAYMAN'S GUIDE TO CAMPUS DISABILITIES

As postsecondary staff and faculty, we should be aware of the wide variety of disabilities for which "enabling accommodations" will provide access to academic, cultural, and recreational facilities. These accessibilities come in the forms of both nonstructural (nondiscriminatory policies, practices, and activity relocations) and structural (architectural barrier removal) "total program" aspects.

The following is a layman's guide to the most common ambulatory, sight, and hearing disabilities appearing on campuses. It is purposely neither technical nor exhaustive, but will provide a basic understanding of impairments affecting a growing number of students, staff, and faculty, ranging from "college age" to a more senior age status.

With this introductory knowledge we are all a bit better equipped to ask the key question of each individual, "With which *functional* limitations should we be concerned to enable your choice of a full campus life?"

* *

DISABILITY	LAYMAN'S DESCRIPTION	TYPICAL, MOST COMMON FUNCTIONAL LIMITATIONS
allergy	oversensitivity of body to certain foreign substances (allergens or antigens) which ultimately trigger antibody production and consequently undesirable reaction	monitor of activity, often with medication to prevent contact with allergens and control reaction
amputation	upper and/or lower limb birth deficiency or surgical removal	hand, arm, ambulation limitations
arthritis	inflammation of a joint(s); local or widespread	limited physical movement or ambulation
asthma	usually an allergenic swelling of bronchiolar wall with mucoid secretions	constricted breathing, coughing, wheezing, difficulty in exhaling and decrease in endurance
autism	a form of childhood schizophrenia in which anxiety is dealt with inadequately	difficulty in forming relationships and dealing with external events
bone fractures	break in bone(s) anywhere in body	temporary or permanent limited physical activity or ambulation
bursitis	inflammation of any bursa (lubricating fluid sac in joints) of body	temporary or permanent limited physical activity or ambulation
cardiovascular limitations	any of a number of heart and circulatory impairments	temporary or permanent limited physical activity or ambulation
cerebral palsy	congenital brain damage resulting in motor, sensory, and perceptual difficulties	coordination impairments of limb(s), speech and/or sight; limitations in many functional activities, especially mobility
cerebrovascular accident (CVA or stroke)	paralysis resulting from interruption of blood supply to brain	lateral limitations of activity, speech, coordination, and/or ambulation

APPENDIX 10-2 (cont'd)

cystic fibrosis	Inherited disease of exocrine glands which pour secretions into or out of the body instead of into the blood	blockage of formation of many organs especially producing respiratory distress
decubitous ulcers (severe bedsores)	skin breakdown over bone protrusions, not uncommon to those with lack of sensation and the wheelchair mobile	temporary limitation of activity with occasional need for plastic surgery
developmental disability	means a disability of a person which— is attributed to (A) (i) mental retardation, cerebral palsy, epilepsy, or autism; (ii) any other condition of a person found to be closely related to mental retardation because such condition results in similar impairment of general intellectual functioning or adaptive behavior to that of mentally retarded persons or requires treatment and services similar to those required for such persons; or (iii) dyslexia resulting from a disability described in clause (i) or (ii) above (B) originates before such person attains age eighteen; (C) has continued or can be expected to continue indefinitely; (D) constitutes a substantial handicap to such person's ability to function normally in society.[1]	
diabetes	most commonly, pancreas fails to produce sufficient insulin to utilize sugar, resulting in high blood sugar levels (opposite: hypoglycemia)	monitor of activity and diet with often needed self-administered insulin injections (requires refrigeration)
dyslexia	partial alexia in which letters but not words may be read, or in which words may be read but not understood	inability to read or read at normal rate
epilepsy	chronic nerve disorder resulting from recurring surge "discharges" of electrical impulses within brain cells	*epileptic attack types* grand mal: marked by varying degrees of convulsion and possible loss of consciousness lasting from a few minutes to several hours Jacksonian: a focal type in which seizure is isolated in one part of the body petit mal: temporary loss or impairment of consciousness without significant convulsions, may last only few seconds psychomotor: alterations in state of consciousness, hallucinations, dream states
gout	arthritic symptoms usually caused by precipitation of uric acid in tissues and consequently painful urate crystals in body joints	temporary or permanent limited physical movement or ambulation
hearing limitations	*two types of hearing loss* conduction deafness--failure of airborne sound waves to be conducted efficiently to nerves of inner ear	loss of hearing ranging from difficulty in hearing to total deafness; possible speech impediment
	nerve or perceptive deafness--failure of auditory nerves to accept, perceive, and transmit messages to brain	loss of hearing ranging from difficulty in hearing to total deafness; possible speech impediment

APPENDIX 10-2 (cont'd)

Term	Description	Limitation
hemiplegia	paralysis to one-half (lateral) of the body, usually as a result of a CVA	limited physical activity or ambulation, possible speech impediment
hemophilia	abnormal clotting of the blood	prolonged bleeding with minimal injury
hypoglycemia	body utilizes too much blood sugar leaving sugar deficiency, especially during fasting periods (opposite: diabetes)	monitor of activity and diet with need for increase in glucose intake or frequency to avoid fatigue, light-headedness, dizziness
learning disability		
multiple sclerosis (MS)	usually progressive degeneration of myelin sheath surrounding central nervous system	sight, speech, hearing, coordination, ambulation and/or general activity impairments
muscular dystrophy (MD)	usually progressive degeneration of muscle fibers and replacement by fatty and fibrous tissue	limited physical activity or ambulation
myasthenia gravis	easily fatigued and weakened muscles especially of eyes, throat, and respiratory areas	limited physical activity or ambulation
osteogenesis imperfecta	weak bones and connective tissue	ease of bone breaks and joint dislocations
osteomyelitis (acute or chronic)	destructive invasion of bone and bone parts by infection	temporary or permanent limited physical movement or ambulation
paraplegia	paralysis which involves both legs and the trunk; when due to spinal cord injury also results in loss of voluntary bowel and bladder control	limited physical activity or ambulation
poliomyelitis	viral infection of spinal cord; accompanied by muscle atrophy and weakness of involved limbs	limited physical activity or ambulation
quadriplegia	paralysis involving parts or all of four limbs and the trunk; accompanied by loss of voluntary bowel and bladder control and decrease in respiratory reserves	limited physical activity or ambulation
scoliosis	lateral curvature of the spine	temporary or permanent limited physical movement or ambulation
sight limitations	*some common causes* amblyopia–dimness of vision from non-use of eye aniseikonia–difference in size and shape of an image perceived by each eye astigmatism–vision distortion resulting from imperfect curvature of the cornea (lens)	loss of sight ranging from difficulty in reading and legal blindness to total blindness

APPENDIX 10-2 (cont'd)

cataract—corneal incapacity

color blindness—inability to distinguish colors

diplopia—double vision

farsightedness (hyperopia)—close objects are blurred, far objects distinct

glaucoma—partial or total blindness (most common adult cause) resulting from intensive destructive pressure of fluids inside the eye

nearsightedness (myopia)—close objects are distinct, far objects are blurred

night blindness (nyctalopia)—imperfect vision in total or partial darkness

retinitis pigmentosa—hereditary disease that degenerates retina, resulting in eye's inability to transmit pictures to brain

specific learning disability — means a disorder in one or more of the basic psychological processes involved in understanding or in using language, spoken or written, which may manifest itself in an imperfect ability to listen, think, speak, read, write, spell or to do mathematical calculations. The term includes such conditions as perceptual handicaps, brain injury, minimal brain dysfunction, dyslexia, and developmental aphasia. The term does not include children who have learning problems which are primarily the result of visual, hearing, or motor handicaps, of mental retardation, or of environmental, cultural, or economic disadvantages.[2]

spina bifida — failure of fusion of spinal column through which one or more neural elements of spinal cord may protrude

temporary or permanent limited physical movement or ambulation

spinal cord injury — damage to spinal cord from accident

temporary or permanent paralysis to lower and/or upper limbs with motor/sensory loss; limited physical activity or ambulation

* *

Sources: Cooley, Donald G., *Better Homes and Gardens Family Medical Guide*, Des Moines, Iowa, Meredith Corporation, 1973.
Myers, Julian, *An Orientation to Chronic Disease and Disability*, New York, Macmillan, Inc., 1965.

Medical Consultant: Murray M. Freed, MD, Director, New England Regional Spinal Cord Injury Center, Chief, Department of Rehabilitation Medicine, University Hospital, Boston, Massachusetts.

Notes: [1]PL 94-103 (42 USC 6001) Developmentally Disabled Assistance and Bill of Rights Act.
[2]PL 94-142 (20 USC 1401) Education of the Handicapped Act.

Compiled by: Alfred H. DeGraff, M.S., S.E.A., Director, Disabled Student Services, Boston University, Boston, Massachusetts, Copyright, 1979.

GLOSSARY

Accessibility – the freedom of a physically disabled person to approach, enter, and use or participate in academic programs, personnel offices, worksites, and public areas.

Adverse Impact – occurs when employment decisions such as hiring, promotion, and termination work to the disadvantage of members of protected groups. Adverse impact focuses on the consequences of employment practices, and as such, the charging party need only establish that an employment practice has the effect of excluding a significant proportion of women or members of minority groups.

Affected Class – any group of employees or former employees who are members of a protected group that has suffered or that continues to suffer the effects of unlawful discrimination.

Affirmative Action – specific actions taken by the institution designed to eliminate the effects of past discrimination in regard to admission of students, special programs for disadvantaged students, as well as recruitment, hiring, or promoting of employees.

Affirmative Action Plan (AAP) – a written plan conforming to *Executive Order 11246* in which an institution analyzes specific problems and identifies areas in which members of protected groups are underutilized. In those areas, the institution must set specific goals and timetables to eliminate this underutilization.

Affirmative Action Program – a generic name referring to the entire institutional affirmative action effort, of which the written Affirmative Action Plan is one part.

Age Discrimination in Employment Act of 1967 (ADEA) – a federal law prohibiting employment discrimination by private employers against persons 40 to 70 years old on the basis of their age, except where age is a *bona fide* occupational qualification (BFOQ). The Age Discrimination in Employment Act is enforced by the EEOC.

American Indian or Alaskan Native – a person with origins in any of the original peoples of North America and who maintains cultural identification through tribal affiliation or community recognition.

Annual Goal – a yearly target expressed as both a number and a percentage, for hiring minorities or females into a job group for which underutilization exists.

Applicant Flow Data - a written log and summary showing the racial and sexual demographics of each applicant for each position open at the institution.

Applicant Pool - all candidates who have applied for a job during the period the job was open from whom a person is selected to fill the position.

Asian or Pacific Islander - a person with origins in any of the original peoples of the Far East, Southeast Asia, the Indian Subcontinent, or the Pacific Islands, including China, Japan, Korea, the Philippine Republic, and Samoa.

Availability - the percentage of women and minorities with the required skills or who are capable of acquiring them within the institution's recruiting area used to determine underutilization.

Black - a person with origins in any of the black racial groups of Africa who is also not of Hispanic origin.

Bona Fide Occupational Qualification (BFOQ) - a job requirement which permits an employer to legally discriminate on the basis of sex, age, or religion. Examples include the requirement that a performer playing the part of a woman be a woman or that a minister of a particular religion be a member of that religion. The concept of BFOQ is interpreted very narrowly by the courts. Although age may be a BFOQ, race is never a BFOQ.

Business Necessity - if institutional practices adversely affect members of a protected group, the institution must be able to demonstrate that the practices challenged are essential to the institution and that no alternative nondiscriminatory practice exists.

Charge of Discrimination - a statement alleging discrimination filed with a government agency.

Charging Party - a person who files a charge of discrimination against the institution with a state or federal agency. May also be called the "complainant."

Civil Rights Act of 1964 - a comprehensive law establishing federal guarantees of civil rights in the fields of voting, public accommodations, use of public facilities, public education, benefits under federally assisted programs, employment, and other fields. Also known as Title VII, the Act prohibits discrimination in employment on the basis of race, color, religion, sex, or national origin. See *Educational Amendments of 1972*.

Class Action Suit - a civil action brought on behalf of an affected class by one or more individuals or by the EEOC to secure a judicial remedy to an unlawful pattern of discrimination by the institution.

Cohort Analysis - a cohort is one of a group of individuals having a statistical factor in common such as race, sex, or date of birth; a cohort analysis may be used in equal pay studies in analyzing comparable members of a department.

Comparable Worth - the concept of equal pay for work of comparable value. Identified by the EEOC as a major issue of the 1980's and as the primary factor in the disparity between average wages of males and females.

Compliance - the degree to which the institution has carried out its mandatory affirmative action obligations.

Compliance Review - a review conducted by the OFCCP to determine whether institutions with federal funds have Affirmative Action Plans acceptable in both format and substance. A review examines the institution's Affirmative Action Plan regarding race, sex, color, religion, national origin, handicap, and veteran status.

Conciliation - the process by which a government agency attempts to settle a complaint of discrimination through agreement with the respondent after a finding of reasonable cause and before bringing a civil action.

Conciliation Agreement - an agreement between an institution found to have substantive Affirmative Action problems and the agency that has identified those problems. May include back pay, seniority credit, promotion, or other forms of relief.

Debarment - an action resulting from an administrative ruling adverse to the institution that makes the institution ineligible to receive further federal funds.

Desk Audit - a review of the written Affirmative Action Plan and supporting documentation submitted to the OFCCP.

Disability - See *Handicapped Individual*.

Disabled Veteran - a person entitled to compensation for disability under laws administered by the Veterans Administration, or a person whose discharge or release from active duty was for a disability incurred or aggravated in the line of duty.

Disparate Effect - applies to specific employment practices such as testing or job requirements which, though applied neutrally, adversely impact on women or minorities. See *Adverse Impact*.

Disparate Treatment - discrimination by which an employer treats certain people differently because they are women or members of a minority group. Comparative evidence, statistical evidence, and direct evidence of motive may be used to prove disparate treatment.

Educational Amendments of 1972 - expanded coverage of the 1964 Civil Rights Act to include faculty in institutions of higher education. (See Congressional hearings chaired by Rep. Edith Green listed in the Bibliography.)

EEO-6 Report - the annual report filed by institutions of higher education with the Higher Education Reporting Committee of the EEOC regarding the sex and minority status of the institution's employees by job category and salary interval. The EEO-6 form is designed to satisfy the informational reporting needs of the EEOC, the OCR, and the OFCCP.

Employment Opportunity Specialist (EOS) - job title for OFCCP reviewer
of institutional Affirmative Action Plans and for EEOC investigators.

Equal Employment Opportunity - admininstering all terms and conditions
of employment without regard to age, color, handicap, national
origin, race, religion, or sex.

Equal Employment Opportunity Commission (EEOC) - the federal agency
mandated to enforce Title VII of the Civil Rights Act of 1964,
the Equal Pay Act of 1963, and the Age Discrimination in Employment
Act of 1967.

Equal Pay Act of 1963 - a federal law, enforced by the EEOC, prohibiting
pay differentials on the basis of sex for similar jobs within an
institution's workforce.

Executive Orders 11246 and 11375 - Presidential Executive Orders
promulgated in 1965 and 1967 which require a nondiscrimination
clause covering employment in all contracts with the federal government for more than $10,000* and also require written Affirmative
Action Plans which comply with Revised Order No. 4.

Gender Harassment - discriminatory behavior directed against individuals
who belong to a gender group the aggressor considers inferior. Such
discrimination is unusually pernicious when it occurs within institutionally established relationships such as faculty and student or
administrator and staff member. Common examples in the classroom
include use of sexist language, illustrations, examples, and gestures.

Goals and Timetables - numerical projections the institution makes as
part of the Affirmative Action Plan; refers to the representation
of minorities and women in job groups in which they have been underutilized. Goals and timetables are not quotas.

Good-faith Effort - actions required by Revised Order No. 4 and those
the institution may voluntarily develop to achieve compliance and
to improve the campus's affirmative action program.

Grievance - filed by a student, employee, or applicant for employment
alleging unfair treatment. Refers to internal institutional procedures as opposed to charges of discrimination filed with outside
agencies.

Handicapped Individual - any person who (1) has a physical or mental
impairment that substantially limits one or more of his or her
major life activities, (2) has a record of such impairment, or (3)
is regarded as having such an impairment. A handicap is "substantially
limiting" if it is likely to cause difficulty in securing, retaining,
or advancing in employment. See also *Qualified Handicapped Individual.*

Hispanic - a person of Mexican, Puerto Rican, Cuban, South American,
or other Spanish culture or origin, regardless of race.

Impact Ratio Analysis - a formula used to determine adverse impact.
Refers to the selection rate for a group divided by the selection
rate for the group with the highest selection rate. Impact ratios
are compared to the 80% rule of thumb to determine adverse impact.

*Change proposed by Reagan Administration.

Infection Theory - a broad view of the applicability of Title IX and Section 504 to college and university programs. Proponents of the theory argue that all programs should be subject to Title IX, not just those which receive federal funding.*

Job Area Acceptance Range (JAAR) - a mathematical formula used to identify possible affected classes as well as concentration and underrepresentation of minorities and women in the institution's work force. JAAR is not the same as the process for determining underutilization, nor is it conclusive proof of discrimination.

Job Description - a written statement detailing the work to be performed by the incumbents in a particular title.

Job Group - one or more positions having similar content, wage rates, and opportunities. Positions grouped together should contain enough employees so that the analysis performed is statistically significant.

Job Qualifications - education, experience, minimum age, and other factors as requirements to being hired, transferred, or promoted into a particular job.

Job-Relatedness - any criterion employed to determine whether a person will be hired, fired, transferred, promoted, or given a salary increase must be directly related to job performance.

Job Title - the particular name or classification of a job.

Letter of Commitment - an agreement by an institution in which it agrees to make substantive changes or increased efforts in its Affirmative Action Plan.

Mediation - a process by which someone whose role is to facilitate resolution of conflict or complaint acts as intermediary between or among parties to a complaint or a grievance to the end of bringing it to a conclusion satisfactory to all parties without the expense and conflict of formal litigation.

Multiple Regression - a statistical analysis of the relationship of one variant with others; a multiple regression analysis may be used to determine why students of one demographic group attend an institution in different proportion than students of other demographic groups.

Negotiation - a means of achieving a solution by which each party gains and hence has a stake in fulfilling the agreement.

Office for Civil Rights (OCR) - the office within the Department of Education responsible for carrying out ED's responsibility as a compliance agency for Titles VI and IX.

Office of Federal Contract Compliance Programs (OFCCP) - the office within the U.S. Department of Labor to which is delegated the responsibility of administering Executive Order 11246 and its implementing regulations, such as Revised Order No. 4.

*See *Seattle University v. HEW*.

On-Site Review - an on-campus review during which the investigator gathers additional information in order to make a determination as to the compliance or lack thereof of the Affirmative Action Plan.

Parity - the employment of women and minority group members in various job categories at rates approximating the rates at which validly qualified members of those groups are available for employment in those job categories.

Progression Line Charts - lists of job titles in a broad job family, generally starting with less difficult, lower-paying jobs and progressing to more difficult, higher-paying jobs.

Protected Class - any group or member of that group protected by the anti-discrimination laws on the basis of race, sex, age, color, handicap, national origin, religion, or Vietnam veteran status.

Qualified Handicapped Individual - one who can perform the "essential functions" of a job with reasonable accommodation.

Quotas - court-ordered hiring and/or promotion ratios of minorities and females into positions from which they have been excluded.

Reasonable Accommodation - alterations, adjustments, or changes in the job, the workplace, academic programs, and/or term or condition of employment which will enable an otherwise qualified handicapped individual or disabled veteran to participate or to perform a particular job successfully, as determined on a case-by-case basis depending on the individual circumstances. Also refers to adjustments made by an employer to accommodate an employee whose religious beliefs forbid working certain days and hours.

Reasonable Cause - a determination made by a government agency, after investigation of a charge of employment discrimination, that there is a basis "to believe that the charge is true." A finding of reasonable cause by the agency is an administrative finding, which is accorded substantial weight by the judiciary.

Rehabilitation Act of 1973 (Sections 503 and 504) - prohibits discrimination against the disabled and requires institutions to take affirmative action to hire and promote qualified disabled persons and to make academic programs accessible to disabled persons. Enforcement by OCR and the OFCCP.

Relevant Labor Market - geographic area used to determine availability.

Revised Order No. 4 - regulation of the U.S. Department of Labor enforced by the OFCCP which sets forth in detail the required contents of affirmative action plans to be developed and maintained by institutions with federal contracts. Such plans must include a utilization analysis and projections of goals and timetables.

Sexual Harassment - an incident in which a person uses his or her position to control, influence, or affect the grade, career, salary, or job of another employee or prospective employee in exchange for

sexual favors. Sexual harassment includes sexual innuendos made
at inappropriate times, perhaps in the guise of humor; verbal
harassment or abuse; subtle pressure for sexual activity; sexist
remarks about a woman's clothing, body, or sexual activities; unnecessary touching, patting, or pinching; leering or ogling of a
woman's body; constant brushing against a woman's body; demanding
sexual favors accompanied by implied or overt threats concerning
one's jobs, grades, letters of recommendation; and physical assault.

Show Cause Notice - a step in the enforcement phase of an OFCCP
Compliance Review which requires the institution to show cause why
its federal funding should not be discontinued.

Standard Deviation - variation above or below the average.

Standard Metropolitan Statistical Area (SMSA) - a specific, defined
geographic area for statistical reporting, designated by Bureau
of Labor Statistics in conjunction with demographic data provided
by the Bureau of the Census; always includes a central city and
surrounding territory.

Statistically Significant - of numerically or other mathematically
sufficient quantity to make a judgment based on statistical analysis.
If, for example, 40 of 100 blacks and 90 of 100 whites taking a
pre-employment test pass it, the numbers are sufficient to determine
whether adverse impact may be indicated. If, however, only five
blacks and five whites taking the test are studied, the numbers
involved are statistically insignificant, and no judgment regarding
adverse impact can be based on the failure rates.

Systemic Discrimination - employment or admission policies or practices
which, though often neutral on their face, serve to differentiate
or to perpetuate a differentiation in admission to the institution
or in employment of applicants or employees because of their race,
color, religion, sex, national origin, handicap, or veteran's status.
Systemic discrimination normally relates to a recurring practice
rather than to an isolated act of discrimination, and may include
failure to remedy the continuing effects of past discrimination.
Intent to discriminate may or may not be involved.

Title VI - prohibits discrimination on the basis of race, color, or
national origin in the provision of benefits or services under programs receiving federal financial assistance. May be applied to
academic programs, admissions, or financial aid. Title VI applies
to discrimination in employment only where the "primary objective"
of the federal grant in question is to provide employment and is
enforced by OCR.

Title VII - prohibits discrimination in employment on the basis of race,
color, religion, sex, or national origin, regardless of whether the
employer is a contractor with the federal government. Coverage was
extended to faculty in higher education by the 1972 Amendments.
Enforcement is by the EEOC.

Title IX - prohibits discrimination on the basis of sex in educational
programs. May be applied to admissions, financial aid, athletics,

or academic programs. The Department of Education argues that
Title IX is applied to discrimination in employment only where
the "primary objective" of the federal grant in question is to
provide employment.* Enforcement is by OCR.

Underutilization - a disparity between the employment of members of a
racial, ethnic, or sexual group in a job or job group and their
availability. Underutilization is determined by conducting an
availability analysis.

Uniform Guidelines on Employee Selection Procedures - were adopted in
1978 by the federal agencies enforcing anti-discrimination laws.
The Guidelines incorporate a single set of principles designed to
assist those who must comply with federal requirements regarding
discrimination based on race, color, religion, sex, and national
origin (see 29 CFR 1607.1A).

Utilization Analysis - an analysis conducted by an institution to
determine whether minorities and women are employed in each major
job group at a rate consistent with the availability of qualified
minorities and women in the relevant labor market for the positions
covered by each job group.

Validation - a procedure by which employee selection devices are demonstrated empirically to be predictive of job performance in the
particular jobs for which they are used. Under the Uniform Guidelines on Employee Selection Procedures, tests or other selection
devices which screen out minorities or women at a greater rate
than others must be validated according to procedures which meet
the published standards of the American Psychological Association.

Veteran of the Vietnam Era - a person who served on active duty for
a period of more than 180 days, any part of which occurred between
August 5, 1964, and May 7, 1975, and was discharged or released
therefrom with other than a dishonorable discharge; or who was discharged or released from active duty for a service-connected
disability if any part of such active duty was performed between
August 5, 1964, and May 7, 1975; and who was so discharged or
released within 48 months preceding an alleged violation of the
Vietnam Era Veterans' Readjustment Assistance Act of 1974, the
affirmative action clause, or the regulations issued pursuant to
the Act.

Vietnam Era Veterans Readjustment Act of 1974 (402) - a federal statute
requiring institutions holding federal contracts of $10,000 or more
to take "affirmative action to hire and advance in employment"
disabled and Vietnam-era veterans. The law is enforced by the OFCCP.

White - a person with origins in any of the original peoples of Europe,
North Africa, or the Middle East who is not of Hispanic origin.

Workforce Analysis - a listing of each job title as it appears in payroll records ranked from lowest paid to highest paid within each
department.

*This question is before the Supreme Court in *Seattle University
v. HEW.*

KEY CASES

The section that follows contains a topical list and an alphabetized summary of the cases affecting affirmative action in higher education. Citations usually are to Commerce Clearing House's *Employment Practices Decisions*. For a more complete summary of appellate and Supreme Court decisions involving equal employment opportunity, the following resource is recommended:

Equal Employment Opportunity Court Cases. The main volume was published in 1979 and the first annual supplement was published in 1980. Copies are available from the U.S. Government Printing Office, Washington, D.C. 20402.

Stock number for the 1979 volume is 006-000-01141-1.
Stock number for the 1980 volume is 006-000-01227-2.

Topical Index

Age Discrimination
    Levine v. Fairleigh Dickinson University

Backpay
    Dyson v. Lauery
    Jepson v. Florida Board of Regents
    Johnson v. University of Pittsburgh
    Joost-Gaugier and White v. Tufts Institution of Learning
    Kunda v. Muhlenberg College
    Schwartz v. State of Florida

Benefits
    City of Los Angeles v. Manhart

Disabled (Discrimination Against)
    American National Insurance Co. v. Fair Employment Practice
        Commission
    Carmi v. Metro St. Louis
    Doss v. General Motors Corp.
    Moon v. Roadway Express
    Rogers v. Frito-Lay, Inc.
    Southeastern Community College v. Davis
    University of Texas v. Camenish

Employment Discrimination
    Carmi v. Metro St. Louis (504)
    Christensen v. State of Iowa
    Cussler v. University of Maryland
    Delaware State College v. Ricks
    Faro v. New York University
    Green v. Board of Regents
    Greene v. Howard University
    Holliman v. Martin
    Jepson v. Florida Board of Regents
    Johnson v. University of Pittsburgh
    Joost-Gaugier and White v. Tufts Institution of Learning
    Kunda v. Muhlenberg College
    Lamphere v. Brown University
    Levine v. Fairleigh Dickinson University
    Lieberman v. Gant
    Mt. Healthy City School District Board of Education v. Doyle
    North Haven Board of Education v. Bell (IX)
    Penalta Federation of Teachers v. Penalta Community College
    Perry v. Sindermann
    Peters v. Middleburg College
    Pickering v. Board of Education
    Powell v. Syracuse University
    Rajender v. University of Minnesota
    Rowe v. General Motors Corp.
    Schwartz v. State of Florida
    Seattle University v. Department of Health, Education and Welfare
      (XI)
    Stukuls v. State
    Sweeney v. Board of Trustees of Keene State College
    U.S. Steelworkers of America v. Weber
    Weise v. Syracuse University
    Wilkins v. University of Houston

Equal Pay and Comparable Worth
    Brown v. William Wood
    Christensen v. State of Iowa
    County of Washington, Oregon v. Gunther
    Cussler v. University of Texas
    Electrical Workers v. Westinghouse Electrical Corp.
    Lemons v. City and County of Denver

Faculty Rights
    Board of Regents v. Roth
    Brenna v. Southern Colorado State College
    Delaware State College v. Ricks
    Faro v. New York University
    Ferguson v. Thomas
    Green v. Board of Regents
    Greene v. Howard University
    Holliman v. Martin
    Jepson v. Florida Board of Regents
    Johnson v. University of Pittsburgh
    Joost-Gaugier and White v. Tufts Institution of Learning
    Kunda v. Muhlenberg College
    Lamphere v. Brown University

Lieberman v. Gant
McKillop v. Regents of University of California
Mt. Healthy City School District Board of Education v. Doyle
NLRB v. Yeshiva University
Penalta Federation of Teachers v. Penalta Community College
Perry v. Sindermann
Peters v. Middleburg College
Pickering v. Board of Education
Powell v. Syracuse University
Rajender v. University of Minnesota
Stukuls v. State
Sweeney v. Board of Trustees of Keene State College
Weise v. Syracuse University

Job-Related Qualifications (Including Testing)
Application of Lombardo
Carmi v. Metro St. Louis
Cussler v. University of Maryland
Green v. Board of Regents
Griggs v. Duke Power
Peters v. Middleburg College
Washington v. Davis
Weise v. Syracuse University

Private Causes of Action
Alexander v. Yale University (IX)
Cannon v. University of Chicago
Carmi v. Metro St. Louis (504)
Clarke v. Felec Services, Inc. (503)
Moon v. Roadway Express (504)
Rogers v. Frito-Lay, Inc. (504)
University of Texas v. Camenish
Weisbord v. Michigan State University

Procedural Issues (Including Due Process and Filing Deadlines)
Carmi v. Metro St. Louis
Delaware State College v. Ricks
Ferguson v. Thomas
General Telephone Company of the Northwest v. EEOC
McKillop v. Regents of University of California
Ramos v. Texas Tech University
Sears, Roebuck and Company v. Equal Employment Opportunity Commission

Promotional/Tenure
Banejee v. Board of Trustees of Smith College
Cussler v. University of Maryland
Green v. Board of Regents
Kunda v. Muhlenberg College
Rajender v. University of Minnesota
Rowe v. General Motors Corp.
Stukuls v. State
Sweeney v. Board of Trustees of Keene College

Religious Discrimination
Equal Employment Opportunity Commission v. Mississippi College
Trans World Airlines v. Hardison

Sex Discrimination
    Cussler v. University of Maryland
    Dyson v. Lauery
    Faro v. New York University
    Green v. Board of Regents
    Jepson v. Florida Board of Regents
    Johnson v. University of Pittsburgh
    Joost-Gaugier and White v. Tufts Institution of Learning
    Kunda v. Muhlenberg College
    Lamphere v. Brown University
    Lieberman v. Gant
    McKillop v. Regents of University of California
    Peters v. Middleburg College
    Power v. Syracuse University
    Rajender v. University of Minnesota
    Schwartz v. State of Florida
    Sweeney v. Board of Trustees of Keene State College
    Wilkins v. University of Houston
    Yellow Springs Exempted Village School District Board of Education
        v. Ohio High School Athletic Association

Sexual Harassment
    Alexander v. Yale University
    Bundy v. Jackson
    Kyriazi v. Western Electric
    Ludington v. Sambo's Restaurant
    Vinson v. Taylor

Statistics (Proof of Discrimination)
    Firestone Synthetic Rubber and Latex Co. v. Marshall
    Hazelwood School District v. United States
    Keco Industries v. EEOC
    McDonnell Douglas Corp. v. Green
    Mecklenberg v. Montana State Board of Regents
    Melani et al. v. The New York City Board of Higher Education
    Wilkins v. University of Houston

Students (Discrimination Against)
    Cannon v. University of Chicago
    Othen v. Ann Arbor School Board (IX)
    Ramos v. Texas Tech University
    Regents of University of California v. Bakke
    Steinburg v. Chicago Medical School
    University of Texas v. Camenish
    Yellow Springs Exempted Village School District Board of Education
        v. Ohio High School Athletic Association

Alphabetical Index

Adams v. Richardson, 356 F. Supp. 92 (D. D.C. 1973)
    The Department of Health, Education and Welfare and Department
    of Labor were directed to institute enforcement proceedings for
    the federal laws prohibiting race discrimination in the educational
    system. Affected southern states which had operated dual systems
    of education.

Alexander v. Yale University, 459 F. Supp. 1 (D. Conn. 1977)
> A Federal District Court held that a female student was entitled
> to bring a private action under Title IX regarding her allegation
> that she received a low grade in a course because she rejected
> her professor's outright proposition "to give her a grade of 'A'
> in the course" if she complied with his sexual demands.

American National Insurance Co. v. Fair Employment Practice Commission,
25 EPD 31751 (Cal. App. 1981)
> A three-judge panel ruled that "handicap" under the California
> Fair Employment Practices Act refers to an impairment of function
> rather than to a medical condition that has lesser effects. Rivard,
> who has high blood pressure, was discharged from a position involv-
> ing door-to-door selling of insurance and collection of premiums.
> The California Supreme Court has granted a hearing of this case.

Application of Lombardo, 240 N.Y. 5 2d 119 (N.Y. 1963)
> A state court ruled the teaching ability, administrative capacity,
> and creative inspiration are relevant but not mechanically measurable.

Banejee v. Board of Trustees of Smith College, 495 F. Supp. 1148 (D.
Mass. 1980)
> The failure of the plaintiff to gain tenure was not the result of
> discrimination on the basis of national origin or race but rather
> because of increased competition for tenured positions in the early
> 1970's.

Board of Regents v. Roth, 408 US 564, 92 S. Ct. 2701 (1972)
> The court ruled that a faculty member with a one-year contract who
> is appropriately notified of nonrenewal is not entitled to notice
> of a reason or an opportunity for a hearing.

Brenna v. Southern Colorado State College, 589 F. 2d 475 (10th Circuit
1978)
> When faced with a bona fide financial exigency, an institution may
> retain a nontenured faculty member and dismiss a tenured faculty
> member without violating the latter's substantive due process rights.

Brown v. William Wood, 16 EPD 8171 (Alaska 1978)
> In this case brought under Alaska's equal pay statute, the court
> held the plaintiff had made a *prima facie* case. There was no
> correlation between plaintiff's evaluations and her raises, "catch
> up" monies were not used to bring plaintiff to level of males, and
> legislative funding did not prevent the university from bringing
> plaintiff's salary to a par with males.

Bundy v. Jackson, 24 EPD 31439 (D.C. 1981)
> The court characterizes sexual harassment as an activity which
> "injects the most demeaning sexual stereotypes into the general work
> environment and ... always represents an intentional assault on
> the individual's innermost privacy." Although sexual harassment
> is extremely serious, an employer can limit liability by taking
> immediate and appropriate corrective action upon learning that
> harassment has occurred.

Cannon v. University of Chicago, 47 USLW 4549, 99 S. Ct. 1946 (1979)
   Congress intended a private right of action to enforce Title IX;
   a plaintiff may bypass the administrative remedies provided by
   Title IX and seek private enforcement directly.

Carmi v. Metro St. Louis Sewer District, 620 F. 2d 672, 23 EPD 30892
   (8th Circuit 1980) Cert. denied 24 EPD 31256.
   The court denied the plaintiff relief because he did not have
   standing to sue; Carmi filed under Sections 503 and 504. The court
   reasoned that federal funds were received for construction, not
   for employment; that since the plaintiff was not employed by the
   district, he lacked sufficient interest to plead due process
   violations; and that the requirement of a physical examination was
   rationally related to employing persons who can perform the job
   without endangering others.

Christensen v. State of Iowa, 563 F. 2d 353 (8th Circuit 1977)
   The university had recently evaluated all jobs, found clerical jobs
   (female) to be of the same value as plant jobs (male), but paid
   lower wages to the clerical employees. The court held that this
   practice did not violate the Equal Pay Act.

City of Los Angeles v. Manhart, 435 US 702 (1978)
   The court held that an employee-operated pension fund that requires
   a 15% larger contribution from females than males violates Title
   VII.

Clarke v. Felec Services, Inc., 23 EPD 32141 (Alaska 1980)
   The Alaska court ruled that a private court action to enforce Section
   503 may be implied.

County of Washington, Oregon v. Gunther, 26 EPD 31877 (1981)
   The Court affirmed a Ninth Circuit decision in the first comparable
   worth case to reach the Supreme Court. The Court ruled that claims
   for sex-based wage discrimination can be brought under Title VII
   "even though no member of the opposite sex holds an equal but higher
   paying job." Such a suit cannot be brought if the wage rate is
   based on seniority, merit, quantity, or quality of production.
   Justice Brennan stated that Congress did not intend the Bennett
   Amendment to restrict Title VII and that a "broad approach" to
   equal opportunity was essential to overcoming the effect of past
   discrimination.

Cussler v. University of Maryland, 430 F. Supp. 602 (Maryland 1977)
   Female professor's denial of promotion to full professor and lower
   pay were due to criticism of her research and publications by qualified colleagues in accordance with normal university procedures
   and to the superior evaluations of the higher-paid male faculty
   members. Title VII is not violated.

Delaware State College v. Ricks, 24 EPD 31393 (1980)
   The Court addresses the issue of when the filing period for a
   charge of discrimination for a faculty termination begins to toll:
   whether from the date the faculty member is first notified of the
   terminal year or whether from the last day of employment. The
   Supreme Court held that the time period begins to toll when the

professor is notified that s/he will not be granted tenure. An amicus curae brief filed by the AAUP argued that by requiring employees to file suit before their appointment actually ends, the Court would close off the possibility that employment disputes could be resolved through a college's internal review procedures rather than through litigation.

Doss v. General Motors Corp., 25 EPD 31761 (DC Ill. 1981)
   The court ruled that the employer had sufficient job-related reasons for rejecting Doss who suffers from a chronic ear infection and that denying him employment was not unlawful discrimination under Illinois state law.

Dyson v. Lauery, 417 F. Supp. 103 (ED Va. 1976)
   The plaintiff won back pay to compensate her at the rate and rank she would have held had she been a male.

Electrical Workers v. Westinghouse Electrical Corp., 23 EPD 31106 (3rd Circuit 1980)
   Title VII prohibitions are broader than those of the Equal Pay Act. Paying women less than men for comparable work violates Title VII sex-bias prohibitions. Review denied by Supreme Court.

Equal Employment Opportunity Commission v. Mississippi College, 451 F. Supp. 564, 24 EPD 31268 (SD Mississippi 1980) Cert. denied 26 EPD 31901.
   The Court ruled that the exemption from Title VII of religious organizations is limited to those practices involving the relation-ship of a church and a minister. The exemption does not extend to instructors at religiously affiliated colleges or to discrimina-tion on the basis of race or sex by religiously affiliated insti-tutions. Review denied by Supreme Court.

Faro v. New York University, 502 F. 2d 1229, 8 EPD 9632 (2nd Circuit 1974)
   The leading case for judicial nonintervention in faculty employment issues, since modified by the Second Circuit.

Ferguson v. Thomas, 430 F. 2d 852 (5th Circuit 1970)
   A U.S. Court of Appeals found that the minimum procedural due process to be provided in a tenure termination hearing for cause is that the teacher be advised of the cause or causes for termina-tion in sufficient detail to fairly enable the teacher to show any error that may exist; that the teacher be advised of the names and the nature of the testimony of witnesses against him/her; that at a reasonable time after such advice, the teacher must be accorded a meaningful opportunity to be heard in his/her own defense; and that the hearing should be before a tribunal that both possesses some academic expertise and has an impartiality toward the charges.

Firestone Synthetic Rubber and Latex Company v. Marshall, 25 EPD 31590 (DC Tex. 1981)
   Firestone had been debarred from government contracts for failure to declare underutilization of women and minorities in job groups and organizational units with fewer than 50 people. Firestone initiated the court action, contending that it had complied with government contractor regulations. A federal trial court in Texas

vacated the Labor Department order of debarment, ruling that the
technical guidance memorandum which attempted to force declaration
of underutilizations in job groups with fewer than 50 employees
had not been issued in accordance with the Administrative Procedures
Act.

Fullilove v. Klutznick, 48 USLW 4979 (1980)
Supreme Court ruled that racial quotas imposed by Congress are
constitutional if Congress's purpose is to remedy past discrimination and if the quotas are kept flexible and temporary. The Court
distinguished the case from *Bakke* by stating that in *Bakke*, the
University was not the proper government body to enact racial
remedies and there was not a past history of racial discrimination.

General Telephone Company of the Northwest, Inc. v. EEOC, 48 USLW 4513
(U.S. May 12, 1980)
The Court ruled that EEOC could bring class actions in Federal
Courts without being subject to the limitations of Rule 23 (class
actions). (Rule 23 requires that a class be sufficiently numerous
and that all members share important interests.)

Green v. Board of Regents, Texas Tech University, 474 F. 2d 594 (5th
Circuit 1973)
The Court ruled that faculty promotions were a matter of professional
judgment and that the university's failure to establish definite
criteria controlling faculty promotion was not fatal to its defense.

Greene v. Howard University, 412 F. 2d 1128 (D.C. Circuit 1969)
The Court held that the employment contracts of faculty include
the hiring policies and practices of the university as embodied
in its employment regulations and customs.

Griggs v. Duke Power, 401 US 424 (1971)
In a landmark case, the Court held that facially neutral employment policies that had a disparate effect upon members of a protected class constituted discrimination under Title VII.

Hazelwood School District v. United States, 433 US 299, 15 EPD 1 (1977)
The implication that discrimination will not be inferred unless two
to three standard deviations are present; standard deviation is a
more meaningful statistical technique than the 80% test.

Holliman v. Martin, 330 F. Supp. 1 (1971)
The Court held that the following are reasons for nonrenewal of
a faculty contract: immoral conduct; incompetency in scholarship,
research, and publishing; and insubordination.

Jepson v. Florida Board of Regents, 22 EPD 30624 (5th Circuit 1980)
The court ruled for a plaintiff in a promotional and salary case.

Johnson v. University of Pittsburgh, 16 EPD 8194 (W.D. Penn. 1977)
The plaintiff won an injunction barring the university from
terminating her employment, but later lost on the merits.

Joost-Gaugier and White v. Tufts Institution of Learning, 421 F. Supp.
152 (1975)
The plaintiff won an injunction and later won on the merits because

a department head with known anti-female biases had served on her tenure committee. The court held that plaintiff was entitled to be judged by a committee free from the influence of sex bias.

Keco Industries v. EEOC, 22 EPD 30759 (6th Circuit 1980)
The Appellate Court ruled that affirmative action plans designed for compliance with Revised Order 4 can be used as evidence of bias in subsequent civil rights lawsuits. Certiorari to the Supreme Court denied.

Kunda v. Muhlenberg College, 463 F. Supp. 294, 22 EPD 30674 14571 (On appeal to the Supreme Court.)
A plaintiff alleging sex discrimination against an institution of higher education won reinstatement, back pay, promotion to rank of assistant professor, and tenure upon completion of her masters degree within two years.

Kyriazi v. Western Electric, 20 EPD 30273 (N.J. 1979)
A female engineer who brought a suit alleging sexual harassment was awarded retroactive benefits and back pay as well as punitive damages against the individual defendants.

Lamphere v. Brown University, 71 FRD 641 (DR 1. 1976)
Lamphere was certified as a class representative, won retroactive tenure and a cash settlement. Claims ultimately totaled $107,000, and Brown spent about one million dollars in attorneys fees.

Lemons v. City and County of Denver, 22 EPD 30852 (10th Circuit 1980)
Cert. denied 24 EPD 31256.
The court declined to impose a compensation system based on other comparable but different city jobs.

Levine v. Fairleigh Dickinson University, 25 EPD 31729 (3rd Circuit 1981)
Although a nontenured employee has no assurance of continuous employment, the university violated the ADEA when it reduced the contract of a 66-year-old professor from a one-year full-time contract to a one-year part-time contract. The university may, of course, evaluate him in light of his ability, the demand for his course, and his department's ability to satisfy its needs.

Lieberman v. Gant, 23 EPD 31164 (2nd Circuit 1980)
The plaintiff failed to prove that her credentials were equal to those of males granted tenure and hence her case was dismissed. Decision upheld on appeal.

Ludington v. Sambo's Restaurant, 21 EPD 30367 (ED Wis. 1979)
The court ruled that allegations of sexual harassment were not actionable unless the employer sanctioned the actions of the supervisors.

McDonnell Douglas Corp. v. Green, 411 US 792 (1973)
A landmark case in which the Supreme Court set down the following requirements for establishment of a *prima facie* case of discrimination: plaintiff must show (1) that s/he belonged to protected class; (2) that s/he applied and was qualified for a job; (3) that

despite his/her qualifications s/he was rejected; (4) that after his/her rejection, the position remained open and the employer continued to seek applicants with complainant's qualifications. Once the plaintiff meets that burden of proof, the burden shifts to the defendant who has an opportunity to show that it had a legitimate nondiscriminatory reason for nonselection. The burden then shifts once again to the plaintiff who has an opportunity to show that this reason for nonselection was a mere pretext on the part of the defendant.

McKillop v. Regents of University of California, 386 F. Supp. 1271 1276 (Ca. 1979)

The California Court applied state rather than federal rules to protect the University's confidential correspondence from discovery by the plaintiff.

Mecklenburg v. Montana State Board of Regents, 13 FEP 462, 13 EPD 11438 (1976)

The only successful class action against an institution of higher education prior to 1980; the arguments focused on determining the relevant labor pool.

Melani et al. v. The New York City Board of Higher Education, 12 EPD 11068 (SD N.Y. 1976)

A class action suit lodged in 1973 involving more than 6,000 women employed by City University of New York since 1968 and alleging discriminatory salaries. The case has become a statistical battle-ground regarding regression and cohort analyses.

Moon v. Roadway Express, 22 EPD 30657 (5th Circuit 1980)

Appellate Court ruled that disabled persons do not have private right to sue under the Rehabilitation Act's affirmative action provisions; was denied certiorari by the Supreme Court.

Mt. Healthy City School District Board of Education v. Doyle, 429 US 274 (1977)

The U.S. Supreme Court held that where a dismissed teacher claimed his conduct was protected by the First and Fourteenth Amendments, but his employer claimed that he was dismissed for other permissible reasons, the trial court should have determined whether the employer had shown by a preponderance of the evidence that it would have dismissed the teacher even in the absence of his constitutionally protected conduct.

NLRB v. Yeshiva University, 48 USLW 4175, 100 S. Ct. 856 (1980)

The U.S. Supreme Court held that a private university's full-time faculty members are managerial employees excluded from coverage of the National Labor Relations Act where their authority in academic matters including course offerings and scheduling, teaching methods, grading policies, and matriculation standards is absolute; where they effectively decide which students will be admitted, retained, and graduated; and where their views have on occasion determined student body size, tuition, and school location.

North Haven Board of Education v. Hufstedler (Bell), 23 EPD 31143 (2nd
   Circuit 1980) Cert. granted.
   The Second Circuit ruled contrary to several other circuits that
   Title IX covers employment discrimination.

Othen v. Ann Arbor School Board, 49 USLW 2569 (ED Mich. 1981)
   The court ruled that Title IX extends only to those educational programs which receive direct federal assistance. On appeal.

Penalta Federation of Teachers v. Penalta Community College, 48 USLW
   3354 (November 1979)
   The U.S. Supreme Court denied review of a California Supreme Court
   decision that upheld a statute preventing community college teachers
   who are employed only 60% or less of full time from acquiring tenure
   by length of service.

Perry v. Sindermann, 408 UW 593, 192 S. Ct. 2694 (1972)
   The U.S. Supreme Court held that at a Texas college, the faculty
   handbook and the state system guidelines were sufficient to create
   the possiblility of *de facto* tenure, and the faculty member should
   be given the opportunity to prove such tenure. If *de facto* tenure
   were proved, it would establish a property interest that would en-
   title him to notice of the reason for his nonrenewal and a hearing
   to rebut the charges.

Peters v. Middleburg College, 409 F. Supp. 857 (D. Vermont 1976)
   Peters' case contained the following indices of sexism: the department chair told her that her involvement in the women's movement
   and her emphasizing the feminist perspective on literature rendered
   her "too political"; the chairman's letter of recommendation stated
   Peters was "a little too assertive" in her teaching; derogatory
   comments about Peters' feminism were made to her by several of the
   department members involved in her employment decisions. However,
   Peters lost because the Court stated, "an evaluation of one's teaching ability is necessarily a matter of judgment."

Petroni v. Board of Regents, 566 F. 2d 1038 (Ariz. Ct. App. Div. 1977)
   An Arizona State Appellate Court held that the department head was
   protected by a qualified privilege in a case where a department
   chairperson prepared an unfavorable but nonlibelous tenure recommendation for use by a tenure committee.

Pickering v. Board of Education, 391 US 563 (1968)
   The U.S. Supreme Court held that a teacher could not be dismissed
   for making public statements upon matters of public concern in
   exercise of First Amendment rights, unless the statements could be
   shown to: (1) impede the teacher's proper performance of his classroom duties; (2) substantially disrupt the regular operation of
   the school; (3) violate an express need for confidentiality; or
   (4) undermine the effectiveness of the working relationship between
   the superior and the subordinate. This is known as the "Pickering
   Rule."

Powell v. Syracuse University, 580 F. 2d 1150, 17 EPD 8468 (2nd Circuit
   1978)
   The Faro Court (2nd Circuit), restating its position in light of

Sweeney, said that the decision in Faro "has been pressed beyond all reasonable limits" and that the courts must be "particularly sensitive to evidence of academic bias."

Rajender v. University of Minnesota, D. Civil No. 4-73-435 (Minn. 1980)
   In the settlement of a major sex discrimination case, the university agreed to pay $100,000 plus attorneys fees to the former chemistry professor who charged failure to promote based on sex discrimination and possibly because of her national origin. By February 1981, at least 16 women had filed sex discrimination claims as a result of the consent decree signed in August 1980.

Ramos v. Texas Tech University, 441 F. Supp. 1050 (ND Texas, Lubbock Div. 1977)
   A U.S. District Court found that a student who applies for admission to a graduate program at a public institution and is rejected on academic grounds has no "property" or "liberty" interest requiring procedural due process.

Regents of University of California v. Bakke, 98 S. Ct. 2733 (1978)
   A special admission program setting aside 16 places in the medical school class for disadvantaged students, chiefly racial minorities, violates the equal protection clause of the Fourteenth Amendment and Title VI of the Civil Rights Act of 1964.

Rogers v. Frito-Lay Inc., 22 EPD 30657 (5th Circuit 1980)
   Private court action to enforce Section 503 not implied; an appellate court ruling that disabled persons do not have a private right to sue under the Rehabilitation Act was denied certiorari by the Supreme Court.

Rowe v. General Motors Corp., 457 F. 2d 348 (1972)
   In Rowe, the Court established the following criteria in regard to promotion: forms used must be relevant to tasks measured; position descriptions must reflect actual jobs; judgmental attitudes must be defined by a manual to be used by the appraiser; and only relevant data should be used.

Schwartz v. State of Florida, 494 F. Supp. 574 (ND Fla. 1980)
   The plaintiff won retroactive back pay and attorneys fees when the court ruled that her qualifications for a faculty position were superior to those of the black male who was hired.

Sears, Roebuck and Company v. Equal Employment Opportunity Commission, 581 F. 2d 941 (D.C. Circuit 1978) and Burlington Northern Inc. v. Equal Employment Opportunity Commission, 582 F. 2d 1097 (7th Circuit 1978)
   The court ruled that investigative materials contained in the files of the Equal Employment Opportunity Commission may not be released even to charging parties because this would "fuel private lawsuits" and might interfere with EEOC's conciliation procedures.

Seattle University v. Department of Health, Education and Welfare, 23 EPD 31039 (9th Circuit 1980)
   The court ruled that HEW was not authorized to issue employment regulations under Title IX. Accepted for review by Supreme Court.

Southeastern Community College v. Davis, 99 S. Ct. 2361, 422 US 397 (1979)
> The U.S. Supreme Court found that a professional clinical training program is not required by Section 504 of the Rehabilitation Act of 1973 to substantially modify its criteria for admissions to accommodate physical handicaps; the applicant must be qualified "in spite of the handicap" rather than "without regard to the handicap," e.g., severe deafness.

Steinberg v. Chicago Medical School, 371 N.E. 2d 634 (Ill. 1977)
> The Illinois Supreme Court found that a contractual relationship between the school and the applicant for admission was created when the private school accepted an application fee; and the school was obligated to evaluate the applicant according to the admission criteria printed in the school's information brochure and its bulletin.

Stukuls v. State, 366 N.E. 2d 829 (Ct. App. N.Y. 1977)
> A New York Appellate Court held that a department chairperson and similar college officials who are communicating with a tenure committee in the proper time, place, and manner are protected by a qualified privilege even though information is false, so long as there is no proven malice.

Sweeney v. Board of Trustees of Keene State College, 604 F. 2d 106 (1st Circuit 1979) (See also 98 S. Ct. 295, 569 F. 2d 169.)
> The first major discrimination victory by a plaintiff who sued an institution of higher education over sex discrimination. Following a trial court ruling in Sweeney's favor (which ordered her promotion backdated to 1975 with appropriate back pay and attorneys fees) the case went to the Supreme Court twice, resulting in the trial court's decision being upheld both times. The Appellate Court discusses judicial responsibility to scrutinize university employment decisions.

Trans World Airlines v. Hardison, 97 S. Ct. (1977)
> An employer must make reasonable accommodations for an employee's religious observance for compliance with Title VII.

U.S. Steelworkers of America v. Weber, 99 S. Ct. (1977)
> The Supreme Court ruled that Title VII's prohibition against racial discrimination does not condemn all private, voluntary, race-conscious affirmative action plans. The Plan approved in Weber included separate seniority lists for black and white employees and/or new training programs designed to increase black representation in the craft category.

University of Texas v. Camenish, 25 EPD 31725 (1981)
> The Supreme Court sent the case back to the Texas district court for a trial on the merits. The remaining issue in the case is who-- Camenish or University of Texas--ultimately will bear the costs for a sign-language interpreter who attended Camenish's classes with him.

Vinson v. Taylor, 22 EPD 30708 (D.C. 1980)
> Employer without knowledge of supervisor's alleged sexual harassment

of an employee is not liable for those actions.

Washington v. Davis, 96 S. Ct. 2040 (1976)
    A test is not unconstitutional solely because it has a racially
    disproportionate impact on members of a racial minority. In Davis,
    the test was facially neutral, served a legitimate governmental
    purpose, and was job-related.

Weisbord v. Michigan State University, 495 F. Supp. 1347 (WD Mich. 1980)
    The Court ruled that Title IX is for the benefit of students and/or
    federally funded research and does not create a private cause of
    action in an employment context.

Weise v. Syracuse University, 522 F. 2d 397 (2nd Circuit 1975)
    The court stated "as the indispensable tools of the scholars'
    trade ... [scholarship and research] should be left to the
    scholars."

Wilkins v. University of Houston, 26 EPD 32101 (5th Circuit 1981)
    The court found that the university did not discriminate against
    female faculty women despite such apparent disparities as average
    salary, mean salary, rank, length of service, and age. The court
    stated that evidence presented did not consider the college in
    which a faculty member teaches the most important factor influ-
    encing salary.

Yellow Springs Exempted Village School District Board of Education v.
  Ohio High School Athletic Association, 443 F. Supp. 753 (SD Ohio
  1978)
    The court found a regulation prohibiting girls from participating
    with boys in contact sports in violation of the due process clause
    of the Fourteenth Amendment.

BIBLIOGRAPHY

A review of the literature for the past decade confirms that the 1970's was the decade of women. Except for the issues of black colleges and desegregating institutions of higher education, very few articles and books were written during this period on discrimination against racial or ethnic minorities. Age discrimination, sexual harassment, comparable worth, and discrimination on the basis of handicap are emerging issues, but are not heavily represented in the literature of the 1970's. This bibliography reflects these trends.

The bibliography is divided into four sections: Employment Discrimination (including age discrimination, sexual harassment, and comparable worth), Affirmative Action in Higher Education, Resources for Affirmative Action Offices, and Bibliographies.

Employment Discrimination

Bartropp, J. "Title VIII and Employment Discrimination in 'Upper Level' Jobs." *California Law Review* 73:1614.
  The author discusses application of the general principles developed in blue collar employment cases to white collar and professional jobs where "judgment, leadership, initiative and sensitivity are important."

Beandry, A., ed. *Women in the Economy*. Washington, D.C.: Conference on Alternative State and Local Public Policies, 1978.
  A legislative agenda for areas affecting women such as employment discrimination, pension benefits, and alternative work patterns as well as highlights of present laws.

Berger, M. *Litigation on Behalf of Women*. New York: Ford Foundation, 1980.
  Examines litigation as a tool in promoting equality for women and concludes that most of the winners in "women's rights" cases have been men and that women have won only when it was not at the expense of men. The author illustrates the courts' reluctance to grant relief even when discrimination has been proved as well as the higher standard of proof applied by the judiciary in discrimination cases.

Braun, L. "Statistics and the Law: Hypothesis Testing and its Application to Title VII Cases." *Hastings Law Journal* 32:59-89 (Summer 1980).
  The author, a mathematician, examines the role of statistics in determining whether employers have engaged in employment discrimination.

The article develops methodology and mathematical techniques relevant to showing whether a particular minority group is represented
adequately in the employer's workforce or whether discrimination can
be inferred based on salaries, increments, or tenure without promotion of these groups. The author suggests that these mathematical
techniques are superior to and more sophisticated than such measures
as the Four-Fifths Rule.

Cruz, N. "Is Equal Employment Opportunity Cost Effective." *Labor Law
Journal* (May 1980), 295-298.
   Suggests that Equal Employment Opportunity regulations are fiscally
   conservative and cost effective because they encourage full utilization of human resources.

Deane, N.H., and Tillar, D.L. *Sexual Harassment: An Employment Issue.*
Washington, D.C.: College and University Personnel Association, 1981.
   The authors review the treatment of sexual harassment by the courts,
   suggest responses available to victims of sexual harassment, outline
   a practical approach for prevention, and include such resources as
   case studies, a list of sexual harassment cases, and a bibliography.

Faucher, M., and McCulloch, K. "Sexual Harassment in the Workplace--
What Should the Employer Do?" *EEO Today* (Spring 1978), 38-46.
   Discusses sexual harassment as job discrimination, the forms it
   may take, the legal context, and the judicial interpretations to
   date. Less serious forms of sexual harassment such as derogatory
   verbal references to women as "girls" or "dumb" are included as
   well as the relationship to cases of racially-based harassment.
   The authors suggest methods for internal investigation of employer
   policies.

Grune, J. *Manual on Pay Equity.* Washington, D.C.: Conference on Alternative State and Local Public Policies, 1980.
   Analyzes job and wage discrimination and identifies growing efforts
   to correct structural wage inequities. The manual describes the
   issue of equal pay for work of comparable value.

Guy, J. "The Developing Law on Equal Employment Opportunity for the
Handicapped: An Overview and Analysis of the Major Issues." *University
of Baltimore Law Review* 7:2 (Spring 1978), 183-278.
   An examination of state and federal law dealing with the obligation
   of employers to provide employment opportunities to disabled persons.
   The author surveys pertinent statutes and implementing regulations,
   concluding that these regulations impose onerous standards for compliance.

Hoyman, M., and Robinson, R. "Interpreting the New Sexual Harassment
Guidelines." *Personnel Journal* (December 1980), 996-1000.
   The authors discuss sexual harassment as a legal question as well
   as a problem that can be prevented by developing a model program implemented by the personnel department. Such a program, supported by
   a strong statement by top management, includes informational systems,
   management and sensitivity training for current and new employees,
   the development of sanctions, and the development of performance
   appraisal programs which monitor employee and supervisory compliance.

Hull, K. "A Major Supreme Court Decision." *Human Rights* 9:1 (Spring 1980), 34-37.
   Examines concepts relating to Section 504 and the Davis case: due process, accommodation, and integration of the disabled into the mainstream of society. The author suggests that the Davis case creates ambiguities about the coverage and enforcement of Section 504.

"Implementing Title IX: The HEW Regulations." *University of Pennsylvania Law Review* 124 (1976), 806-842.
   An overview and legal analysis of Title IX regulations; includes citations to legal history of Title IX, legal cases, and other relevant literature.

Jackson, D. "Affirmative Action for the Handicapped and Veterans: Interpretative and Operational Guidelines." *Labor Law Journal* 29:2 (February 1978), 107-117.
   Describes the origins and requirements of the Vietnam Era Veteran's Readjustment Assistance Act which extended affirmative action in employment to disabled and Vietnam-era veterans.

Jacobs, R. "Employment Discrimination and the Handicapped: Some New Teeth for a 'Paper Tiger'--the Rehabilitation Act of 1973." *Howard Law Journal* 23:3 (1980), 481-519.
   An analysis of the Rehabilitation Act of 1973 and the leading cases arising out of that law, concluding that federal legislation is needed to extend Title VII coverage to disabled persons.

Johnston, J., and Knapp, C. "Sex Discrimination: A Study in Judicial Perspective." *NYU Law Review* 46 (1971), 675.
   In a careful examination of the role of the judiciary in cases involving professional and occupational restrictions, labor regulation, places of public accommodation, jury qualifications, public sentencing, and criminal sentencing, the authors conclude that "... by and large the performance of American judges in the area of sex discrimination may be succinctly described as ranging from poor to abominable...." The authors also delineate and discuss similarities between race and sex discrimination.

Kantor, R. *Men and Women in the Corporation*. New York: Basic Books, Inc., 1977.
   A landmark study of the role of men and women in organizations that not only analyzes the problems tokens face but proposes practical ways organizations can improve the success rate of their women and minorities. Kantor suggests that "clustering"--integrating jobs or areas with several members of protected groups--removes many of the problems tokenism creates for both the token and the organization.

Kreps, J. *Sex in the Marketplace*. Baltimore: Johns Hopkins University Press, 1971.
   An analysis of women's employment and earnings focusing on the literature and enunciating some of the questions yet unanswered. The author examines the supply and demand forces accounting for the concentration of women in selected occupations and their acceptance of lower pay and concludes that more must be learned

about the opportunity cost of woman's participation in the market, the value of nonmarket work, and about the structural and institutional system by which women are excluded from certain occupations. A bibliography is included.

Livernash, R., ed. *Comparable Worth: Issues and Alternatives.* Washington, D.C.: Equal Employment Advisory Council, 1980.
This study of the concept of comparable worth was funded by the conservative Business Roundtable and concludes that implementation of comparable worth would have disruptive and undesirable consequences. The study suggests, in the alternative, that pay inequities can best be rectified by the accelerated promotion of women, particularly within the managerial and professional hierarchy.

Lloyd, C., and Niemi, B. *The Economics of Sex Differentials.* New York: Columbia University Press, 1979.
The authors dispel many of the myths and misconceptions about working women and then amplify that information with theory, data, and analysis. Thoroughly researched and based on careful and proper use of data and a broad knowledge of sources and research.

Milk, L. "But Can They Do the Job?" *Human Rights* 9:1 (Spring 1980), 16, 49-50.
Discusses the impact of compliance reviews, complaint investigations, and court action on employment rights of the disabled.

Neugarten, D., and Shafritz, J., eds. *Sexuality in Organizations: Romantic and Coercive Behaviors at Work.* Oak Park, Ill.: Moore Publishing Company, Inc., 1980.
The editors have gathered articles pertaining to sexuality in organizations from a variety of sources, reflecting the sexual dynamics inherent in the work setting, the nature and scope of sexual harassment, the organizational responses to the problem, and the legal issues of sexual harassment.

Obee, J., and Cooper, J. "Age Discrimination in Employment--the Bonafide Occupational Qualification Defense." *Wayne Law Review* 24:4 (July 1978), 1339-1368.
An examination of the ADEA, the BFOQ defense, and the similarity to Title VII. The authors suggest that the problem of determining medically the functional age of individuals should be addressed administratively. Concerned with public safety and the older worker.

"Sex Discrimination and Intercollegiate Athletics." *Iowa Law Review* 61:420 (1975).
An analysis of sex discrimination in athletics under the equal protection clause and Title IX; includes historical and social information on sex discrimination.

Seymour, W. "Sexual Harassment: Finding a Cause of Action under Title VII." *Labor Law Journal* 30 (March 1979), 139-156.
The author discusses the degree to which sexual harassment is a problem and the remedies available under Title VII. Key cases in the area are cited and analyzed.

Smith, R., ed. *The Subtle Revolution: Women at Work*. Washington, D.C.:
The Urban Institute, 1979.
A product of the research program on Women and Family of the Urban
Institute, this book contains articles on subjects ranging from the
movement of women into the labor force to institutional responses
to the income tax and social security system. The authors demonstrate that the expansion of the female labor force will lead to
important changes in the American family such as working women
marrying at a later age and an increasing number of families in
which both partners work for pay.

Somers, P., and Clementson-Mohr, J. "Sexual Extortion in the Workplace."
The Personnel Administrator 24 (April 1979), 23-28.
A comprehensive discussion of the extent and ramifications of sexual
harassment. The authors include a working definition, an examination of myths and facts, studies, resources, a review of the legal
context, litigation references, proposed remedies, and excerpts
from personal experiences with sexual harassment.

Vanished Dreams: Age Discrimination and the Older Woman Worker. Cleveland, Ohio: National Association of Office Workers, 1980.
A discussion of the problems faced by older women workers and the
impact of the Age Discrimination in Employment Act. The authors
recommend that age considerations become part of race and sex
investigations by government agencies as a key to encouraging
organizations to improve their treatment of older women workers.

Wolff, M. "Protecting the Disabled Minority: Rights and Remedies Under
Sections 503 and 504 of the Rehabilitation Act of 1973." *St. Louis
University Law Journal* 22:1 (1978), 25-68.
An analysis of Sections 503 and 504 and their implication for federal
contractors. The author considers judicial review and administrative
enforcement as well as the major provisions under the law.

Affirmative Action in Higher Education

Abramson, J. *The Invisible Woman: Discrimination in the Academic
Profession*. San Francisco: Jossey Bass, 1975.
A portrayal of the author's discrimination suit against the Univer-
sity of Hawaii which denied her tenure and eventually fired her.
Contains an analysis of academic procedures and processes.

Astin, H., and Bayer, A. "Sex Discrimination in Academe." *Educational
Record* 53 (1972), 101-118.
The authors examine the academic reward system, using salary, rank,
and tenure as indicators, and propose a reevaluation of this system.

Astin, H.; Carter, A.; and Hirsch, W., eds. *Women--A Challenge to
Higher Education*. New York: Praeger, 1977.
Scholars, examining the role of women in higher education, trace
the educational leadership of women from the founding of women's
colleges to the establishment of women's studies programs; summarize
employment patterns of women; and discuss issues of social responsibility and public policy as they relate to women.

Bayer, A., and Astin, H. "Sex Differentials in the Academic Reward
    System." *Science* 188 (1975), 796-802.
        Using the variables of academic rank, tenure status, and base
        institutional salary, the authors estimate the extent to which
        equity has been approached since 1968-69.

Belcher, L. "Dispute Settlements--Grievance and Arbitration Procedures"
    in D.H. Blumer, ed. *Legal Issues for Postsecondary Education: Brief-
    ing Papers II*, pp. 61-78. American Association of Community and Junior
    Colleges, 1976.
        Considers means of dispute resolution between the institution and
        the faculty; includes suggestions for formal grievance procedures.

Bernard, J. *Academic Women*. University Park: Pennsylvania University
    Press, 1964.
        A major study of the contribution of women to "the total academic
        enterprise in the United States." Chapters consider discrimination
        and the differences between academic men and women. Appendices
        contain the results of several studies.

Berry, M., ed. *Women in Higher Education Administration*. Washington,
    D.C.: National Association of Women Deans, Administrators and Counsel-
    ors (NAWDAC), 1980.
        A collection of essays on such topics as women college and uni-
        versity presidents, the community college woman administrator,
        survival strategies, women discriminating against women, barriers
        in administrative opportunities, job satisfaction, and upward mo-
        bility.

Bienem, L.; Ostriker, A.; and Ostriker, J. "Sex Discrimination in the
    Universities: Faculty Problems and No Solution." *Women's Rights Law
    Reporter* 2 (March 1975), 3-9.
        A study of discrimination in higher education suggesting that
        discrimination means that *less* qualified people are being hired,
        promoted, and paid in preference to more qualified candidates.
        References studies in which males are rated higher than comparably
        qualified females.

Boulding, E. "The Global Macroproblem: Prospects for Women and Minori-
    ties." *Liberal Education* 62 (1976), 185-207.
        Examines the attitude of white middle-class males, particularly
        in colleges and universities, and the impact of this attitude on
        the advancement of minorities.

Chalmers, E. "Achieving Equity for Women in Higher Education Graduate
    Enrollment and Faculty Status." *The Journal of Higher Education* 43
    (1972), 517-524.
        Examines reasons for the disproportionate representation of women
        in higher education: lower levels of female expectation, criteria
        for success better adapted to the needs and lifestyles of men,
        and the unfair application of fair criteria.

Clark, D. "Discrimination Suits: A Unique Settlement." *Education Record*
    (Summer 1977), 233-249.
        A description of a negotiated settlement of a sex discrimination
        suit filed against Montana State University that had a positive

effect on both the institution and on the women involved.

Crowfoot, J., et al. "Whatever Happened to Affirmative Action?" *Integrated Education* 14:6 (November-December 1976), 5-7.
Discusses the socialization role of institutions of higher education and lists tactics used in higher education that detract from and blunt efforts to implement affirmative action programs.

Davidson, M. "Affirmative Action's Second Generation: In the Matter of Vilma Herandez." *Change* 11:8 (November-December 1979), 42-46.
Recounts on three levels the mid-career review of a faculty member hired for affirmative action reasons: as a confrontation of ideological positions, as a complicated set of historical events, and as a basis for posing questions about affirmative action.

Divine, T. "Women in the Academy: Sex Discrimination in University Faculty Hiring and Promotion." *Journal of Law and Education* 5:4 (1976), 429-451.
Summarizes the anti-discrimination legislation between 1964 and 1974 and analyzes two models of university hiring: the ordinal model and a new model termed the "skill pool" model. The author discusses the merits and faults of each model and makes a case for the conceptual and legal superiority of the skill pool model for university faculty recruitment.

Downey, P., and Endy, D. "A Struggle for Academic Equity." *Graduate Woman* (November-December 1981), 10-15.
The Cornell 11, seeking equity from a university that has allegedly denied tenure to deserving women and paid inequitable salaries to women, are the subject of this article. The authors review the origins of the case, discuss the particulars of several of the women's actions, cite statistics about representation of women on the faculty at Cornell and elsewhere, and analyze the impact of tenure denial because of sex discrimination on a scholar's career during a time of belt-tightening at most colleges and universities.

"Eliminating Sex Discrimination in Educational Institutions: Does Title IX Reach Employment." *University of Pennsylvania Law Review* 129:417-451 (December 1980).
This note examines the plain language, the legislative history, and the purposes behind Title IX and argues that the Supreme Court in *Seattle U. v. HEW* should rule that the Department of Education did not exceed its statutory authority by issuing regulations reaching employment discrimination. The note suggests that Congress was particularly concerned about the adverse impact that employment discrimination has in an educational setting and that only the threat of fund termination can eliminate sex discrimination from the educational system.

Faia, M. "Discrimination and Exchange: Double Burden of the Female Academic." *Pacific Sociological Review* 20:1 (1977), 3-20.
Examines such subtle forms of sex discrimination as discrimination not only in terms of salary, but also in terms of prestige of institution, rank, tenure status, and the personal costs of attaining and keeping an academic career.

Farley, J., ed. *Sex discrimination in Higher Education: Strategies for Equality*. Ithaca, N.Y.: Cornell University, 1981.
  Based on papers presented at a conference held at Cornell University, this book features examinations of the problems of litigation, building mentorships, redressing grievances, and implementing change in higher education.

Farnsworth, M. *The Young Woman's Guide to the Academic Career*. New York: Rosen Press, 1974.
  Discusses coping mechanisms and survival skills for young women wishing to succeed in academia.

Feldman, S. *Escape from the Doll's House: Women in Graduate and Professional School Education*. New York: McGraw-Hill, 1974.
  An analysis of women in graduate and professional school education which concludes that although inequities clearly exist, they are not the same thing as discrimination. Inequities exist because of socialization, childbearing, pre-graduate school preparation, and the quality of women's relationships with their major professors.

Ferber, M., and Westmiller, A. "Sex and Race Differences in Nonacademic Wages on a University Campus." *Journal of Human Resources* 11:3 (Summer 1976), 366-373.
  Tests the hypothesis that when other variables are considered, race and sex are not statistically significant in explaining wages in different occupations. The results, using data for the nonacademic workforce of a large university campus, do not support that hypothesis and indicate that discrimination is a factor in determining rewards by occupation.

Ford, L. "The Implications of the Age Discrimination in Employment Act Amendments of 1978 for Colleges and Universities." *Journal of College and University Law* 5:3 (1978), 161-209.
  An exhaustive examination of the ADEA amendments and related cases and their impact on tenure, mandatory retirement, and higher education role in complying with the law. The author suggests that higher education's resistance to and evasion of applicable laws and regulations may result in a loss of higher education's credibility in the public eye.

Franklin, P., et al. *Sexual and Gender Harassment in the Academy*. New York: The Modern Language Association of America, 1981.
  The authors discuss sexual harassment of students and employees focusing on the legal situation and the institution's responsibility to provide a harassment-free environment. Containing Codes of Conduct and Grievance Procedures from several institutions, the authors take sexual harassment a step further, applying the legal principles to gender harassment, a phenomenon which has received little attention but which serves as a bar to a healthy learning environment. Specific cases illustrate gender-based discrimination by male faculty members against individual female students as well as against women as a group.

Freeman, R. "The New Job Market for Black Academicians." *Industrial and Labor Relations Review* 30:2 (January 1977), 161-174.
  Suggests that the historic employment pattern of black academicians

has changed significantly as a result of federal affirmative action
requirements. Black faculty members receive more job offers than
comparable white faculty members, in 1973 had a 7% income advantage
over white faculty with comparable skills and productivity records,
and had lowered standards applied to them.

Furniss, W., and Graham, P., eds. *Women in Higher Education.* Washington,
  D.C.: American Council on Education, 1975.
  Papers from the 1972 Annual Meeting of the American Council of
  Education were selected by the editors "to capture a moment in the
  history of colleges and universities when the shift from ideological
  to technical issues is sufficiently far along that action can be
  taken without the need to review yet again the fundamental principles
  on which it is based." Sections include women in higher education,
  the woman student, the woman professional in higher education,
  academic programs, affirmative action, and contexts for decision-
  making.

Gappa, J. *Improving Equity in Postsecondary Education.* Washington,
  D.C.: U.S. Government Printing Office, 1977.
  Educational leaders who met to discuss equity in postsecondary
  education concluded that efforts to achieve equity have been limited
  and often ineffective.

Gelwick, B., ed. *Up the Ladder: Women Professionals and Clients in
  College Student Personnel.* Cincinnati, Ohio: American College Personnel Association, 1980.
  Addresses the problems of women's professional advancement and
  provides information on how to publish, administer, and have an
  impact on campus.

Ginensky, A., and Rogoff, A. "Subjective Employment Criteria and the
  Future of Title VII in Professional Jobs." *University of Detroit
  Journal of Urban Law* 54:165.
  An examination and comparison of Equal Employment Opportunity
  Commission decisions and court decisions regarding blue collar
  jobs, white collar jobs, and professional jobs. The professional
  category includes higher education faculty discrimination cases.

Gittell, M. "The Illusion of AA." *Change* (October 1975), 39-43.
  An examination of efforts in the early 1970's by prominent academicians to oppose affirmative action through such organizations
  as the Committee for a Rational Alternative and the Committee on
  Academic Non-Discrimination and Integrity.

Goldstein, J. "Affirmative Action: Equal Employment Rights for Women
  in Academia." *Teachers College Record* 74:3 (1973), 395-422.
  Examines the relationship between institutions of higher education
  and the federal government in the area of sex discrimination, and
  the implications of that relationship for higher education in the
  future.

Green, E., et al. *Discrimination Against Women: Hearing before the
  Special Subcommittee on Education of the Committee on Education and
  Labor, House of Representatives, Ninety-First Congress, Second Session,*

on Section 804 of HR 16098. Washington, D.C.: U.S. Government Printing
Office, 1970.
   A two-volume transcript of House hearings conducted in 1970 by
   Representative Edith Green; a very useful compilaton of material
   on discrimination against women.

Groszko, M., and Morgenstern, R. "Institutional Discrimination: The
Case of Achievement Oriented Women in Higher Education." *International Journal of Group Tensions* 4:1 (1974), 82-92.
   This article, one in an issue treating the subject of sex-based
   discrimination, examines institutional discrimination against women
   which reinforces such female stereotypes as fear of success and which
   fails to encourage traits leading to achievement and competence.

Haber, B. "Why Not the Best and the Brightest: Equal Opportunity vs.
Academic Freedom." *Forum* (January 1981), 19-31.
   An exploration of the use institutions of higher education have
   made of the concept of academic freedom to counteract affirmative
   action. The author considers the Blaubergs and Rajender cases as
   well as federal investigations of the University of California,
   Berkeley.

Haslam, C. "Age Discrimination and Campus Employment." *Human Rights*
4:321. Reprinted in *Journal of College and University Law* 2:236 (1975).
   Discusses application of the ADEA to institutions of higher education with analyses of key cases illustrating the significant impact
   this law may have on higher education.

Higginbotham, L. "From Racism to Affirmative Action: Will Universities
Span the Gap?" *The Black Law Journal* IV:2 (1974), 230-239.
   The keynote address at a conference considering equal employment
   opportunity, affirmative action, and the availability of the benefits of higher education to members of minority groups and nonminority women. This entire issue of the *Journal* is devoted to
   proceedings from this conference.

Hochscheld, A. "Inside the Clockwork of the Male Careers" in *Women and
the Power to Change.* New York: Carnegie Commission on Higher Education, 1975.
   The author argues that the university is a meritocracy based on
   the life patterns of traditional male academics and their families.
   The academic reward system is thus keyed to a pattern in direct
   conflict with the careers of most women, whose primary childbearing
   years coincide with the years in which the male academic is establishing a "reputation" and who, not having "wives," must juggle
   both a career and household responsibilities.

Jackson, J. "Reparations are Justified for Blacks." *AEI Journal on
Government and Society: Regulation* (September-October 1978), 24-29.
   Explores myths associated with the *Bakke* case and University of
   California special admission program: that Bakke's qualifications
   would have gotten him into the University of California's medical
   school but for the special admission program, that whites were
   arbitrarily excluded because of a rigid quota, and that the "regular" admittees had better credentials and outperformed the "special"
   admittees.

Jastram, P.S., and McCombs, G.C., III. *Access for Handicapped Students to Higher Education*. Washington, D.C.: Department of Education, 1981.
The resources contained in this handbook are the result of a series of seminars sponsored by the AAUP and HEATH with a view toward improving faculty responsiveness to disabled students in their classrooms and laboratories. The handbook contains workshop presentations on such topics as pre-admission inquiries, learning disabilities, and attitudes and behaviors; scenarios from role-playing situations; a bibliography; and a list of resource persons and their special areas of expertise with various kinds of disabilities.

Kaplin, W. *The Law of Higher Education*. San Francisco: Jossey Bass, 1978.
A comprehensive guide to the legal implications of decision-making in higher education administration; contains discussions of many landmark cases; emphasizes basic legal principles relating to faculty, students, and the community.

Kramer, S., and Vladech, J. *Labor Relations and Equal Opportunity in Higher Education*. New York: Practicing Law Institute, 1977.
A handbook for use as a reference on collective bargaining in universities, litigation under Title VII, and other federal affirmative action requirements.

Kuk, L. "Beyond Affirmative Action." *College and University Personnel Association Journal* 29:3 (1978), 17-20.
Suggests that individual institutions must themselves create a climate in which women faculty members are able to realize their full potential.

Lanoue, G. "Tenure and Title VII." *Journal of College and University Law* 1:3 (Spring 1974), 206-221.
An examination of the impact of Title VII applied to the tenuring process at colleges and universities. The author concludes that a well-administered tenure system utilizing collegial judgment is not necessarily inconsistent with Title VII and that institutions should take steps to see that tenure is awarded in a nondiscriminatory manner.

Lewis, L. *Scaling the Ivory Tower*. Baltimore: The Johns Hopkins University Press, 1975.
An examination of the concept of merit and its impact and effect on academic careers. Chapters are included on professional evaluation, the appointment process, and the effect these processes have on women and minorities.

Linnell, R., and Gray, P. "Faculty Planning and Affirmative Action." *College and University Personnel Association Journal* 28:6-9 (Spring 1977).
The authors suggest alternatives for increasing representation of members of protected groups in academic departments during "steady state" periods in institutional growth.

Liss, L. "Affirmative Action Officers--Are They Change Agents?" *Education Record* (Fall 1977), 418-428.
A discussion of the characteristics of affirmative action officers, their roles on campus, and the problems encountered and created as a result of affirmative action.

Lussier, V. "Academic Collective Bargaining: Panacea or Palliative for
   Women and Minorities?" *Labor Law Journal* 27:9 (1976), 565-572.
      Examines areas in which colleative bargaining has aided or rein-
      forced affirmative action goals and areas in which the principles
      of affirmative action and collective bargaining potentially con-
      flict with one another. Seventeen contracts from selected academic
      institutions are reviewed in light of nondiscrimination, equal
      pay, seniority, tenure, and arbitration.

Making Affirmative Action Work in Higher Education. A report by the
   Carnegie Council on Policy Studies in Higher Education. San Francisco:
   Jossey Bass, 1975.
      A review of the impact of affirmative action on academic policies,
      federal laws affecting higher education, and affirmative action
      requirements interspersed with an analysis of discrimination in
      higher education.

Marcus, L. "Has Advertising Produced Results in Faculty Hiring?"
   Educational Record 57:4, 247-250.
      An analysis of advertising compared to the network approach as
      means of generating female and minority applicants for open faculty
      positions. The author concludes that advertising has produced results
      in faculty hiring but that the network approach remains the primary
      means of recruitment.

Mazia, J., and de Ita, N. "Sex Discrimination in Academia: Representing
   the Female Faculty Plaintiff." *Golden Gate University Law Review* 9:
   481-506 (1979-80).
      The authors explore the means and difficulties inherent in repre-
      senting female faculty plaintiffs, discussing the applicable laws,
      individual v. class actions, the litigation process, and negotia-
      tion of the class settlement in *Lamphere v. Brown University.*

McDonald, B. "Equal Pay for Coaches of Female Teams: Finding a Cause
   of Action Under Federal Law." *The Notre Dame Lawyer* 55:5 (June 1980),
   751-776.
      Examines the equal pay problem of coaches of female teams, an
      atypical type of discrimination because it is not based on the gender
      of the coaches but on the gender of the teams. The author suggests
      an amendment to Title VII as the best means of closing this legal
      loophole.

Mickelson, S. *Women Graduates*. Washington, D.C.: Women's Equity Action
   League, 1975.
      The tables included in this statistical survey of the proportion
      of women earning degrees in higher education in the United States
      show data such as the proportion of Bachelors, Masters, and Doctoral
      degrees earned by women by major field of study and selected sub-
      field; the proportion of first professional degrees earned by women;
      Bachelors, Masters, and Doctorates earned by women by major field
      and as a percentage of all degrees earned by women between 1960-
      61 and 1971-72.

Millett, J. *New Structures of Campus Power*. San Francisco: Jossey Bass,
   1978.
      An examination of such models of institutional governance as dual
      organization, academic community, political process, organized
      anarchy, and bureaucracy. Through 30 case studies, the author
      examines the relationship among faculty, students, administration,

and, belatedly, professional support staff.

Minority Women and Higher Education, No. 1. Washington, D.C.: Association of American Colleges, Project on the Status and Education of
   Women, 1974.
   A study examining the myths concerning black women and suggesting
   that minority women experience both race and sex discrimination
   and will not have equal economic or educational opportunity until
   both types of discrimination are eliminated.

Mitchell, S. "Civil Rights--Handicapped Discrimination." *Cumberland
   Law Review* 8:3 (Winter 1978), 977-989.
   A historical review of discriminatory treatment of the handicapped
   including an examination of recent cases in education, transportation, and employment opportunities.

Novak, M. "Questions for the Court." *AEI Journal on Government and
   Society: Regulation* (September-October 1978), 34-36.
   In light of *Bakke*, the author suggests that economic and educational
   differences rather than racial inferiority determine the time of
   entry of migrating groups into the American mainstream.

O'Neil, R. *Discriminating Against Discrimination: Preferential Admissions
   and the DeFunis Case.* Bloomington: Indiana University, 1975.
   Examines the *DeFunis* case and related issues; argues in favor of
   special admission programs for minorities, considering and rejecting various nonracial alternatives.

Parkhouse, B.L., and Lapin, J. *Women Who Win: Exercising Your Rights
   in Sport.* Englewood Cliffs, N.J.: Prentice-Hall, Inc., 1980.
   This resource book provides concrete information for recognizing
   and combatting discrimination in athletics, for implementing change,
   and for filing charges of discrimination. *Women Who Win* provides
   some savvy suggestions for women administering women's athletic
   programs, and for working within the athletic department, professional organizations, and the university hierarchy.

Reese, K., ed. *Teaching Chemistry to Physically Handicapped Students.*
   American Chemical Society, 1981.
   Focuses upon the special arrangements that may be necessary for
   handicapped students in laboratory science classes. The handicapped student should be personally involved in discussions of
   special arrangements, and usually is a capable source of information because of his or her knowledge of what has proved practical
   previously. The booklet contains illustrations of an adjustable-
   height wheelchair and of a platform chair, both homemade designs
   that permit good mobility around the lab.

Reul, M. "Did You Ask Me If I Love My Job? Equal Employment Opportunity
   in Higher Education." *Equal Opportunity Forum* (October 1980), 11-13.
   An analysis of the mix of law, regulation, and explosive feelings
   that affect the job of an Equal Employment Opportunity officer.
   The author examines the job requirements and expertise needed for
   the position.

Roberts, S. *Equality of Opportunity in Higher Education--The Impact
   of Control Compliance and the Equal Rights Amendment.* Washington,
   D.C.: National Organization for Women, 1972.
   HEW's higher education guidelines, issued in October 1972, called

for nondiscriminatory practices in hiring and promotion of women
and minorities in higher education, and affirmative action programs
to assure that any discriminatory practices in existence would be
eradicated. Because women are neither hired, promoted, or paid
commensurate with their male counterparts, institutional refusal
to rectify injustice can result in legal proceedings.

Rossi, A. "Women in Science: Why So Few?" *Science* 148 (May 1965), 1196-
1202.
   Various social and psychological obstacles restrict women's choice
   and pursuit of careers in science: the priority of marriage in
   women's aspirations, out-of-date views on the undesirable impact
   of maternal employment on children, early family influence, and
   social norms which hinder the development of certain intellectual
   abilities in girls.

Sandler, B. "Affirmative Action on Campus: Progress, Problems and Per-
plexity" in *Affirmative Action in Employment in Higher Education.*
Washington, D.C.: U.S. Commission on Civil Rights, 1975.
   Discusses affirmative action as a concept criticized largely because
   it has been misunderstood. Affirmative action has often been badly
   administered, and the federal requirements have been misinterpreted.
   The author argues that affirmative action, by increasing the pool
   of applicants for positions, *increases* the likelihood that the
   best-qualified person will be hired for the job and that hiring
   less-qualified people because of race or sex is illegal.

Sandler, B. "Sex Discrimination, Educational Institutions, and the
Law: A New Issue on Campus." *Journal of Law and Education* 2:4 (October 1973).
   The author analyzes the laws affecting campus women who are either
   employees or students, summarizes federal policy concerning employment, and discusses such issues as goals and quotas.

Shoemaker, E., and McKeen, R. "Affirmative Action and Hiring Practices
in Higher Education." *Research in Higher Education* 3:4 (1975), 359-
364.
   Examines institutional recruitment activities. The authors conclude
   that qualified minority and female candidates are available for
   employment and are making progress and that white males are not
   being "closed out" of the hiring process.

Smith, L. *The College Student with a Disability: A Faculty Handbook.*
Washington, D.C.: Heath, 1980. (GPO #19800-327-505:QL4.)
   Prepared as an introductory review of the disabilities that affect
   learning in higher education, this booklet suggests variations,
   provides a general guide to the instruction of disabled students,
   and is designed for the faculty member to facilitate interaction
   between professor and disabled student.

Solomon, L., and Keeter, J. "Affirmative Action in Higher Education:
Towards a Rationale for Preference." *Notre Dame Lawyer* 52:1 (October
1976), 41-76.
   Explores the conditions in higher education which necessitated
   promulgation of the 1972 HEW Higher Education Guidelines, analyzes
   the requirements they impose, and examines the impact of the Guidelines on the conditions they were designed to correct, on the individuals and institutions affected, and on the goals and values
   inherent in societal notions of morality, civil liberty, and
   academic excellence.

Sowell, T. "Affirmative Action Reconsidered." *The Public Interest* 42
(Winter 1976), 47-65.
Using ACE surveys, the author concludes that almost all of what has
been achieved since 1970 had been achieved prior to affirmative
action. Changes resulted from civil rights legislation, demonstra-
tions, and changes in American public opinion rather than from
affirmative action regulations.

Sowell, T. "Affirmative Action Reconsidered: Was It Necessary in
Academia?" in *Affirmative Action in Higher Education*. Washington,
D.C.: U.S. Commission on Civil Rights, 1975.
A discussion of women, blacks, and other racial minorities and
the factors which affect their availability, their publication
records, and their salaries in higher education. The author asserts
that numerical underrepresentation does not automatically indicate
discrimination.

Sowell, T. "Landmark or Curiosity?" *Regulation* (September-October
1978), 30-34.
In light of *Bakke*, the author suggests that economic background
for blacks and marital status for women account for salary
differences between demographic groups and that affirmative action
also creates incentives *not* to hire minorities and women.

Steele, C., and Green, S. "Affirmative Action and Hiring: A Case Study
of Value Conflict." *Journal of Higher Education* 47:4 (1976), 413-435.
The authors, through a case study, examine the conflict between
university compliance with the values of affirmative action and
resistance to the federal mandate requiring compliance with
affirmative action regulations.

Taylor, E., and Shavlik, D. *Selecting Professionals in Higher Education:
A Title IX Perspective*. Washington, D.C.: Health, Education, and Welfare (no date).
Developed under a contract between the Resource Center on Sex Roles
in Education and Health, Education and Welfare, this book is one
of a series of technical assistance materials developed to assist
education agencies and institutions in complying with Title IX.
The authors address selection methods and search committees and
suggest means of improving the likelihood that women will be selected for key positions.

Till, F. *Sexual Harassment: A Report on the Sexual Harassment of
Students*. Washington, D.C.: National Advisory Council on Women's
Educational Programs, 1980.
Provides an insightful overview of the conditions of campus sexual
harassment, along with working definitions, methods and strategies
for coping with institutional harassment of students, and recommendations for federal action.

"Title VI, Title IX and the Private University; Defining 'Recipient'
and 'Program or Part Thereof.'" *Michigan Law Review* 78:608-625 (February 1980).
This note discusses the *Bob Jones* and *Grove City College* cases and
federal aid to private colleges and universities, concluding that
the best definition of "recipients" is "those with discretion to
choose among potential beneficiaries." The note also discusses
whether federal funding should be terminated when noncompliance is
found in a particular program, contrasting the "pinpoint" provisions
with the "infection" theory.

Vladech, J., and Young, M. "Sex Discrimination in Higher Education: It's Not Academic." *Women's Rights Law Reporter* 4:2 (1978), 59-78.
A discussion of judicial treatment of females in higher education, including suggestions for developing a case and for educating the judiciary in the problems of women in higher education.

Wagner, L. "Tenure and Promotion in Higher Education in Light of Washington v. Davis." *Wayne Law Review* 24 (November 1977), 95-132.
The author examines the impact of *Washington v. Davis* on promotion and tenure in higher education and suggests that because of the limitation on the use of statistics to prove discrimination in individual discrimination cases, promotion and tenure cases should be brought as contract actions (*Peters*) or as class actions (*Mecklenberg*).

What Constitutes Equality for Women in Sports? Washington, D.C.: Project on Equal Education Rights, 1974.
Examines equal opportunity for women in sports, emphasizing the educational value of sport; attitudes toward women in sport; the legal mandate of equality for women in noncompetitive programs; what constitutes mixed teams in competitive athletics; single sex teams vs. mixed teams in competitive athletics; the funding of competitive athletic programs; separate-but-equal administrative structure in athletic and physical education departments and governing associations; and what constitutes equality for women employees in sports.

Yurko, Richard. "Judicial Recognition of Academic Collective Interests: A New Approach to Faculty Title VII Litigation." *Boston University Law Review* 60:473-541 (1980).
The author analyzes the relationship between the courts and academic decision-making, exploring both the increase in the volume of litigation and the recent shift in judicial attitude. The judicial approach historically has been a unilateral acceptance of procedurally correct university decisions. A line of cases has developed suggesting a closer judicial assessment of the discriminatory impact of those decisions upon members of protected groups as well as a more thorough examination of the subjective decisions that characterize academic hiring and promotion.

Resources for Affirmative Action Offices

There is a plethora of information, handbooks, and conference proceedings available for the use of Directors of Affirmative Action and their staffs. Many are expensive and some are of marginal quality. Items indicated * are particularly recommended. Addresses of publishers or organizations are listed at the end of the bibliography.

AAUP Policy, Documents and Reports. Washington, D.C.: American Association of University Professors, 1977.
Contains policy statements on academic freedom, tenure, due process, institutional governance, collective bargaining, professional ethics, student rights and freedom, research and teaching, and collateral benefits.

Affirmative Action Compliance Kit. New York: Executive Enterprise, Inc.
Designed for federal contractors who must comply with Revised Order
4, the Kit contains a step-by-step guide for writing a Plan for
review by the Office of Contract Compliance and is divided into a
Working Manual, a Reference Guide, a Glossary, and a Forms Package.

Affirmative Action for the Handicapped. Washington, D.C.: U.S. Government Printing Office, 1980.
A publication designed primarily for the use of compliance officers
as a learning resource and reference guide, it contains five
chapters written by authorities in their fields.

Affirmative Action Recruitment Kit. Washington, D.C.: Department of
Labor, 1978.
Contains materials for recruiting women primarily for professional,
technical, and managerial positions. Includes workforce data, recruitment sources, legislation affecting employment of women, and
compilations of women's professional organizations and caucuses.

Anyone's Guide to Filing a Title IX Complaint. Washington, D.C.:
Project on Equal Education Rights, 1980.
An informative guide to filing a charge of discrimination with the
Office of Civil Rights.

Bode, E. "Auditing Affirmative Action Through Multiple Regression
Analysis." *Labor Law Journal* 31 (February 1980), 115-120.
Recommends the statistical technique of multiple regression as one
allowing a sophisticated objective analysis for purposes of affirmative action audits.

Civil Rights Directory. Washington, D.C., 1981.
A comprehensive listing of private groups and government agencies
involved in civil rights, the revised edition of the *Directory* is
available free from the U.S. Commission on Civil Rights. The
Directory includes brief descriptions, as well as addresses and
telephone numbers of over 900 such organizations, and capsule
summaries of major civil rights laws and executive orders. Write
to USCCR Publications Warehouse, 621 N. Payne St., Alexandria,
Va. 22314.

Cleveland, M. *Age Discrimination in Employment: A Guide to the Law.*
New York: Executive Enterprises Publications Co., 1979.
A summary for the lay reader of the ADEA requirements and their
application to the employer/employee relationship.

The College Administrator and the Courts. North Carolina: College
Administration Publications.
A looseleaf binder with quarterly supplements containing case briefs
and commentary on legal issues facing higher education. Decisions
affecting Equal Employment Opportunity, tenure, and employment
rights of nontenured employees are among those discussed clearly
in language that can be understood by non-lawyers.

Competitive Athletics: In Search of Equal Opportunity. Washington,
D.C.: Government Printing Office, 1976.
Developed by the Resource Center for Sex Roles in Education, contains assessment tools, a bibliography, and suggested strategies
for ensuring equal opportunity in higher education athletic programs.

Compliance Manual: Equal Employment Opportunity Commission. Chicago: Commerce Clearing House.
> A looseleaf manual detailing principles and procedures used by the Equal Employment Opportunity Commission in investigating and conciliating discrimination charges. Regular updates.

Downey, P. "The Invisible Woman--Where is (s/he)?" *Graduate Woman* (March/April 1979), 8-13.
> An exploration of the generic use of masculine pronouns which has the effect of rendering women invisible.

"Employment Dispute: Arbitration Rules." *The Arbitration Journal* 33:3 (September 1978), 25-29.
> Contains the arbitration procedures developed by the American Arbitration Association for employment discrimination cases. A Suggested Submission Agreement is included.

Employment Practices Decisions. Chicago: Commerce Clearing House.
> A series of bound volumes containing court decisions in the field of Equal Employment Opportunity since 1965. Purchase includes a bi-weekly supplement and a four-volume looseleaf service, *Employment Practices Guide.*
>> The supplements often duplicate information in the *Fair Employment Reports*; however, supplements include the actual cases which are eventually bound in the EPD volumes. If the campus does not have a law library or legal office where the cases are readily accessible, this is an excellent resource. Copies of major Supreme Court decisions are received within days of their announcement by the Court.

Fair Employment Practices Manual. Washington, D.C.: Bureau of National Affairs.
> Looseleaf reporting service similar to the Commerce Clearing House's *Employment Practices Decisions* described above. An Affirmative Action Office without easy access to a law library should purchase either the EPD or FEPM.

Fair Employment Report. Silver Springs, Maryland: Business Publishers, Inc.
> A bi-weekly, eight-page report highlighting the most recent developments in affirmative action in government, industry, and education. If an office can afford only one resource, this is likely to prove the most valuable.

Federal Contract Compliance Manual (FCCM). Washington, D.C.: U.S. Government Printing Office, 1979.
> This comprehensive manual gives detailed instructions to compliance officers on principles and procedures to be used in enforcing Executive Order 11246, which applies to government contractors. Quarterly updates.

Federal Laws and Regulations Prohibiting Sex Discrimination. Washington, D.C.: Women's Equity Action League.
> A chart showing procedures, provisions, and enforcement of regulations.

Filing a Faculty Grievance. Washington, D.C.: Women's Equity Action League.
> A guide on grievances for faculty members.

Galvan, R. "Handling Title VII Charges Before the EEOC." *Arizona Bar Journal* 16 (August 1980), 16-40.
  Reviews the procedures followed by the EEOC since the transfer of Equal Pay and Age Discrimination responsibilities to that agency.

Gray, M., and Scott, E. "A Statistical Remedy for Statistically Identified Discrimination." *Academe* (May 1980), 174-181.
  This article comments and extends Scott's salary evaluation *Kit*, which provided a method of statistical analysis for determining what females and minorities would be paid if they were evaluated the same as white males. The article suggests that flagging salaries of females falling below the line may result in reverse discrimination charges filed by males who are also below the line as well as a search for reasons as to why the women aren't paid as well. Because the females whose salaries fall above the line may also have been discriminated against, the remedy is to raise the salaries of the entire class. (See also Scott.)

Grievance Guide. Washington, D.C.: Bureau of National Affairs, 1972.
  A basic guide to grievance procedures, arbitration, disciplinary procedures, and such specific problems as absenteeism, misconduct, personal leave, and work sharing.

Guide to the Section 504 Self-Evaluation for Colleges and Universities. Washington, D.C.: National Association of College and University Business Officers, 1978.
  One of the most useful single resources available on the regulations regarding the handicapped, this guide contains a clear explanation of the regulations as well as sections of the regulations pertinent to that explanation. Discussions and comments are presented on program accessibility; student programs, activities, and services; employment; and implementing the Plan. A comprehensive list of sources of additional information and technical assistance is included as well as a directory of state vocational rehabilitation agencies and a bibliography.

*HEATH Hotline. Washington, D.C.: Higher Education and the Handicapped.
  Sponsored by a consortium of higher education associations, consumer organizations of handicapped persons, private foundations, and the government. Known as Higher Education and the Handicapped (HEATH), the hotline is open between 1 and 5 p.m. EST on Tuesdays, Wednesdays, and Fridays. (202) 293-6447. HEATH was formed to encourage creative and constructive responses to the federal requirements mandating equal access to higher education for handicapped students and employees.

Higher Education and the Handicapped. Washington, D.C.: Higher Education and the Handicapped.
  This document contains updated information on the regulations and current resources available for developing campus programs to remove discrimination against the handicapped. Of particular value is the 1980-81 *Resource Directory*.

Higher Education Kit. Washington, D.C.: Women's Equity Action League.
  Contains information on federal laws and regulations.

How Federal Regulatory Agencies Work. New York: Executive Enterprises, 1980.
  A review of the Office of Federal Compliance Commission and the

Equal Employment Opportunity Commission and how these agencies are structured and perform their regulatory responsibilities.

In the Running. Washington, D.C.: Women's Equity Action League.
A newsletter focusing on equal opportunity in sports published by the WEAL fund.

McCarthy, J., ed. *Resolving Conflict in Higher Education.* San Francisco: Jossey Bass, 1980.
Discusses mediation as a tool to problem-solving and conflict resolution in higher education, focusing on the roles of the AAUP and the AAUA in negotiating settlements acceptable to the parties to a conflict. Conflict is viewed as an inevitable fact of academic life and as an opportunity for growth. Nonadversarial approaches to conflict resolution are viewed as an alternative to government regulation and litigation of conflict situations.

*Miller, C., and Swift, K. *The Handbook of Nonsexist Writing for Writers, Editors and Speakers.* New York: Lippincott and Crowell, 1980.
The authors present a well-researched, well-documented, and thorough study of sexism in the English language, citing studies and using quotations, history, etymology, and common sense to argue convincingly against language purists opposed to change.

More Hurdles to Clear: Women and Girls in Competitive Athletics. Washington, D.C.: Clearing House Publications, 1980.
Presents an informative history of women and girls in athletics by charts, graphs, and narrative; shows the impact of Title IX on female athletic participation and analyzes the current status of Title IX enforcement.

*NEXUS. Washington, D.C.: American Association for Higher Education.
Sponsored by the American Association for Higher Education, NEXUS is a toll-free information and referral service for people who are involved in improving higher education. NEXUS provides information about programs for compliance with Section 504 including information regarding programs other colleges and universities have tried.

On Campus with Women. Washington, D.C.: Project on the Status and Education of Women.
A quarterly newsletter on equity for women, particularly in higher education focusing on the problems and issues associated with the education and employment of women in the academic community. In addition the Project develops and disseminates papers on such subjects as financial aid, minority women, sexual harassment, rape on campus, and women in higher education administration; monitors federal regulations, statutes, policies, and enforcement and serves as liaison between women, institutions, the government, and other women's organizations.

PEER Newsletter. Washington, D.C.: Project on Equal Education Rights.
A quarterly newsletter focusing primarily on leverage for change in K-12 schools.

Recruitment, Admissions and Handicapped Students. Washington, D.C.: Office for Civil Rights, Department of Education, 1978.
This guide, a publication of the American Association of Collegiate Registrars and Admissions Officers and the American Council on Education, was developed primarily for the use of admissions officers.

The guide suggests how the law applies to recruitment, publications, application forms, admission tests, financial aid, orientation, registration, and grievance procedures. A checklist to assist in reviewing institutional policies and practices regarding handicapped applicants, a directory of national organizations for handicapped persons, a directory of state administrators of vocational rehabilitation, and a directory of clearing houses for useful information are included.

Resource Kit for Title IX. Washington, D.C.: U.S. Government Printing Office.
Developed by the Resource Center for Sex Roles in Education, the *Kit* includes detailed information about the regulations and manual for institutional self-evaluation.

Ross, M., et al. *Science for Handicapped Students in Higher Education*. Washington, D.C.: American Association for Advancement of Science.
Focusing on the barriers, solutions, and recommended strategies for change, this guide contains a directory of consumer organizations for handicapped persons and additional resources not mentioned in other bibliographies.

Sahlein, S. *The Affirmative Action Handbook*. New York: Executive Enterprises Publications Co., 1978.
A guide for dealing with day-to-day supervisory problems such as may occur with hourly employees. The book summarizes employment practices, discusses types of discrimination, and relates these issues to one another through case studies.

Scott, E. *Higher Education Salary Evaluation Kit*. Washington, D.C.: American Association of University Professors, 1977.
Suggests a method for data collection grouping to flag women and minorities for whom salary inequities may exist. Contains lists of colleges and universities at which salary studies have been performed, studies by professional societies of salaries within their disciplines, and bibliography of general studies of salary inequities in academe. (See also Gray.)

Seyfarth, et al. *Complying with Equal Employment Regulations for Handicapped Persons*. New York: Executive Enterprises Publications, 1979.
A guide explaining employer responsibilities for hiring disabled employees. Case studies are used to clarify employment procedures that comply with the law.

Shaeffer, P., and Lynton, E. *Corporate Experiences in Improving Women's Job Opportunities*. New York: Conference Board, 1979.
A survey of 265 major companies regarding gains for women in "female intensive" industries and "male intensive" industries. The authors compare "successful" experiences with "disappointing" ones in an effort to discover what efforts are effective in equalizing job opportunities for women. Commonalities of successful experiences were: careful analysis of job requirements, career planning or "pathing," and alerting supervisors of their Equal Employment Opportunity responsibilities.

Shepard, I. *A Compliance Guide to the 1978 Amendments to the ADEA*. Washington, D.C.: College and University Personnel Association, 1978.
A reference tool for campus administrators managing employee benefit plans, intended to provide assistance in review and audit

of institutional policies and practices. Includes a compendium
of state age discrimination laws.

Sports Kit. Washington, D.C.: Women's Equity Action League.
A kit for analyzing sports and Title IX.

*SPRINT Hotline. Washington, D.C.: Women's Equity Action League.
A hotline sponsored by the WEAL Fund for questions and problems
about equal opportunity in sports. (800) 424-5162.

Student Guide to Title IX. Washington, D.C.: U.S. Government Printing
Office.
Developed by the Resource Center for Sex Roles in Education, the
guide enumerates the rights to a nonsexist education in admissions,
financial aid, academic programs, physical education, and athletics.

Summary of the Regulations for Title IX. Washington, D.C.: Project on
Equal Education Rights, 1980.
A brief summary of the Regulations prepared by Project on Equal
Education Rights.

Title IX and Physical Education: A Compliance Overview. Washington,
D.C.: U.S. Government Printing Office.
Developed by the Resource Center on Sex Roles in Education, this
resource contains a checklist for evaluating Title IX compliance
progress in physical education, a review of the Title IX requirements, and suggestions for ensuring institutional compliance.

Title IX Grievance Procedures: An Introductory Manual. Washington, D.C.:
U.S. Government Printing Office.
Developed by the Resource Center on Sex Roles in Education, this
resource reviews basic information about grievances and grievance
procedures, Title IX requirements, and effective procedures that
comply with those requirements.

Update on Title IX and Sports #3. Washington, D.C.: Project on the
Status and Education of Women, 1980.
Contains tables summarizing the key provisions of the Department
of Education's policy interpretation on Title IX and intercollegiate
athletics.

Van Bowen, J., and Riggins, C. "A Technical Look at the Eighty Per Cent
Rule as Applied to Employee Selection Procedures." *University of
Richmond Law Review* 12:4 (Summer 1978), 647-656.
An examination of the use of the "eighty percent rule," regarded
by federal enforcement agencies as evidence of adverse impact.
The authors advocate use of a rule based on binomial distribution
which makes use of the standard deviation, a statistical approach
accepted by the Supreme Court in *Hazelwood School District v. United
States*.

Warschaw, T. *Winning by Negotiation*. New York: McGraw-Hill Book Company,
1980.
Discusses negotiating styles and recommends strategies for "Win-
Win Negotiating" which offers the maximum in achievement and effectiveness with the minimum of abuse and put-down of others. Written

in popular style but has a wealth of substantive information.

What Constitutes Equality for Women in Sports? Washington, D.C.: Project
on Equal Education Rights, 1974.
   Examines equal opportunity for women in sports, emphasizing the
   educational value of sport; attitudes toward women in sport; the
   legal mandate of equality for women in noncompetitive programs;
   what constitutes mixed teams in competitive athletics; single sex
   teams vs. mixed teams in competitive athletics; the funding of
   competitive athletic programs; separate-but-equal administrative
   structures in athletic and physical education departments and
   governing associations; and what constitutes equality for women
   employees in sports.

Bibliographies

Astin, H.; Suniewick, N.; and Dweck, S. *Women: A Bibliography on Their
   Education and Careers*. New York: Behavioral Publications, Inc., 1971,
   1974.
   An annotated bibliography of empirical studies, containing introductory overview of those findings.

Barabas, J. *Women: Their Educational and Career Roles*. New York:
   Columbia University, 1972.
   An annotated bibliography dealing with the realistic and creative
   contributions of women who have been hindered by traditional employment patterns and social institutions. Divided into women in the
   society, counseling women, women in academia (as students), continuing education for women, career choice and development for
   women, and women in the world of work.

Barrie, A. *An Annotated Bibliography on Sexual Harassment in Employ-
   ment*. St. Paul, Minn.: Minnesota Department of Equal Employment
   Relations, Equal Opportunity Division, 1980.
   An annotated bibliography on sexual harassment available from the
   Minnesota Department of Equal Employment Relations, 444 Lafayette
   Road, St. Paul, Minn. 55101, (612) 296-8307.

Forrest, K., and Chang, W. *Affirmative Action and Equal Employment:
   A Bibliography*. San Jose, Calif.: San Jose State University Library,
   1977.
   A bibliography of equal employment resources including pamphlets,
   articles, speeches, books, and articles.

Livernash, R., ed. *Comparable Worth: Issues and Alternatives*. Washington, D.C.: Equal Employment Advisory Council, 1980.
   An annotated supplemental reading list on wage discrimination and
   job evaluation.

McCarthy, J. *Resolving Conflict in Higher Education*. New Directions for
   Higher Education, 32. San Francisco: Jossey Bass, 1980.
   Resources for those wishing to learn more about the theory of conflict, dispute resolution procedures, and mediation and negotiation
   strategy.

Moore, K., and Wollitzer, P. *Women in Higher Education: A Contemporary Bibliography*. Washington, D.C.: National Association of Women Deans, Administrators and Counselors (NAWDAC), 1979.
   A well-annotated bibliography, comprehensive and organized into subject areas such as discrimination, minority women, college women and sports, women in specific majors, and demographic studies.

Robinson, L.H. *Institutional Analysis of Sex Discrimination: A Review and Annotated Bibliography*. Washington, D.C.: ERIC Clearinghouse on Higher Education, 1973.
   A bibliography to aid information gathering by cross-comparison between institutions, by locating analytical approaches, and by highlighting issues of sex discrimination.

Westervelt, E.M., and Fixter, D. *Women's Higher and Continuing Education: An Annotated Bibliography with Selected References on Related Aspects of Women's Lives*. Princeton, N.J.: College Entrance Examination Board, 1971.
   Annotated bibliography of works dealing with women in higher education; includes pre-1970 citations.

Women in Higher Education: A Selected Bibliography. Harrisburg, Penn.: General Library Bureau, 1975.
   This bibliography emphasizes material of use to affirmative action officers in institutions of higher education.

Addresses of Publishers

American Association for the Advancement of Science, 1776 Massachusetts Avenue, N.W., Washington, D.C. 20036

American Association of Higher Education (AAHE), Suite 780, One Dupont Circle, N.W., Washington, D.C. 20036; (202) 785-8480, (800) 424-9775

American Association of University Professors (AAUP), Suite 500, One Dupont Circle, Washington, D.C. 20036; (202) 466-8050

Bureau of National Affairs, Inc. (BNA), 1231 25th Street, N.W., Washington, D.C. 20037

Business Publishers, Inc., P.O. Box 1067, Blair Station, Silver Springs, Md. 20910

Clearing House Publications, U.S. Commission on Civil Rights, Washington, D.C. 20425

College Administration Publications, Inc., P.O. Box 8492, Asheville, N.C.

College and University Personnel Association (CUPA), Suite 120, 11 Dupont Circle, Washington, D.C. 20036; (202) 462-1038

Commerce Clearing House (CCH), 4025 W. Peterson Avenue, Chicago, Ill. 60646

Conference Board, 845 Third Avenue, New York, N.Y. 10022

Executive Enterprises, Inc., 33 West 60th Street, New York, N.Y. 10023

Higher Education and the Handicapped (HEATH), Resource Center, American Association of Higher Education/American Council on Education (AAHE/ACE), Suite 780, One Dupont Circle, N.W., Washington, D.C. 20036

National Association of College and University Business Officers (NACUBO), Suite 510, One Dupont Circle, N.W., Washington, D.C. 20036

National Association of Women Deans, Administrators and Counselors (NAWDAC), Suite 624-A, 1625 Eye St., N.W., Washington, D.C. 20006

Project on Equal Education Rights (PEER), 1112 13th Street, N.W., Washington, D.C. 20005; (202) 332-7337

Project on the Status and Education of Women, Association of American Colleges, 1818 R Street, N.W., Washington, D.C. 20009; (202) 387-1300

Technical Assistance Unit, Office of Program Review and Assistance, Office of Civil Rights, 300 Independence Avenue, S.W., Washington, D.C. 20201

U.S. Government Printing Office, Superintendent of Documents, Washington, D.C. 20402

Women's Bureau, Department of Labor, 200 Constitution Avenue, N.W., Washington, D.C. 20210

Women's Educational Equity Act Publishing Center (WEEA), Educational Development Center, 55 Chapel Street, Newton, Mass. 02160

Women's Equity Action League (WEAL), Suite 822, 805 15th Street, N.W., Washington, D.C. 20005; (202) 638-1961

BIOGRAPHICAL INFORMATION

Lois VanderWaerdt is an attorney, director of Affirmative Action at the University of Missouri-St. Louis and an Assistant Professor of Business Law. She has worked for the Office of Federal Contract Compliance Programs (OFCCP) and for the Federal Mediation and Conciliation Service.

Ms. VanderWaerdt is the author of several articles on discrimination against faculty, staff and students in higher education.